# THE DAY THE STARS STOOD STILL

A MEMOIR ABOUT

## LOGAN FLEMING

THE FORMER TOP WAX ARTIST
OF MOVIELAND WAX MUSEUM

BY SUZANNE SUMNER FERRY
as told by LOGAN FLEMING

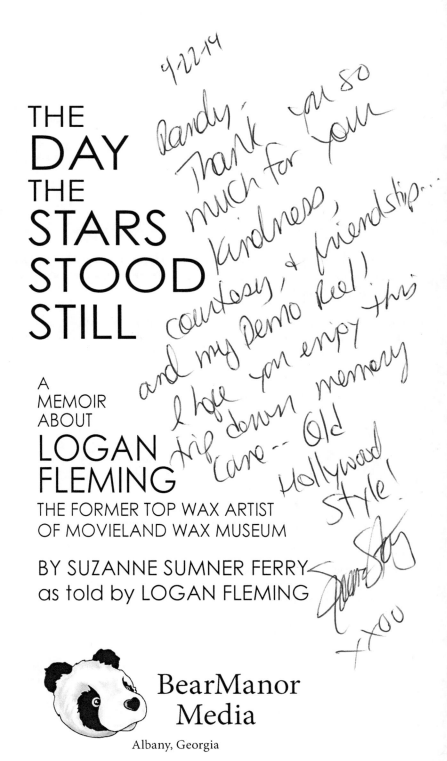

*7-22-14*

*Randy,*
*Thank you so much for your kindness, courtesy, + friendship... and my Demo Reel! I hope you enjoy this trip down memory lane -- Old Hollywood Style!*

*XXOO*

### BearManor Media

Albany, Georgia

Published in the USA by:
BearManor Media
PO Box 1129
Duncan, OK 73534-1129
www.BearManorMedia.com

ISBN 1-59393-698-2

Printed in the United States of America

Design and Layout by Allan T. Duffin.

**ALSO BY SUZANNE SUMNER FERRY**

*Corinna the Christmas Elf*

# Table of Contents

DEDICATION by Suzanne Sumner Ferry                                  ix
IN MEMORIAM by Miles Fleming                                        xi
FOREWORD by Suzanne Sumner Ferry                                    xiii
ACKNOWLEDGEMENTS by Suzanne Sumner Ferry                            xv
INTRODUCTION                                                        xvii

PART ONE: MOVIELAND WAX MUSEUM

| | | |
|---|---|---|
| 1. | Logan Fleming and His First Visit to Movieland | 1 |
| 2. | The First Test: Slim Summerville | 5 |
| 3. | Getting Hired and Proving Myself | 9 |
| 4. | Beginning my New Career | 13 |
| 5. | My Own Studio and the Palace of Living Art | 15 |
| 6. | Adventures in Paris and London | 17 |
| 7. | A Bigger Studio; Hiring for P.R. | 21 |
| 8. | The *Star Trek* Gang | 23 |
| 9. | Remodeling Movieland and More | 31 |
| 10. | The King of Comedy, Mr. Jerry Lewis | 33 |
| 11. | Sammy Davis, Jr. | 37 |
| 12. | Museum Pranksters | 43 |
| 13. | Romancing a Wax Figure and Gina Lollobrigida | 45 |
| 14. | Dick Martin: "Come As You Are Dressed" Party | 49 |
| 15. | Dan Rowan | 53 |
| 16. | The Oldies But Goodies | 55 |
| 17. | Buster Keaton | 57 |
| 18. | Mary Pickford and the Museum Dedication | 59 |
| 19. | Vincent Price and His Antics | 61 |
| 20. | Burt Reynolds; Christopher Reeve | 65 |
| 21. | Cliff Robertson | 71 |
| 22. | Stars Hall of Fame, Orlando, Florida | 73 |
| 23. | Robert Stack; Frankenstein's Photo Booth | 75 |
| 24. | *The Poseidon Adventure* and Special Effects | 79 |
| 25. | Keystone Pranks | 81 |
| 26. | Nancy Sinatra and Authenticity in the Museum | 85 |
| 27. | Smothers Brothers | 89 |
| 28. | The Clampett Clan Takes a Trip | 91 |

| | | |
|---|---|---|
| 29. | The Gift of Having Original Costumes | 97 |
| 30. | Chuck Connors, *The Rifleman* | 99 |
| 31. | Finding the Right Horses for Ben-Hur | 101 |
| 32. | Slim Summerville and Zasu Pitts | 103 |
| 33. | Danny Thomas Day | 105 |
| 34. | Laurel & Hardy | 107 |
| 35. | The Great Sophia Loren | 111 |
| 36. | Newer Set Additions and Collaboration | 113 |
| 37. | More on *Spartacus*; The Douglas Boys | 117 |
| *38.* | *Bonanza* | 121 |
| 39. | Paul Newman, Robert Redford and Gene Kelly | 123 |
| 40. | Lawrence Welk | 127 |
| *41.* | *Gone with the Wind* | 135 |
| 42. | Western Sets | 137 |
| *43.* | *Sanford and Son* | 143 |
| 44. | Touching Moments | 147 |
| 45. | "The Great Sexpot," Mae West | 151 |
| 46. | Ann-Margret | 165 |
| 47. | Opening the Stars Hall of Fame | 167 |
| 48. | Hair Today, Gone Tomorrow | 171 |
| *49.* | *The Little Rascals* | 173 |
| 50. | A Great Daredevil | 175 |
| 51. | Bob Hope | 177 |
| 52. | Carol Burnett and the Slip-Up | 179 |
| 53. | Hulk Hogan; Tom Selleck | 183 |
| 54. | Many More Stars; Golden Globes | 185 |

PART TWO: PALACE OF LIVING ART     191

PART THREE: MORE MOVIELAND FACTS     205

AFTER MOVIELAND     211

EPILOGUE: FINAL THOUGHTS ON MY CAREER     215

Final Words of Praise by Mr. Shannon Shrum     219

Index     221

# Dedication

I would like to thank my family for their patience and support,
especially my wonderful husband, Mike,
as well as the entire Fleming family.

This book is dedicated to all the talented stars that stood still
for Mr. Logan Fleming.

From left to right, the Flemings: Craig, Liz, Kevin, Logan and Miles

# In Memoriam...

## Logan Fleming – 1923 - 2011

The making of this book has been truly a labor of love. My Dad always wanted to share his illustrious career and unique experiences with a wider audience. While he wasn't able to hold on until the book was released, he did get to see the prototype, thumb through the pages and pictures, and know with assurance that his final dream to share his story would come to pass.

It was his sincere hope that you, the reader will gain an appreciation for a truly dying art...that of making a wax figure from scratch without the use of computer technology; and perhaps laugh or even shed a tear as you learn a few things you never knew about some of our most beloved Hollywood movie stars.

*Miles Fleming — Son*

# Foreword

Every now and again you meet someone who can tell a great story and, when they do, it leaves an impression forever. And as we know, truly great stories not only transport you into the story itself, but can move you and provoke thought. These stories usually come from experience or imagination.

Having lived next door to a nice gentleman named Logan Fleming and his charming wife Liz for over seven years, I had no idea how many amazing life experiences were holed up in Logan's mind, just waiting to be shared. Nor did I imagine how dynamic Logan's job had been over the years, what an exciting life he and his wife had lived, or what a great storyteller he was. But I feel truly fortunate to have found out, like I stumbled upon a huge, important secret that needed to be shared.

I was curious and wanted to hear more when Logan first approached me about writing his memoir. However, I was not sure I would have enough time to attack such an endeavor when I hardly had time to handle my own priorities. Yet, when I finally sat down with Logan and heard his stories for the first time, I couldn't get enough. I was intrigued and compelled to finish this book for him.

After getting to know Logan and his wife Liz over the past few years, my drive was to see him pick up the first copy of his book, inspect it proudly, and be able to read and enjoy his own memories. I was drawn to his unique stories, transported back to a time and place I had only dreamt of in the past. Logan had worked with many movie and television stars and he knew how to work with them. He had worked in the wonderful world of Old Hollywood for many years and had numerous stories to share.

I knew that I would learn a lot from Logan about his experiences, the history of Old Hollywood, and the lives and personalities of many of our favorite stars of yesteryear. I knew in my heart that it would be a great honor to write this book for him. Lucky for me, I not only knew how to multi-task, but I was pretty adept at managing my time and meeting tough deadlines. So I wrote this book while my children napped, on weekends, evenings, and whenever I could squeeze in some time. I became very resourceful with my precious pockets of writing time, working it around my even more precious family time. It took a couple of years to get through the manuscript, do the research, have numerous meetings and accomplish what was necessary. There were times when Logan and I would pass notes about the book back and forth through our mailboxes. It sure came in handy that Logan Fleming is my next-door neighbor. I've always said, "Whatever works, works." And it did.

Logan certainly has earned and deserved the opportunity to share his story with you. He has lived a long and exciting life. These stories, based on Logan's career experiences with Movieland Wax Museum and the Palace of Living Art in Buena Park, California, as well as the Stars Hall of Fame in Orlando, Florida, plus the numerous other wax museums for which Logan created wax likenesses later in his career, all bring imagination and wonder to those who love movies, glamour, and art. They help bridge the gap between fantasy and reality. They are your stories now.

# Acknowledgments

The author would like to thank the following individuals for their assistance with this project: Sarah Star for your design work; Miles Fleming for your editorial support and fact-checking; Liz Fleming for your patience, availability for questions, and kindness; Kevin Fleming for taking my many calls and messages, editorial support, and the title idea; Actor Jon Huertas (*Castle*, ABC) for your rave review and love of Old Hollywood; Peter Larsen, Pop Culture Reporter, *Orange County Register*, for giving us your time, interview and sharing your thoughts about Logan; Lt. Colonel John H. Tomlinson USMC (retired), former day manager at Movieland Wax Museum and former operations director at Stars Hall of Fame in Orlando, for spending time with me on the phone and answering my questions; Jo Ann (formerly Gordon) Oxsen, former hostess/greeter at Movieland Wax Museum, for taking time to share your memories with us; Ms. Ida Myers for sharing your memories and visiting Logan and Liz Fleming with me; Ian Schapel of Adelaide, South Australia, for also sharing your memories of Movieland along with many of your wonderful photographs. I also want to thank Brad L. Johnson, author of *Tynk* (2011), *The Slightly Whacked Vegetarian Cookbook for Real People* (2007), and *The Comic Collector's Handbook* (2005), for your advice and creative assistance.

I am extremely grateful for: the use of the Internet and other forms of social media for research, including Wikipedia and the Internet Movie Database; for editorial assistance by Bob Sumner, author of *Hiking Nevada's County High Points*; for watching some of Logan Fleming's personal videos taken inside Movieland (provided by the Fleming family); and countless other resources for fact-checking, date-checking, and other items that Logan mentioned for which I needed further interpretation.

I also want to thank my family for sacrificing time while I worked on this book. Your sacrifices allowed me to put my heart and soul into this project for Logan and his lovely family.

# Introduction

Logan Fleming had a very eclectic past. Born in Long Beach, California, his mother was an extremely talented concert violinist and his father was a successful real estate agent. His father would drag Logan to church meetings at the age of three and four. Being an active young child, he found it quite difficult to sit still. To keep his son quiet and engaged, Logan's father would hand his son little business cards and a pen. Logan would draw double-winged planes doing dogfights. These were exceptionally detailed and advanced drawings for a three year-old, as you can see from the photo of these sketches. So from an extremely early age it was quite clear that Logan had a unique artistic talent for drawing, and a great eye for detail.

Logan Fleming's sketches of fighter planes at around 3-1/2 years of age.

Logan ended up having a long, rewarding and successful career as the top wax artist and creative director for the extremely famous Movieland Wax Museum, which was founded on May 4, 1962 in Buena Park, California. It was the largest wax museum in the United States. Movieland was developed just a few miles away from Disneyland and Knotts Berry Farm, which helped put it on the map of tourist attractions. It was created and owned by Mr. Allen Parkinson.

Mr. Parkinson, interestingly enough, was the owner of the Sleep-Eze sleeping pills. He purchased a Canadian company called "Persomnia" and changed the name to Sleep-Eze. Having suffered from insomnia himself, he had always been interested in herbs and medicinal remedies. He had traveled extensively and discovered a particular herbal remedy on one of his travels in Africa that he was told could make people sleep. He took some of this substance home and started experimenting. As Logan explained, Mr. Parkinson once took some of the pills he developed at one location (using himself as a guinea pig) to see if he could drive home before falling asleep. He almost totally passed out before he made it onto his property, and fell fast asleep in his car for several hours. So when Mr. Parkinson became the owner of Sleep-Eze sleeping pills, he made quite a fortune. He sold Sleep-Eze in 1959, using some of his profits to help develop Movieland Wax Museum. It had been a pipe dream of his for a long time. Isn't it funny how a little pill made to knock people out awakened an entire new subculture of Hollywood entertainment?

During Movieland's lifespan, Mr. Parkinson saw traffic of over one million visitors per year who came to enjoy the more than two hundred wax figures of Hollywood's most popular, beloved movie stars that graced the museum building (and the silver screen). Logan Fleming was extremely instrumental in making these stars come to "life" within the Movieland arena as well as bringing the artful masterpieces of the world to life in the Palace of Living Art and later on, to many other wax museums. These creations were made for the public to adore, and adore they did.

Logan was their most talented wax artist who eventually became the museum's creative director, and his story is an exceptionally fascinating one. He started out fighting to prove how much of an asset he could be for the museum, to finding his niche, gaining respect as a wax artist, and developing an amazing career. Eventually, he found himself immersed in the world of Hollywood and movie stars, and enjoying two months off in the summers during their busiest years. Long summer vacations for Logan and his family became a regular luxury, so they traveled a lot. All the hard work, the dedication and the perseverance would pay off greatly in many ways.

From making himself into a talented wax artist with no experience creating wax figures under his belt at all, to coming up with a very innovative way to launch his career, to meeting Hollywood's top celebrities in their own private residences and laughing it up with the big boys of Hollywood, Logan's story is inspiring, entertaining and most importantly, historical.

As this book unfolds, it will become very clear to the reader that the title could also be called, "The Day the Stars Sat Still." The results of these "sitting still sessions" are reflected in the successful wax figures brought to life by the hands of Logan Fleming. These sessions were such an integral step in the process of creating wax figures for Movieland that, if skipped, could prove to be disastrous.

Don't forget: it was Logan Fleming's eyes, hands, personality and artistic vision that created the eternal wax likenesses of some of our favorite and most beloved movie stars of Old Hollywood for the world to enjoy forever. To have your wax figure created was an amazing honor back then. And no one's hands could do you better justice than Logan's.

An original brochure from Movieland Wax Museum.
Photo by Ian Schapel, Adelaide, South Australia.

The front of Movieland Wax Museum and Palace of Living Art in Buena Park, CA.

# Part One
# Movieland Wax Museum

# Chapter 1

## Logan Fleming and his First Visit to Movieland Wax Museum

**M**y name is Logan Fleming and I was born in Long Beach, California in 1923 and grew up at the height of the Great Depression. As I was artistically inclined at an early age, it became quite apparent that I would evolve as an artist of some kind or another. The great magazine illustrators of this period (Norman Rockwell, J.C. Leyendecker, Albert Dorne, John Whitcomb and other notables) were the highest paid artists of their time. I naturally sought to have a career like these great illustrators, as I grew older. My folks saw to it that I had ten years of private art classes before I was drafted into the United States Army. As I was drafted, World War II progressed.

In the army, I had a stint of being an army cartoonist and eventually ended up with three years in the Army Air Corps. After the war, I tried in vain to get a job in one of the big art agencies of Los Angeles. After graduating from the Herbert Jepson Art Institute, I ended up working for a small art service group for about a year before I applied for a position at the Pacific Outdoor Advertising Company in Los Angeles.

My dreams of becoming a magazine illustrator were dimming because photographers were coming in and taking the jobs of the illustrators away from the magazine companies. This was discouraging to me but I did not let it stop my progress towards getting paid to make art and express myself creatively. I knew deep down that in order to be truly fulfilled in my work, I must find a career as an artist.

I finally got the job at Pacific Outdoor Advertising, as I had learned from an early age that perseverance pays off. This perseverance would prove to be the conduit to my wonderful career with Movieland. I started in the "dark room" (a room where they did the preliminary work for artists, like patterns and such, for the large, outdoor billboards). After working for a nice gentleman who was an experienced billboard artist for a year or so, he sadly passed away. I took over his job in the dark room.

Back in those days we had to use an opaque projector with three glass slides, projected from one side of the room to the other, to help get the patterns for the images ready for the billboards. It sounds archaic but it worked just fine. Those billboards we were creating ("outdoor bulletin boards" they were called back then) were about forty feet wide. It took about three jumps with the projector to jump over and draw the three perspectives.

We drew the patterns from the projected images on the glass slides, right onto the great big boards inside the dark room. The images were on paper rolls extending the length of the board, three or four rolls high, drawn with indelible pencils. Then we would "pounce" it. By pouncing it, we would take a sock and fill it full of charcoal and then "pounce" it on top of the paper after it was perforated. It was perforated with an electric needle on an electric board. That is how we got the patterns. Then we'd take an indelible pencil and go over all of it, wipe it off and we were ready to go.

Finally, it was ready for the outdoor man to paint it onto those large boards to create the actual billboard. Eventually after two or three years of having done this, I became one of the top pictorial men in the company. The giant Marlboro cutouts came in a little later. I was very instrumental in creating the original Marlboro billboards. I also did a lot of the large cowboy cutouts for the Marlboro billboards. The cowboys would stick up over the boards up to twenty feet high. I was the one who hand-painted those Marlboro men. They had huge heads made from cardboard photographs, which were the best photographs of that time. They came out extremely realistic as you can see from photographs I have, which were taken when I was working on them. That is what I did for fifteen years at Pacific Outdoor Advertising.

Around this time, a very good friend of mine whom I've known since childhood named Arthur Cox had been out to visit the brand-new, giant wax museum in Buena Park, California. Movieland Wax Museum had been founded on May 4, 1962. The museum had been there for about a year. He knew I was artistically inclined and loved artwork. Arthur had a feeling that I would get a kick out of going to that new wax museum.

So Arthur and his wife took my wife Liz and me out for a nice dinner one night, and then they took us to the wax museum. I walked into the museum not knowing at all what to expect (wax museums were a new concept back then), and I saw that it was pretty nice.

In fact, this museum would go on to become the largest wax museum in the United States. I could tell that the guests in the museum were pretty impressed. I was quite intrigued, to say the least. But I was not exactly impressed.

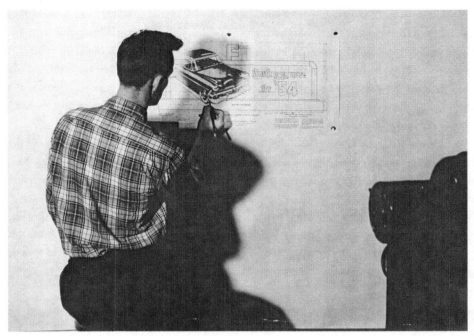

Logan sketches projected images before drawing to scale, creating billboards.

Logan works on a billboard for Pacific Outdoor Advertising. Note the model sitting in the chair as they draw to scale. *Photo by Pacific Outdoor Advertising Agency.*

Having always had an artistic talent, especially for drawing faces, I carefully looked at the faces of the wax figures throughout the museum. Closely scrutinizing the faces there, I was actually quite disappointed with what I discovered and with how unrealistic they appeared. Some of the stars' wax figures had fairly good likenesses (you could tell which Hollywood stars they were supposed to represent, alright), but they did not look real and they did not have any beards, proper details, or correct flesh tones. They really looked like wax. They looked bad. They were anything but realistic looking.

Especially Clark Gable (1901-1960). I was sad about seeing Clark Gable with no roughness or manly edge about him. I could not get it out of my system. I just knew I could do better for him. So I kept thinking about it and thinking about it, long after my visit that day.

I went home thinking to myself that I knew I could improve on Clark Gable's face. I dwelled on it for two weeks. Finally, I got my gumption and called up the museum. Mind you, I had never done any waxwork in my life. I knew nothing about it. I had just done pictures, drawings and some modeling with clay.

Logan works on his drawings for the Pacific Outdoor Advertising Company billboards. *Photo by Pacific Outdoor Advertising Agency.*

# Chapter 2

## The First Test: Slim Summerville

I called Movieland Wax Museum and was able to reach the owner: Mr. Allen Parkinson. Allen was quite famous because he was the owner of Sleep-Eze, an over-the-counter sleep aid. Sleep-Eze was at one time the largest selling non-prescription drug on the West Coast. That was how he got the money to build the museum.

I made an appointment to see Mr. Parkinson. When I got there, he made me wait at least thirty minutes before he would see me. I looked around the museum while I was waiting. In my head I knew what I would say and offer to do to help him.

I finally was invited into Mr. Parkinson's office. He asked me for samples of my work. Well, I did not have any samples or any knowledge about wax sculpting or museums. I just had my instinct and my artistic ability. I told him I could help this museum; I just had the strong feeling that I could make things better for him. Mr. Parkinson was a bit taken aback by my bold suggestion, especially without any physical samples to show him. In fact, he got downright upset and was slightly insulted about what I was offering, particularly because I had nothing to show him or any credentials to back up what I wanted to do.

He was upset that I would take his time and trouble him for a job when I had nothing to show him. He could not believe it and was quite sore with me. He finally came to the conclusion that he was going to put me on the spot to make me prove to him that I had some type of talent. He was a hard man to please at first, and this would be my first test.

Mr. Parkinson called over his "Girl Friday"(which used to be the term that was used to describe someone's faithful secretary, personal or executive assistant, and a term which I may use throughout this book because it was used during my career) to join us in his office. Her name was Mona Poe and she ran the place for him. He said, "Mona! Mona! Do you have any of those pictures we just got from Hong Kong of Slim Summerville?" Mona went immediately and brought those pictures over to him.

He showed me the pictures of the old comedian, Slim Summerville (1892-1946). George "Slim" Summerville had been a silent film comedian and former Keystone Kop before doing many more commercial comedies for studios such as Fox. He had a distinctive, potato-shaped nose and a slim upper lip, which made him funny to watch. There were some good side views, three-quarter views and other angles of him from the pictures. Mr. Parkinson asked me if I could make a wax figure of Slim's head from these pictures to look just like him. I told him yes, I knew I could do it, without hesitation. I told him I wouldn't be there if I didn't think I could do it. So he told me to take the pictures and make him a clay model and bring it back when it was finished. I thanked him, took the pictures and left.

As I left Mr. Parkinson's office, I felt like I had at least been given a chance. To me, a chance at something was a small victory in itself. I was motivated. I drove home and thought over how I would execute this project. I was excited and optimistic. I had no studio at home and in fact, my wife Liz and I were right in the middle of a major remodel. We were adding a second floor to the house and the entire top floor was unfinished and under major construction. There was a roof on the second floor, but no closed walls yet. My mother-in-law was going to move in and we had more children planned, thus the need for more room.

Well, I eventually decided to hole up on the second floor of our unfinished house to work on this Slim Summerville sculpture for Mr. Parkinson. I really had nowhere else to do it. I worked on it for a week, mostly in the evenings after my day job. I used basic clay and dining utensils (forks, spoons and knives).

After a few days, I saw some progress and was getting excited about it. I had never done a three-dimensional sculpture like this. After one week, I had a credible image of old Slim. I was happy with what I had created thus far.

Next I had to figure out how to present my clay head of Slim Summerville to Mr. Parkinson. I truly wanted to impress the heck out of him. I went to an army surplus store and got a small barracks box – about a foot wide – just the right size. I used black velvet to line the entire inside of the box. I also put a little latch with a spring inside, so the figure would stand upright inside the box with black velvet and the white clay figure inside. When I pressed the button, the top of the box would open up and the white figurehead would be exposed against the classy black velvet. I thought it was a pretty striking presentation, with a great color contrast. I had learned from my days at art school that presentation was very important.

I called Mr. Parkinson after about a week and made arrangements to come in with my Slim Summerville figurehead. I brought my little presentation box with me to his office. He asked to see my sample and I plopped it down right on his desk in front of him. Without a moment's hesitation, I pressed the button and the box top dropped open and the gleaming white face of Slim against the black velvet background instantly appeared before him.

Mr. Parkinson was not prepared for this and was visibly shocked. He backed up his chair quite forcibly. I could tell that he was quite taken by this. He called for Mona and right in front of me, asked her opinion of my model. Mona was obviously very impressed and thought the figure head was much better than the one they had received from Hong Kong. She did not hesitate to say so. Mr. Parkinson actually agreed with her.

Mr. Parkinson became just slightly nicer to me after that. He wanted some time to think about giving me an employment opportunity with his museum. I told him I was working for the Pacific Outdoor Advertising Company as a pictorial artist doing the large Marlboro billboards.

He wanted to know why I thought I could do wax sculpting for the museum. I told him I had really enjoyed the model project for Slim Summerville. I also told him that I felt confident enough with my artistic inclinations and experience where I could do a great job for him and improve the quality of his museum, and learn quickly. I had no experience in sculpting but I told him about my art training and painting background. He was pretty impressed and asked me to call him in a few days and to come back to see him then.

# Chapter 3

## Getting Hired
## and
## Proving Myself

I came out several days later to discuss an offer that he had come up with for me to work in his museum. I was doing pretty well financially already, and was not desperate. I wanted the opportunity to grow into something better where I could double my current salary and have an enjoyable challenge.

Mr. Parkinson had lots of grand ideas about having me redo all the figurines and make them much more realistic with better props and backgrounds. I knew it would be a lot of work and I needed it to be worth my while. He was somewhat shocked that I wanted to double my salary, but he thought it over and asked me to come back in four days.

Mr. Parkinson told me when I returned that it was a deal. I was quite enthusiastic and optimistic. However, Mr. Parkinson did not really have an actual studio set up at the museum facility just yet because his wax statues were being imported to him from various parts of the world. There was also no on-site wax artist at the museum at the time. The only ones he used had their own home studios.

Mr. Parkinson gave me a little corner area near the janitor's closet to set up as a studio area. There was some paint thinner, sand paper, and other basic materials. I brought my own paints. I told him that I could not sculpt the figures in that little space but if he wanted me to change the faces on the sculptures and reshape them, I'd have to find a way to do it. He was afraid I would ruin them if I tried to re-sculpt them.

I asked him if he had any figures that just needed a little touching up first, maybe some color and some character added. I wanted him to give me some smaller projects to start with so I could prove myself and gain his confidence. I told him I could do a lot with paint but not with sculpting just yet. He told me to start out in the evenings and to pick some of the figures that I felt I could improve with just paint, and to start working on them.

I had not yet quit my billboard job because I was not one hundred percent sure that I would be hired on permanently with Mr. Parkinson. So I would take off from my billboard job in the afternoons and drive out to Buena Park to the wax museum. It was kind of a trial period, and very time consuming. My wife was very supportive and ran the household and took care of the children with her mother's help during this time.

For two or three weeks I painted near the janitor's closet. I took the heads and touched them up and made them come to life with more realistic features. To help me do this work, I used actual photographs of the celebrities that Mr. Parkinson would give me. My little system was working slowly but surely. I was putting beards on men, and just bringing the figures to life and giving them much better likenesses. After about three weeks, I asked Mr. Parkinson if I could re-sculpt an actual head of one of the wax figures. He was still a bit hesitant and not ready to let me do that just yet.

The next head he gave me to retouch, Alan Ladd (1913-1964), was the very handsome star that appeared in many films including *Shane* (1953). This sculpture was nowhere near the actual actor's image. Alan Ladd was a very handsome man with a straight, smallish nose. The wax figure of his likeness had an extremely long nose like Fu Manchu! Yet, Mr. Parkinson wanted me to only use paints to fix the face. I felt this task was nearly impossible but this is what my boss wanted. So I told him I'd give it my best try. I was worried that he would fire me if I could not do it. This was a make-or-break test.

I got out there in the evening and had to work on the set itself because the head would not come off. It was uncomfortable because many museum patrons would be coming through the museum and walk right past me while I worked, watching me paint with the bright lights on. Luckily, I had turned the figure at a three-quarters angle, so Alan Ladd did not look as bad to the guests as they walked by. I would only do one side of his face at a time for this reason, which made it even more challenging.

On top of the facial challenges, Mr. Ladd's hairline was much too high on the original wax figure. There was very little hair to work with, so I had to paint hair onto him and make his hairline appear much more realistic. When I was finished, it actually looked much improved. But the nose was still a real problem. Paint was just not working. So I made an executive decision to do something else about the nose. I did not want to be fired, but I truly wanted to make the figure better.

I decided on my own to take a huge risk. This risk turned out to be a pivotal point in my career. I got out my pocketknife and began to chisel down Alan Ladd's nose without Mr. Parkinson's permission. As I cut into the face with my pocketknife, the face was in a shambles. It looked macabre and quite frankly, I thought it was ruined and that my gamble was failing. Chips were all over the floor, and the set looked wrecked. Just as this was happening of course, Mr. Parkinson came out of his office to see the results. He almost hit the ceiling. My knees were shaking and I thought the jig was up.

He screamed, "What are you doing? Ruining my figure that I paid a lot for? I told you not to try remodeling my figures! And just look at this mess! I said to just use paint, and look at what you've done. You've wrecked my figure and messed up my set." He was absolutely furious.

My Irish temper began to boil over and I told him, "This set is the only place I can work, and as I said before, I can help a figure with paint only, but you gave me a figure that looks like Fu Manchu with a long, skinny nose. And you expect me to change it into a handsome actor? And to make matters worse, working on the set in front of all the museum guests coming through is next to impossible!" When I finished saying this, a red-faced Mr. Parkinson stomped his foot quite hard, turned and charged back into his office.

Now, the realization flooded over me that I had no choice but to make this thing into Alan Ladd or I was finished. After getting myself back on track and calming down, I proceeded to go back to work to see if I could salvage the job. Upon close examination, I could see under rough cuts on the cheeks and nose that I was a bit closer to getting a likeness than I had thought. I cut a little more and then smoothed down the roughness and believe it or not, the thing started to look like Alan Ladd.

After smoothing the face down, I applied paint and by copying the photograph carefully, I began to see success. I finished painting the face and putting all the finishing touches on Mr. Ladd. It really started coming to life after that. One of the museum patrons walked by and actually said, "Hey, that's the best figure in here!" I thought then that maybe there was some hope. A few more people walked by and made very favorable remarks on Mr. Ladd's sculpture. This was music to my ears, even though the set was still a mess.

As the sculpture came to life even more, Mr. Parkinson came out with both barrels loaded, ready to really give it to me. He looked at Alan Ladd's sculpture again and he almost flipped. He said, "My God, what have you done to it?" I told Mr. Parkinson that I had made the sculpture look like Alan Ladd. After a moment, he replied, "You sure as hell did! For God's sake, this is unbelievable!" Relief washed over my face like a spring shower.

I told him how many patrons had walked by and told me that Mr. Ladd was the best figure in the museum. Mr. Parkinson did not know what to say. Finally, he just said, "OK. Good. Fine. Clean up the mess here and you should go home." But I could tell that he was very happy. I cleaned up the mess and went home that night, feeling confident.

My wife Liz had been a little concerned about whether or not I would land the job with the museum after putting in so many late hours. When I came home later than usual that evening, she asked me what had happened. I think she half-expected me to tell her I had been fired. I told her I was still employed and I recapped the night's events. She was positively thrilled, just as I was. We had a nice little celebratory dinner with some wine that night as the kids slept, just the two of us. That was a very special moment between us, which

I still recall fondly. It was as if we knew we were on the horizon of something really big, and we just wanted to have a special moment to cherish before things started to get extremely busy. This was a turning point in my life.

As mentioned earlier, my wife has been so very supportive throughout my entire career over the years and deserves everything my career's success has brought us. If it weren't for Liz, I probably would not have had these opportunities with the museum. All the blessings that have come our way from my career are as much due to the support I got from my wife Liz as to my talent.

Logan Fleming and his wife Liz at their 50<sup>th</sup> wedding anniversary.
*Photo courtesy of the Fleming Family.*

# Chapter 4

## Beginning
## My New Career

So this was the beginning of my career with Mr. Parkinson and how I got my start working as a wax figure artist. Little by little, as I did more and more, Mr. Parkinson's faith in my abilities grew. He would only give me certain figures to work on; not any of the big-name celebrities just yet, except for Mr. John Wayne (1907-1979).

John Wayne's figure had arrived looking so poorly made that Mr. Parkinson was not afraid of me wrecking it. He told me to go ahead and see what I could do with John. I honestly had no idea what I would do; Mr. Wayne was just not right. He was a mess! I had to add things, not just cut down things. I needed to find a way to model him up. I had never used wax to remodel the figures up to this point; I knew nothing about how to build with wax, or how to work with it. I had just chiseled down from things that existed or painted and retouched figures. This would be a new challenge for me, and although a bit daunting, it would give me another chance to prove my skills to Mr. Parkinson.

I thought about this problem a lot. As a child, I had done a lot of work on cars. I had used automobile body putty quite a bit to smooth out bumpers on cars. Well, I figured I'd try the auto body putty and see if it would stick to the wax on John Wayne's figure and see if I could kind of work with that. I'd experiment a bit. Maybe I could sand it down a little if need be and work with some paint thinners. Frankly, I did not have too many other options at the time. So I decided to give it a go.

I bought six tubes of Green Bull Body Cement and I used that on John Wayne to build his nose up properly. In fact, I used a lot of this auto body cement on Mr. Wayne's face. When I was finished and his face was painted and sanded down, Mr. John Wayne really looked like himself. Best of all, Mr. Parkinson was extremely pleased with the results of

John Wayne's figure. This figure turned out to be one of my favorites, and my best piece of work ever. It is one of the most highly photographed wax figures. Oftentimes, a person cannot tell by photographs of this wax figure that it is not the real John Wayne himself. So he was really the model who gave me an opportunity to begin to learn how to actually build and model as a wax artist. For that I owe John Wayne a great deal.

Next, Mr. Parkinson started giving me all kinds of projects and liberties to take to greatly improve his cache of wax figures. I had approximately 175 figures to work on and bring to life! Some of them needed only a little touch-up, and others needed a lot of waxwork to improve their likenesses. I used the Green Bull auto body cement for only a few of the wax figures. This is because one of the female wax artists that Mr. Parkinson had hired to work out of her studio showed up at the museum one day. She brought with her a bowl of wax in a Dutch oven or double broiler type of device. She also had a portable hot plate heating device with her. I observed her closely as she worked and took mental notes, asking her questions. As she heated the wax and got it soft enough to work with (but not too liquefied -- kind of like soft, thick butter), she would use a regular kitchen knife to work up with the wax on the sculpture figureheads. This was quite an education for me, to see a wax artist in the flesh (no pun intended) at work right before my eyes, for the very first time. I realized I was not too far off the mark with my instincts. She used the knife, sand paper and paint thinner to work up the wax and mold it into the proper figure. Then she painted it, too.

From this moment on, I had a much better idea of how to work with the wax itself. I bought similar supplies to those she had, and began to work directly with wax for my figures, corrections and models. It worked out very nicely for me. I gradually picked it up and quickly became very efficient, improving my wax artistry skills constantly.

Finally it became time to fix up some of the wax figures that Mr. Parkinson had set aside for a while because they needed lots of work with re-sculpting. I was ready for this now. This was in the middle of 1964. By this time, I had been there for several months, and I was really getting good at sculpting. I did not know it yet, but this was the beginning of an amazing, rewarding and fascinating career for me and the benefits were felt by each of my family members, too.

# Chapter 5

## My Own Studio
## and
## The Palace of Living Art

I had taught myself to repair and redo the wax figures if they needed help by using wax the proper way. I was still having trouble, however, because I did not have a proper place to work at within the museum. There was no available space in the museum set aside for an artist like myself, so I continued to work in the janitor's supply closet. We also used this room as a break room for coffee and such. It was cluttered with tools and whatnot.

Finally, Mr. Parkinson realized that I needed a proper place to work on the wax sculptures. He was realizing my value and potential and wanted to accommodate my professional needs. This gave me even greater confidence.

What he did was to go ahead and build a completely separate studio for me. This was a huge compliment. It was about fifteen feet wide by about thirty feet long. This became my art studio. The studio was actually outside of the museum, although adjacent to it through the garage. The way I accessed my new little art studio was through the back garage and storage room doors. I could also access the main museum through the back door of the building, and this was how I got to the break room for coffee breaks and such.

Having this new working space helped me a lot both professionally and creatively. I did a lot of my work there for over a year or so. After that, there was a big change to take place at the museum. This change was born out of a brilliant idea that Mr. Parkinson had conceived of many years before and now it was time to make it a reality.

This change I am referring to was The Palace of Living Art. "Living Art" was the process of taking a classical painting and recreating it in three-dimensional form. Incredible care and detail was taken to create exact likenesses and body positioning along with sets that realistically depicted the background from the painting. The Palace was to become a grand tribute to some of the greatest masters of art the world has known with beautiful, 3D representations of their most famous works. Each work of art had a display of the painting to the side so that you could move your eyes from the canvas to the set and truly see how it came to life. There were also many famous sculptures that were brought to life in wax as well. In order to execute this idea, we added a wing called Palace of Living Art. The sign in front of the museum was changed to read accordingly, "Movieland Wax Museum and Palace of Living Art."

Mr. Parkinson had worked on the Palace of Living Art for quite some time before I started working on it with him. He had people overseas in Europe working with him, including some folks in Pietrasanta, Italy. There was still just a limited amount of rare Carrara marble left over from the days of Michelangelo and ancient Rome from the same quarry. The Pantheon had been constructed of Carrara marble. This was a gorgeous, veinless and seamless marble that was used to make the Pietà in the beautiful St. Peter's Cathedral.

Mr. Parkinson had found out that there was enough uncut, unused marble left in the quarry used by Michelangelo to create some of the things he wanted to do for the Palace of Living Art. One of the things in particular that Mr. Parkinson wanted to accomplish was to build an exact replica of the Pietà. It took several artisans a few years to sculpt a copy of the Pietà, but the end result was a recreation for the Palace that looked amazingly like the original.

They also had enough marble left to make some other spectacular pieces. They made a recreation of the *Statue of David* like the one in Florence, Italy created by Michelangelo for the front entrance of the Palace of Living Art. The results were stunning and wondrous. The Palace was truly an amazing work of art through and through.

Building the Palace allowed a second floor to be created for the museum. This second floor in turn created more space to be added adjacent to the wax museum for offices and a brand new, larger studio for me. This was a huge bonus for me as an artist.

The Palace of Living Art eventually opened to the public in 1968. It was a great addition to the wax museum. It had its own, beautiful entrance with the previously mentioned *Statue of David* made with the lovely, and flawless Cararra white marble, and a gorgeous Italian statue called *The Bronze Boar* that was very famous in Europe. I'll describe more about The Palace of Living Art later on. For now, I will continue to focus on Movieland Wax Museum.

# Chapter 6

## Adventures

## in

## Paris and London

Several things happened to me after my hire at Movieland until I started working on the Palace of Living Art. After the process of getting hired, repainting wax figures that needed some "wax surgery," learning to use the wax properly, getting a separate studio of my own to work in, and working to improve the museum in general, I gradually started to completely rework *all* of the museum wax figures that were on the floor.

While this was going on, Mr. Parkinson was in the process of traveling quite a bit and arranging for the construction and completion of the sculptured copies that he had ordered from the Louvre, the British Museum, Michelangelo's marble quarry, and a few other places for the Palace of Living Art. In about a year's time or so, the new studio for me to work in and the actual design and construction of the building which would become the Palace of Living Art, including some additional offices, were being completed. When the Palace was being built and the overseas work that had been ordered for the Palace was getting done, I was beginning to spend more and more of my time at the Palace. This went on until the artwork and the entire Palace project was completed with its grand opening in the late 1960's.

With that under our belt, Mr. Parkinson was in the process of having art and mannequin work done for him in small mannequin factories outside of Paris for the Palace. He invited my wife Liz and me to accompany him to Europe so that I could give the mannequin builders the proper information to improve their work that would be sent to us in the United States. It was almost as if I was being asked to train these Parisian artists as my apprentices, and I took this as a huge honor.

It was arranged that Mr. Parkinson would stop at our home on his way to the airport and pick us up. Mr. Parkinson was a tall man who carried himself with dignity, grace and class. When he arrived at our home that morning, my middle son Miles went right up to him and inquired, "Mr. Parkinson, are you honest to gosh a real millionaire?" Mr. Parkinson stated directly, "Yes, I am, Miles." And with that, we were off to Paris.

The minute we got to the airport in Paris, Mr. Parkinson took Liz and me to a small café to drink some of that great, dark French coffee. It was stronger than any coffee we'd ever had. And boy, it really popped us awake. We were on French time immediately upon consumption of their incredibly strong coffee.

Instead of going directly to our hotel, we immediately took full tours of the Palace of Versailles, Hall of Mirrors, the Grand Theatre and other key places. As we drove around, we got our first glimpses of beautiful French women carrying large loaves of fresh bread, flowers and fresh food from the local farmers markets. The City of Lights was packed with beautiful pieces of history, sights, sounds and smells at every corner.

We stayed at a quaint hotel called Hotel du Rond-Point des Champs-Elysées. This hotel is located near one of the Parisian streets known by heart by the French people and visitors from all over the world, Champs-Elysées. We had a delightful, savory dinner that evening at Fouquet's. Fouquet's was founded in 1901 and is perfect for people-watching. With its lovely aged luster and history, it is a very popular Parisian restaurant. It is a celebrity favorite that has attracted the likes of Chaplin, Chevalier, Dietrich, Churchill, Roosevelt, and Jackie Onassis. This classy cafe on the Champs-Elysées sits behind a row of lovely potted flowers at the edge of the sidewalk. This makes it perfect for watching the Parisian scenes unfold. We enjoyed every moment of this.

The next morning, Mr. Parkinson had made plans for me to visit a mannequin-manufacturing house near Pereire, a small settlement on the outskirts of Paris. Pereire was opened on 23 May 1910 when the Metro line was extended from Villiers. The station is named after the Boulevard Pereire and the Place du Maréchal Juin. While I headed there, Liz had ample time to enjoy the sights of the city, go shopping and immerse herself in Paris for a day. I was instructed to take the Metro to this very small, primitive-yet-quaint town. A pleasant gentleman met me there and guided me to a factory where mannequins were assembled. Once at the factory, another gentleman who spoke minimal English met me; this was the factory foreman. He was supposed to help me get headed back to Paris that night after we did some work.

I was assigned to show them without words (being that I did not speak French) what to improve upon regarding the work that they sent us before it was shipped out to Movieland. It was extremely challenging for me to explain everything I wanted to say because there was quite a language barrier.

There was an artist in this factory working on a large bust of a woman, and I found out from the foreman that this was, interestingly enough, Elizabeth Taylor's bust. Then the foreman asked me if I thought the "cowboy" would win the Governor's job in California, in his choppy English. I told him that I thought Reagan would get the job. I was somewhat surprised to hear that they knew all about Ronald Reagan.

I tried to help them as much as I could during that afternoon in the factory with our limited language commonality. It had started to rain, and the streets there were not paved. As it grew darker, the workers gradually began to disappear, and I finally realized that the foreman had forgotten all about directing me back to my hotel (or at least to the Metro station). It was raining hard and quite dark outside. The night watchman realized my predicament, and tried to find someone who spoke English to help me, but to no avail. He tried to find me a taxi but there were none available so far on the outskirts of Paris.

I finally realized that I was on my own, and no one around me could speak English. I knew I was in for an adventure that evening. Luckily, I had a heavy raincoat with me and so I headed outside into the rain. The watchman tried to stop me but I kept going, knowing that the only way I would make it to the center of Paris and back to my hotel was to seek out the closest Metro station. I had to find the terminal on my own, and there were no streetlights at all. A few single bulbs hung sparingly in some local shop windows that I passed, and they became my only source of light. The rain clouds completely covered the moonlight. I would have welcomed the normally stunning Parisian moon and stars.

Every time I would reach an intersection, I would try to find someone. When I did, I would ask them for guidance by simply saying "Pereire" or "Metro," but they just kept speaking in French, pointing this way and that, and I could not make heads or tails out of their directions. Fortunately, I finally happened upon an open-air barbershop. It had a ceiling but no front façade, so I could actually see the barber inside, hard at work. It was the only place around that had a bright light. The client in the barber's chair was covered with foamy white barber's soap, and I could see exactly where portions of his face had already been shaved baby-clean. I walked up to the barber and said as apologetically as I could, "Pereire Terminal?" and he bent down to his client and said something in French. His client nodded and then the barber walked away from the client.

The barber was wearing only a thin, white T-shirt. He walked right outside without hesitation into the intense, cold downpour of rain. I followed him directly and we walked a little ways to an intersection that had five turnoffs. He pointed to one of them and said, "Pereire." He then nodded and headed back towards his barbershop and his waiting client. I thought that was such a kind and neighborly gesture for the barber to take time out from his work and his client to help a stranger find his way on a dark, stormy night, wearing just a thin shirt.

I eventually found the correct terminal, which I so desperately needed, and finally reached the Metro. I sat down inside, taking a little rest. It was so nice to get back to Liz and Mr. Parkinson after such a long, tiring and eventful day.

The next day we bid farewell to Paris and Mr. Parkinson took us over to London, which we enjoyed immensely. After getting us settled in our new hotel and surroundings, Mr. Parkinson flew back to the United States on his own, giving us a few extra days in London to enjoy as we pleased. This was a real treat, and we had a fantastic time exploring the city. We did all the traditional sightseeing including Big Ben, Parliament, Saint Paul's Cathedral, Westminster Abbey, Buckingham Palace, Hyde Park and many other wonderful sights. We were also very fortunate to see Queen Elizabeth in a state parade while we were there. A police officer knew we were tourists and told us how to get a good photograph of the Queen. He told us to wait until she got to a particular point near us. When she got there, Liz was instructed to yell out, "Hello! Hello!" and the Queen would turn her head in our direction, which would enable us to take a great picture of her.

Sadly, Liz did not do as she had been instructed and the Queen did not turn her head until I yelled out a belated, "Hello! Hello!" and sure enough, the Queen turned her head towards us. We got a good picture after all, although it did not go as smoothly as it could have. I later asked Liz why she did not yell at the Queen when the timing was right. Liz told me that she just could not bring herself to yell at a Queen because it seemed like such a vulgar and impolite thing to do. I'm sure she was quite right about that.

After seeing all of the beautiful churches in London and the tourist sights, we headed back home, feeling as if we had experienced a wonderful and adventure-packed trip. We felt very grateful to Mr. Parkinson for taking us with him to Europe out of appreciation for my hard work at Movieland, and in my efforts in helping finish the Palace of Living Art, which was a milestone for the museum. Additionally, I was very flattered that he had me serve as a teacher of sorts for some of the Parisian artisans and sculptors. Now it was time to get back to work at Movieland and start working on many new sets for the museum.

The Eiffel Tower in Paris, where Liz and Logan traveled to with Allen Parkinson so Logan could share his wax artistry knowledge with French artisans. *Photo by Suzanne Sumner Ferry.*

# Chapter 7

# A

# Bigger Studio, Hiring for P.R.

The newly added second floor of the wax museum allowed Mr. Parkinson to create a better, larger art studio that I could use to work in and create my wax figures. This beautiful new studio had skylights, lots of room, and was a great space for my work to be done. The old studio was taken down completely. I never missed it for a moment!

I started out in my new studio in about 1965. That is where I worked from then on out during my career. I was completely undisturbed up there; I cannot say enough about how great the lighting was for my artwork. It really made a huge difference for me in how I could do my work and in the quality of my work experience. It helped me blossom in my career and greatly improve my skills as a wax artist. I was very grateful to Mr. Parkinson for this working space. I cannot stress enough that as an artist, a comfortable studio space is an essential element for an artist's journey. Having the right work environment can truly make or break your creativity.

About that time, we knew that we needed some new wax figures created. I had spent a lot of time working on and touching up the existing ones and it was now time to liven up the museum with some "fresh blood."

We were fortunate enough to gain a publicity agent around the same time. Her name was Lovetta Kramer. Lovetta did so much work for us in arranging to get the movie stars and their agents on board, to get photographers lined up, set up measurement meetings, and so much more. She proved to become a huge asset for the museum.

When we would go out to meet with a star to take measurements and photos, we intentionally wanted to make a memorable first impression and therefore went in style.

Mr. Parkinson owned a studio Rolls Royce and Jack Collins, our head "Keystone Kop" and resident chauffeur would drive us up to the star's home or another designated location in this beautiful car to make our grand entrance. The usual team for these initial meetings was me, Lovetta, and a photographer.

I mentioned earlier that in addition to being the resident chauffeur, Jack Collins was also our head Keystone Kop. He and his team of security guards kept order in the museum, which obviously was a serious and necessary job that had to be done. However, most of our patrons just saw them as comical characters dressed in their Keystone Kop uniforms milling about the museum. These fellows had so much fun interacting with the guests and really added so much to the "Classic Hollywood" atmosphere at Movieland. Later in the book I will share some of the many interesting and humorous stories and pranks they played on unsuspecting visitors. For a little background on Keystone Kops, these men were a group of characters who starred in a bunch of silent film comedies. They were lovable but totally incompetent policemen known for their hilarious antics such as running around frantically in all directions, clutching at their hats, leaping up high in surprise, and taking some extreme pratfalls. They were physically very talented and fit entertainers, known for making their audiences laugh a lot.

Some of the many Keystone Kops perform in front
of the Palace of Living Art for their fans.

# Chapter 8

# The
# Star Trek
# Gang.

The first gig Lovetta got for us was part of the *Star Trek* (1966-1969) group. This television series created by Gene Roddenberry was about a Captain named James T. Kirk and his crew of the Starship Enterprise who explored outer space and worked hard to defend the United Federation of Planets. Surprisingly, they had just been knocked out of their first big run on television after many great episodes. They were very famous already but for some reason their run on television appeared to be over (of course we know that later on this wasn't the end of the story).

Lovetta finally got William Shatner's number from an agent. William Shatner (1931 – present) played Captain James T. Kirk, the captain of the Starship Enterprise and the leading character in *Star Trek*. Lovetta contacted him and left word for Mr. Shatner to call her back. She was hoping he would want to be in the museum, as it was conceived to be a great honor to do so for the stars.

Mr. Shatner returned the call and started the conversation by introducing himself as William Shatner, Esquire, returning the call for Lovetta Kramer. She replied, "This is Lovetta Kramer, Esquire. How can I help you, Mr. Shatner, Esquire?" They both laughed and started out on a good note. This developed into having Mr. Shatner agree to an interview with us. It was an extremely interesting interview.

We met with Mr. Shatner quite early in the morning at his request. He loved to get up early. Mr. Shatner had a gorgeous home in the canyon with a lovely view. We drove up to his house in our Rolls Royce Limousine, driven by our chauffeur. We showed up at the door and Mr. Shatner answered himself. He showed us inside and was extremely cordial. His home smelled lovely, like chicory coffee and fresh-baked cookies. To our delight, his wife had made us wonderful, steaming mugs of coffee and had baked us a huge array of delicious, homemade cookies. Mr. Shatner insisted that we just sit down outside on the porch (which had an amazing view) and have some coffee and cookies for the first thirty minutes while we got acquainted. We could get to business after that.

I have a crooked finger on my left hand that I got while playing baseball years before. Mr. Shatner noticed this immediately and showed me that he had the same crooked finger on his right hand. He had gotten his playing ball as well; at least I recall that is what he told me. We had a nice conversation. I asked Mr. Shatner if he was planning on making more *Star Trek* episodes. He was hoping that the show would continue but he was not too sure. We just spent a little time making small talk and getting to know each other.

It was clear that Mr. Shatner was afraid the studio felt that the *Star Trek* Series was saturated and overdone and would not continue. I told him I was disappointed and felt there were a lot of people out there who still had a lot of interest in seeing more of the *Star Trek* series. He felt that this was the case as well, and some of his coworkers felt this way, but what could they do? He just did not feel certain it would happen. I was quite hopeful that the series was not finished.

We talked about many things with Mr. Shatner that day. It was a gorgeous morning, the fog lying so low over the valley that it was like a warm, thick blanket keeping the city below cozy and sleepy. It was a wonderful hour of enjoyable conversation with Mr. Shatner and the time flew by.

We finally got to work and took his measurements and pictures. I had him pose in a wicker chair to simulate Captain Kirk in his chair on the Starship Enterprise. I told him we'd move the chair around for different angles to get the different views of his face and body. We did not have an actual swivel chair to work with. Mr. Shatner was extremely cooperative and stood up over and over, moving his wicker chair in the same direction ever so slightly each time, while trying to assume the same pose and expression each time. I got eye-level photographs of each pose, two, three-quarter views, side views, a perfect profile, and all the way back around to the front. I took many more photos of his body, seated, and with different angles as well.

I carefully noted his precise eye color, hair color and all body dimensions and measurements. On every figure we did, I got specific dimensions, including hairline to the chin (if the hairline was receding, I would get one measurement with the receding hairline to the chin and then I would also get the measurement of a line directly across the eyebrows down to the chin). This would help with precision on all of my wax figures each time by taking the same type of measurements and by making sure the complete height and width with calipers of the face were done. It helped me get perfect side views, and every imaginable angle of the head. We successfully finished our measurements with Mr. Shatner using all of my standard protocol.

We also concurred after this meeting that we should never assume that movie stars want to be called by their first name unless they invite you to do so. Otherwise, we must address them appropriately as Mister, Misses or Miss So-and-So and nothing else unless we are told ahead of time, or they tell us directly what they wish to be called. If you put yourself in a star's shoes, imagine having a total stranger walk up to you and call you by your first name, acting as if he or she knows you personally. It would make you feel uncomfortable at the very least, especially with the history of celebrity stalkers out there. The sittings were always more relaxed when we called a celebrity by his or her first name, but this was just a matter of their personal preference and not up to us. This was crucial information that we had gathered and would prove to be priceless down the road on many occasions. We always think we know the stars because we've seen them so many times, but we are actually perfect strangers to them.

We graciously thanked Mr. Shatner for a wonderful time and great conversation, the fantastic cookies and Chicory coffee, and for his professionalism. He and his wife had been so very accommodating and gracious. The cookies will enter into our story more later on, because Mr. Shatner's wife was an amazing cookie baker. We bid Mr. Shatner goodbye and returned to the museum, getting quickly back to work. That was one of the first sittings we did with a star after the Palace of Living Art was completed.

Next we come to the other characters of *Star Trek*. In order to do a full, impressive exhibit we needed all the major characters from the show. We received permission and continued with this project. First we did Walter Koenig (1936 to present), who played Chekov on the show. I went to Mr. Koenig's home with our publicist, photographer and driver of our Rolls Royce. The homes that these stars lived in at that time were nothing compared to what they must live in today after *Star Trek's* tremendous, ongoing success. We set up everything and got the session going with him. I mentioned to Mr. Koenig that I had numerous photographs of Mr. Shatner, including publicity stills and other pictures.

When working on a wax sculpture, my approach was to not only use detailed measurements and photographs of the stars from every imaginable angle for the sculpture, but to also collect other photographs of the star. I'd get publicity stills from the motion pictures they had been in, publication shots from books in bookstores and magazines and any other pictures I could get my hands on. All of these pictures would help me out when working on a project.

I recalled from my work with Mr. Shatner and in the photographs I had collected that he was not a very large person. He had a nice build and was somewhat slender, but in some of the pictures he looked very large, almost overweight. I had no idea what created the illusion that Mr. Shatner looked larger in some photographs. Sometimes he appeared to weigh over 200 pounds and other times he appeared quite slim. It was all across the board and rather confusing.

I asked Walter Koenig about the variances in Mr. Shatner's weight and why he looked to be different sizes in these photographs. Mr. Koenig looked down, somewhat embarrassed, and in defense of Mr. Shatner explained that he was not sure but he supposed many of us had ups and downs with our weight issues. I could tell I was not going to get any more information about this matter from him. All in all, we had a very nice measurement session with Walter Koenig.

I went back to my office at Movieland and got back to work. By this time, I had gotten to the point where I felt I really belonged there. It had been a long time since I had done the outdoor billboard advertising. It was a good feeling that I took great pride in and I was truly enjoying my new career.

We continued our routine wax sculpting. The next interview we set up was for James Doohan (1936 to present), the actor who played the engineer of the Starship Enterprise named "Scotty." Mr. Doohan was the only original member of the *Star Trek* series not to provide his voice for the animated version of the show, although he did write some episodes for it and enjoyed writing for television during his career, including an episode of Star Trek. Mr. Doohan was extremely nice and cooperative when we did his interview, measurements and photo session. Everything seemed to go extremely well. At the end of the interview I asked him, "How shall I make Mr. Shatner's body? Sometimes he seems very large in photographs and sometimes he looks slender. What do you think? Shall I have him perceived as larger or slender?" Mr. Doohan looked a little defensive of Mr. Shatner and he would not help me out either.

Up next was DeForest Kelley (1920-1999) who played Dr. McCoy ("Bones"). His wife (Carolyn Dowling) was there, too, and she was expecting a baby at the time. This interview also went smoothly. He was an extremely pleasant fellow. I later found out that DeForest Kelley was born in Atlanta, Georgia but had spent a bit of time with his uncle in Long Beach, California, before deciding to move to Hollywood permanently to become an actor. I decided to ask him about Mr. Shatner's body size, hoping he would be the one to acquiesce and help me out. Up to this point, none of Mr. Shatner's co-stars would help me out. I just wanted to know what size to make Mr. Shatner's wax figure! It was a simple question. But again, Mr. Kelley was tight-lipped about the issue and shrugged out of the question.

As the crew of the Starship Enterprise was interviewed, measured and photographed, no one wanted to come forward and help give me any direction with regards to what size to make Captain Kirk's body. Large, robust? Thin, slender? I was puzzled, because I had seen it so many different ways.

Next up was Mr. Leonard Nimoy (1931 to present), who played Spock (or S'chn-T' Gaii Spock, son of S'chn-T' Gaii Sarek -- of Skon and Solkar -- of Vulcan). Mr. Nimoy played the role of a Vulcan (an alien) from the planet Vulcan. We went to his house. Mr. Nimoy was quite nice and I felt comfortable talking with him from the get go. I told him that I was interested in how the ears were put on him. He told me that he had a pair of the ears in his home and in fact, he'd put them on ME! So Mr. Nimoy proceeded to put the Vulcan ears on yours truly. I looked in the mirror and saw myself with Vulcan ears. It was a great moment for me to look in the mirror and see myself as a Vulcan! I just needed the bowl hair cut. I wish I had a picture of this priceless moment.

Mr. Nimoy, being such a gracious host, gave me lots of great information about how things worked on their set, and the intricacies of it all. I brought up the subject of Mr. Shatner again. Leonard Nimoy and William Shatner were very close friends. This time, I got a different response. Mr. Nimoy just started laughing, and quite heartily. Then he asked me if I was going to interview George Takei, who played the character named Sulu. He told me to check with Mr. Takei and left it at that. I felt that Mr. Takei would be my last chance to get a real answer before having to go back to the source, or make an executive decision.

George Takei (1937 to present) played Lieutenant Sulu and was very warm and friendly during our interview. I asked him about Mr. Shatner's physique after measuring and taking his photographs. I told him he was my last resort to find out about what size to make Mr. Shatner's figure. I told him my dilemma was based on the fact that I had seen so very many photographs of Mr. Shatner in various media and on television, yet they all appeared to vary greatly in size. Sometimes he looked smaller and slender, other times he looked large, even quite muscular, almost looking to be over two hundred pounds. I explained that I was not sure which way to go with Captain Kirk's wax figure and needed his help.

Mr. Takei started laughing his head off. He said he would tell me. I was thrilled! "You just happened in on the great secret of the Star Trek team," Mr. Takei chuckled. I was confused. He repeated that this was the great secret of the show. He then proceeded to divulge to me that Mr. Shatner was hooked on cookies. He loved to drink coffee with these wonderful cookies that his wife would bake. He was so into cookies that he just couldn't stop himself. He was a bona fide cookie-aholic!

We both laughed heartily at this information. I asked Mr. Takei how the directors allowed Mr. Shatner to let his weight go up and down so much due to his cookie habit. Mr. Takei said that they did not allow it, and that it was not fine with them. They had to put a stop to it because it would halt production for a few weeks at a time. He said that although Mr. Shatner was able to drop large quantities of weight rather quickly whenever necessary, it was becoming too much of a problem.

I asked Mr. Takei how Mr. Shatner could get cookies all day if the directors were trying to monitor his weight and food intake for his role. He replied that Mr. Shatner had cookies stashed all over the Starship *Enterprise*'s bridge! Mr. Takei said, "There were boxes of cookies everywhere: cookies in corners, cookies in drawers, cookies in all of our boxes where we stored our characters' instruments; cookies just everywhere. He sneaked them in and there you have it." Mr. Takei started laughing again at divulging to me the "Great Secret" of the *Star Trek* set. I laughed as well and was pleased that I finally knew the reason his weight fluctuated.

Then George Takei went on to advise me that I should make Mr. Shatner's wax figure with a more slender shape, the way the show's directors wanted him portrayed. That should keep everyone happy. Mr. Takei wanted his friend to look good, so he had told me the secret for Mr. Shatner's benefit. I agreed to this wise advice and thanked him.

The set came off without a hitch. Everyone looked great, and in fact, later on, a larger and more elaborate set of the Enterprise bridge was built. A commercial was filmed there at one time and the cameraman told me that he could not tell the figures were wax when looking through the camera's lens. That was a great compliment to me, one that I will never forget. And of course, *Star Trek* went on for many, many more years with great success including several motion pictures and other retail items. It was and continues to be a huge hit, never to be repeated. Trekkies are everywhere! After we finished *Star Trek*, we went back to our regular business of tending to the museum.

The impressive wax likenesses of the crew and Movieland set of the Starship Enterprise's bridge from the Star Trek TV series, which brought Logan many compliments including one from the director of the series itself.

Logan visiting the Movieland tourist attraction where you could take a photo with the wax likeness of "Spock" from *Star Trek*. *Photo taken at Movieland Wax Museum.*

Some of the major stars of *Star Trek* and their wax likenesses at Movieland, with Mr. Gene Roddenberry, standing with Mr. Joe Prevatil, one of the managers of Movieland; *Photography by Norton.*

Another great photo showing William Shatner and Leonard Nimoy
and how closely they resemble their wax likenesses that Logan created.
*Photography by Norton.*

# Chapter 9

## Remodeling Movieland and More.

When you first walked in to Movieland, you would see the famous film director who directed dozens and dozens of major motion pictures, D.W. Griffith (1875-1948). Mr. Griffith's wax figure was revolving around on a turntable with his arms out as if he were directing movies around the museum. Instead of one giant room full of sculptures, Mr. Parkinson had decided to make it appear as if Mr. Griffith were directing various films around the room with the various wax sculptures in different sets around the space's circumference. In the center, however, it was just a large, open, carpeted space. You could see everything all at once from the center.

In addition to the vast improvements to the wax figures that I made, Mr. Parkinson had finally decided to make the museum a much more interesting place for the spectators. By putting in walls of mirrors around each set, it created a type of labyrinth. A person would go through each set and see it with all the mirrors reflecting the different angles for that individual set. This made the museum much more intricate and compartmentalized -- a true adventure for the museum guest. It was easier to focus on each set and each sculpture individually. It also created the illusion of a larger museum and a bigger space. That was the beginning of the modern Movieland Wax Museum.

When having sittings with celebrities in preparation for creating their wax figures, there are many important factors involved. You need their specific clothing size, body measurements, as well as weight and height measurements for costumes and for the wax figures. Accurate measurements and information are vital. Ideally, you also need a tailor or seamstress who has experience working with each particular actor and who knows these actors' idiosyncrasies. If the star's measurements are not up-to-date or available, it is necessary for me, the wax artist, to take his or her measurements.

The many celebrities whom I had the pleasure to meet were always very cooperative when I needed to take their measurements for the creation of their wax figures. Of course, they are very familiar with all the personal and physical attention that goes with their trade and they are used to being pampered and fussed over in many ways. They work with hairdressers, makeup artists, tailors, personal trainers and the like on a regular basis. They get measured, fitted, photographed, made up with many different looks, their hair gets twisted and cut and colored and sometimes covered with wigs or hats, and they partake in intense, rigorous physical routines and workout programs on an ongoing basis. They work hard at their physical appearance. This is just part of their job. And this made it a little easier for me to work with them when it was necessary to take their measurements, photographs or to confirm the measurements I already had.

When taking measurements, things can get interesting and even tricky with the stars. People often asked me which specific measurements the stars were most interested in having taken. Well, of course they wanted the wax figure to look the best it could look. They were very forthcoming with giving us measurements, but what they gave us may not always have been the most current or accurate information.

If a female star at one point had a super-tiny waist, this was the waist measurement she would usually give us for her wax figure (whether or not she had gained a few – or more – pounds since her waist was at its tiniest). Same thing with chest measurements on males and females; the largest measurements they ever had (within reason) were usually given to us for their wax figures, regardless of whether they were currently valid.

Due to these discriminating measurements, it was always best and most accurate if we could physically measure the stars ourselves before partaking in their wax figure sculpting, or we could try to get the star's more current measurements from a tailor or seamstress who had recently measured them. When done correctly with the proper body proportions and measurements to fit the head/face of the star, you could turn the wax figure all the way around and you could still tell from the side or from behind which star you were looking at. Everyone had his or her own unique look from every angle. Even accuracy in the wax figure's hands, feet, and legs were unique and crucial for believability. Specific birthmarks, veins, and freckles; all those things and more were significant for each unique individual's look. It took much more than sculpting a face to make a wax figure!

Many times if you went out to the star's home or location of choice to take his or her measurements and approached them in a very professional, business-like manner, you would continue to be treated with respect for the duration of the working relationship. Obviously, their physical appearance in many instances had a lot to do with their celebrity status. As a result, it was usually not too overbearing for a star to have separate measurements taken for their wax figure to be sculpted. In fact, many found it quite a flattering occasion.

# Chapter 10

## The King of Comedy, Jerry Lewis

One of the most interesting fittings we had was for Jerry Lewis (1926 to present), known by many as "The King of Comedy." We went with the publicist and our photographer and Jack drove the Rolls Royce to Jerry Lewis' estate. As we entered his enormous home, we realized he was living in the famous producer Louis B. Mayer's (1884-1957) former home. The entrance hall itself was beyond belief with an amazing spiral staircase. Mr. Mayer is generally cited as the creator of the "star system" within Metro-Goldwyn-Mayer (MGM) in its golden years. The star system means a movie star (cine star or film star) is well-known (a celebrity), or famous, for his or her starring or leading roles in motion pictures. So basically, Mr. Mayer created the term "star" referring to a famous person in the movie industry, which was the subject of most of our wax figures.

We were met by Jerry's representative. Lovetta always made the arrangements for the star's representative to meet us at the pre-arranged location. His representative told us he would come downstairs momentarily. We waited a few moments and sure enough, Jerry Lewis started to come down the stairs to greet us, dressed in a very impeccable and classy suit. Halfway down the stairs, Jerry Lewis stopped and said, "How would you like me to be dressed for your pictures?"

We confirmed with him that we had already agreed beforehand through his representative that he was to be portrayed in his wax figure as *The Nutty Professor* (1963) aka Professor Julius Kelp. So we told him to dress like *The Nutty Professor*. He went back upstairs and shortly after that, he came back down to us. This time, it was *The Nutty Professor* that we saw before our eyes. He had his false teeth in place, and everything was just right to a tee.

Jerry was more than ready to get started for his pictures; we found an appropriate location and had our photographer get started. This particular photographer named Mr. Klein was the one who regularly took visitors' photographs with Frankenstein on the Frankenstein set at the wax museum. He was a very folksy fellow and made the error of calling Jerry Lewis "Jerry." That was a big mistake.

Mr. Lewis did not say much but after a while, after being called "Jerry" so informally over and over, he got up and looked at the photographer's beloved camera. Looking the photographer square in the eyes, Mr. Lewis said, "Now where did you get this piece of junk? This is a cheap camera for what you need to do today. It's almost an embarrassment for me to have you use the likes of this camera on me today for this photo shoot! Couldn't you have done better than this for me?" He made the photographer wilt rather quickly.

Mr. Lewis sat down and they finished the photo shoot in near silence. This was the photographer's first lesson in how to treat a star. He learned the hard way that you do not call a star by his or her first name. By contrast, I addressed him as "Mr. Lewis" the entire time and he treated me equally with the utmost respect and gratitude.

After the photo shoot was finished and we were waiting for Jerry Lewis to return to say goodbye and wrap things up, I went and looked around the entrance hall of his home. Just taking a quick peek into some of the adjacent rooms, I noticed that Mr. Lewis had the most incredible collection of clown figurines that I could have ever imagined. I was staring at hundreds of clown memorabilia, very funny, of all shapes and sizes, everywhere. It was unbelievable. His home was definitely unique and stunning, down to the swimming pool and grounds.

Mr. Lewis also agreed to give us some of the props that went along with his costume for our final wax sculpture. He came back downstairs dressed in regular clothes this time, and handed us quite a selection of items from *The Nutty Professor* for our museum and sculpture, including false teeth, a tie, and other items. These were parts of the original costume and we thanked him profusely.

When Mr. Lewis showed up for the dedication/opening there was a huge group of fans there to meet him. He brought his wife and a friend. He got on the set next to his figure, made some jokes, posed and just had a lot of fun. The crowd really enjoyed this opening very much. There was always a large banner outside, in front of the museum announcing what the dedication/event was for that day, which star it was in honor of, the details and the time. When Mr. Parkinson first started doing set dedications, the crowds were a bit sparse. However, as time went on and the set dedications became a more popular event, the crowds grew larger and larger and the events were quite impressive. Every time we finished a big sitting and opening for a star's wax figure, we looked forward to finding another star.

Mr. Jerry Lewis with his wax likeness that Logan created
from the movie *The Nutty Professor.*

# Chapter 11

## Sammy Davis, Jr.

Not long after the sitting with Jerry Lewis, we got word from Lovetta Kramer that she had confirmed with Sammy Davis, Jr.'s (1925-1990) representative that Mr. Davis was interested in having his wax figure in the museum. Arrangements were made and I was told that we had been given a date to go for a sitting with Mr. Sammy Davis, Jr.

We got a different photographer to do this particular sitting and we all went out in our limousine to Mr. Davis' house. His home was heavily guarded with uniformed, armed guards at the front entrance. They checked us out and got the approval to let us through, and we went into his estate. This was quite a place. We were met at the front door by Mr. Davis' lovely agent, who invited us inside right away. We went inside and we were offered a nice drink while we waited for Mr. Davis. This was a very early morning appointment because of how busy Mr. Davis was at that particular time.

His home was full of wealth and class. In particular, we noticed that he had the newest type of home entertainment which consisted of a mirrored, projection-type television which was recessed below the floor and would rise up on a mechanism when he wanted to watch it. This was certainly cutting edge technology for the time. The giant screen, when projected upon the wall, made it feel as if you were in a movie theatre. He also had gorgeous furniture throughout his home.

Mr. Davis' agent went away for a moment and when she returned we were told he'd be joining us very soon. It took quite a long time and several trips back and forth to his private rooms for his agent to get Mr. Davis to actually show up for us to do the pictures and measurements. As we found out later, she had tried without success to wake him up several times because he had painted the town the night before and was quite hungover! He was not pleased about being awakened from his hangover one little bit that morning.

Now when he joined us, Mr. Davis was clearly grumpy. He was trying to put in his glass eye and was somewhat uncomfortable about it, not getting it in quite right. He looked very disheveled and exhausted. We could tell that he could definitely have used a few more hours of sleep. He told Mrs. Kramer, our publicity representative, to have us leave. He turned to her and without hesitation said, "Get them outta here! Please get them all out! No way!"

Mrs. Kramer was very good at her job. She stayed extremely polite and pleasant and tried to calm him down, knowing how he felt the entire time and handling it delicately. She told him gently that he, his agents and everyone had all agreed with this sitting for his wax figure to be made and placed at Movieland. She reminded him of the honor it was and how much he wanted this to happen, and how many of his fans would be thrilled about this. The entire time, she addressed him respectfully as "Mr. Davis" to which he responded positively. She was very diplomatic and it worked like a charm.

She also reminded him that everyone had made arrangements to come out very early that morning to accommodate *his* schedule, and that everyone had waited patiently while he slept late, without complaint. Mrs. Kramer also reminded Mr. Davis that the entire sitting would not take very long at all, after which he could return to his rest. We all agreed to do things as quickly as possible to accommodate Mr. Davis. He finally agreed after everyone treated him very nicely, despite his previous outburst.

I decided to do the fitting in one of the rooms that led off of one of the long hallways. It was a gorgeous room lined with exquisite furniture and was somewhat private, but wide enough to get the task at hand finished.

Mr. Davis went back to his room and finally returned a little while later. He was still trying to get his glass eye into the right position and still not having much luck. He said to me, "What do you want?" and I said, "Mr. Davis, we have agreed that your wax figure will be on the stage with Mr. Sinatra and you'll be laughing, cracking jokes and hanging out like old buddies do. What would you be doing if that were the situation?"

He did not say a word. He eyed me square on, walked right past me down to the end of the hallway and past all of his very beautiful furniture, to the end of the room. There at the end of the room was a spectacular, classy bar. The bar was positioned so if you came inside this room from the outdoor patio and pool area, you could approach it and have a drink. It was set up just beautifully, fully stocked, crystal; the works.

Mr. Davis went to the bar and fixed himself a Manhattan. He made the drink with precision, using the perfect glass for such a drink and mixing the ingredients with practiced hands. He took his drink, and walked toward me; in fact, he walked right at me. I was wondering what he was going to do next. I was almost uneasy because the moment was so unpredictable. Mr. Davis kept coming and coming right at me, steady as could be under the circumstances. He walked right up to me, completely even with where I was standing, and quickly turned, breezing right past me, not saying a word. He kept his eyes on me the entire time. It was the strangest feeling that came over me.

He went right back to the exact spot where he had been initially standing when I asked him what pose he would be in if he was in the situation that I'd described with Frank Sinatra onstage. He stood there, faced me and got himself right into the exact, perfect position that he would have been in had he been hanging out with the Rat Pack, cracking jokes and shooting the breeze. He looked as if he were right in that moment, just perfectly.

The photographer was ready, jumped over and quickly started snapping pictures. Mr. Davis got himself positioned just exactly right with the glass in his hand as if he were making a toast. He assumed a very relaxed position and looked to be enjoying himself very much. He kind of put a slight, half-smile on his face. It looked nice but I very politely asked him if he could just give me a tiny bit more of a smile for the photographer. Mr. Davis turned his head, ever-so-slightly, and looked me square in the eyes again. He said directly to me, "That's all you get!" It must be said that he had followed directions as to the full round of pictures that we needed to complete the sitting.

Mr. Davis' tailor had given us his measurements, so we did not take any more of his time that day besides some very basic measurements. We took pictures of his entire body and face during the session. We took pictures of the star's face while he sat in our swivel chair, with all the different angles necessary. When we took body measurements, we would have the star stand up just the way we wanted it. They would have to hold the position and slightly turn and we'd also get all angles of their body dimensions. This worked extremely well and Mr. Davis cooperated once we got him started. The whole situation worked out very smoothly. His wax figure eventually turned out to be one of the very best and most realistic ones that I ever created.

With that, we took whatever pictures we could get and went on our merry way. The pictures worked out just perfectly. I figured out later why Mr. Davis did not want to smile anymore. He had practiced smiling so much in his career, over and over, just to look natural. You have to remember, Mr. Davis had a glass eye. He could only smile so much with his eyes squinting before there was a distorted or fake look that would overcome his face due to his glass eye. So he was actually doing all of us a big favor by not stretching his smile any further that day. He knew how to look natural, and I figured it out later on down the road. He knew his limitations and without saying it, he had showed me what they were as well. His tailor had cooperated with us perfectly. Mr. Davis always ordered larger neck sizes than he needed in order to add the illusion of a few extra pounds. And most importantly, his wax figure turned out splendidly.

There has been a lot written about the legendary Rat Pack. One of the stories that really stands out for me is when Frank Sinatra threatened to not perform unless they let Sammy stay at the Sands Hotel along with the rest of The Pack. In those days they did not allow black people to stay at the Sands, much less even walk through the front entrance of the hotel.

Of course they had no problem with Sammy performing there but he would have to stay elsewhere. It always impressed me that Mr. Sinatra stood up to the management and insisted Mr. Davis be treated with the utmost respect and no differently than anyone else. The management agreed. Mr. Davis was accepted and included with them, and the rest is history.

I happened to be on vacation with my family when the opening of Mr. Davis' wax figure was scheduled. I heard it went off wonderfully and he had an extremely large crowd there to see Mr. Davis and his wax figure dedicated. One of the guests in the audience that day was none other than Mr. Davis' father who he absolutely revered and adored. His Dad had raised him and had also been the one to help him become successful in his career, having come from a career in Vaudeville himself. He had quite a successful two-man act for many years. Sammy grew up watching his father from the sidelines, learning how to perform.

Being constantly on the move, Sammy never got the opportunity to go to school, not even Kindergarten. Everything he had ever learned about life and performing was learned on the road alongside his father.

As Sammy grew up, his Dad began to see how multi-talented he was and ultimately became one third of his father's Vaudeville act. They became the Will Mastin Trio which included Will Mastin, Sammy Davis, Sr. and Sammy Davis, Jr. They performed singing and dancing during the 1920's through the 1960's. Since they started in the 1920's, in order to overcome the child labor laws, Sammy was often presented to the public as "Silent Sam the Dancing Midget." He would walk around backstage with a cigar in one hand and a girl under his arm.

Sammy literally grew up on the stage and picked up all the key nuances from Vaudeville, gaining invaluable experience as a regular performer in the Trio. As mentioned earlier, he had multiple talents. He could play the piano, horns, drums and many other instruments. He could also imitate famous actors so well that you would swear the person was there. He was also an expert dancer and soft shoe man. In fact, Mr. Davis (and others) did the dance step that was later called the "Moonwalk" many, many times on the stage. He also had quite a great voice and became a singer in his own right. He was a star on his own, and broke away while his father continued to do his act. Through it all, Sammy Davis, Jr. and his father remained close and supportive of each other.

Getting back to the Movieland dedication, when Sammy Davis, Jr. saw his figure on the stage with his Manhattan glass in his hand, he grabbed another Manhattan glass from Movieland's bar and got himself into the same pose as his wax likeness up on the stage. He told someone to bring his father in so he could show the figure off. He asked his father, "Well Dad, what do you think of this figure?"

The old man looked at him carefully, and looked at the two Manhattan glasses in their hands, and he turned to his son and said, "Well, son, if this wax figure could sing Mr. Bo Jangles, you'd be out of business!" The crowd erupted in laughter, right along with Mr. Davis, Jr. and his father. It was quite a special night for the museum and also for two Sammys. Truth be told, I was very honored and complimented by Mr. Davis, Sr.'s comments about how realistic he thought his son's wax likeness was.

The real Sammy Davis, Jr. (left) stands next to his wax likeness, created by Logan.

The wax likenesses created by Logan of Frank Sinatra and Sammy Davis, Jr. stand side-by-side, as if performing, at Movieland.

# Chapter 12

## Museum Pranksters

In between the measurements and sittings, the Movieland life went on and was very enjoyable for everyone who worked there or was associated with it. Everyone I have ever spoken to who worked at Movieland Wax Museum back in the day remembers what a wonderful experience it was.

Back then, we had such a wonderful group of supportive and extremely nice people to associate with on many occasions. We just had a ball, and believe me, you just never knew what to expect when you were involved with the entertainment industry. So many interesting things happened at any given moment. You truly never knew what would come next.

One unsuspecting day I was walking through the museum while heading towards the rear of the building when I heard a terrible, horrific noise. A young woman was screaming at the top of her lungs and running wildly through the museum! She had her hands in the air, flailing about. She ran right past me in a blur at top speed.

I became worried myself because I had absolutely no idea what was going on. I rushed to the front of the museum. I got there just about the same time she did. She did not stop or say anything. Her screams pierced my spine, they were so chilling. This poor lady ran right out the front door of the museum, still screaming, apparently scared to death. I had no idea what had happened to her to cause such fear. I was bewildered and very concerned.

Mr. Perez, one of our managers at the museum, came hurrying around to the museum front trying to follow her out but she had left the building too quickly. He said, "Where did that woman go, Logan?" I pointed to the parking lot. She continued screaming her head off as she disappeared into the parking lot and left in her car with a screech before we could even have a chance to talk with her. Mr. Perez tried to catch her but to no avail.

I turned to Mr. Perez and asked him what in the world had scared that poor woman to death. Mr. Perez proceeded to explain to me that some young teenage prankster had really pulled off a good one. He said, "You know the scary set of Dracula back there with Helen Chandler and Bella Lugosi? The one with the old rough trees, dark moonlight and shadows with tombstones?" I knew of the exact set and nodded. This particular set had a huge, ominous casket lying right on the ground. It was a very eerie set. There were many shadows and dark corners, with tombstones lurking all about.

Well, apparently some young punk kid had discovered this set and had decided that he was going to use it to his advantage and have some fun. He had laid himself down near the casket where Bella Lugosi's wax figure stood. The boy had taken off his hat and cocked it over one eye so as to look spooky, and proceeded to stay on the ground quietly, next to the casket. He laid there as if he were a dead person, very still and silent.

A couple of innocent and older, female patrons of the museum were walking by. It was intentionally darker in this part of the museum to create an eerie effect for this particular set. As these women approached the Dracula set, they stopped to look things over. It was almost as if Bella Lugosi was right beneath their feet as they stood there, checking things out. Suddenly, the young man let out a very low, deep, groaning moan. Then he sat up and made a very scary face, beckoning to them with his arms. They freaked out and this is when one of the ladies started screaming her head off, running straight out of the museum with her arms up in the air.

They did catch the young prankster and gave him a hard time, telling him he was not supposed to be messing around on the museum sets. He admitted his wrongdoing but also admitted that the opportunity to do what he had done was just too much fun and too good to pass up; it was a made-to-order deal. But he apologized sincerely and we sent him off on his way. To be this scared and upset, we at the museum reasoned that this woman had probably gone through a terrible experience dealing with death recently and it just hit her hard.

Although there was a bit of humor about the situation, we all felt badly for these poor ladies. We warned the young fellow to not do it again or we'd have to call the Keystone Kops on him. He got the picture after that.

# Chapter 13

## Romancing a Wax Figure
## and
## Gina Lollobrigida

One of our Keystone Kops used to do rounds at the end of each business day and check out the museum to make sure everything was in order before we closed up. When you turned the lights off in the museum at night, it became a very frightening place. You had Frankenstein and lots of eerie figures, especially with all the mirrors. It was quite spooky at night.

One bank at a time, section by section, they would turn the lights off, finally ending at the beautiful Gina Lollobrigida (1927 to present) set. Gina's figure had on a very sexy, black negligee. The set was from a scene in one of her great pictures, *Strange Bedfellows* (1965). This was a hilarious love story that she played next to Rock Hudson (1925-1985). Gina was a gorgeous Italian bombshell.

On one particularly interesting evening, a Keystone Kop and I were walking through the museum together talking and joking as the lights were being turned off. We were not alone.

It turned out that a very inebriated man was wandering around the museum, unbeknownst to us at the time. This drunken fellow had just passed by the John Wayne set, which was directly next to and around the corner from the *Strange Bedfellows* set of Gina Lollobrigida.

We continued turning off the lights at this point. The drunken gentleman continued stumbling his way through the museum, making his way out much more slowly than the lights were being turned off.

As our inebriated "friend" turned the final corner while the lights continued to go off, he saw the sexy Gina Lollobrigida wax figure lying very suggestively in her sexy, black lingerie on a dramatic chaise lounge. This man was just tipsy enough to think that Gina looked like she was enticing him over. He then walked right on to the set and had the nerve to lie right down beside her on the chaise lounge! He was practically spooning the wax figure, putting his arm around her. To this day we are not sure exactly how long this romantic interlude went on before we interrupted it.

As the Keystone Kop and I came around the corner to complete the night's closing, we saw the drunken man's back leg right up next to Gina Lollobrigida's wax figure. When we walked up closer to the set, we at first could only see the man's legs. Eventually, as our eyes adjusted to the darkness, we could see the man was actually snuggling up to her and trying to take Gina's wax figure's lingerie off with his hands down her clothes. He had also raised her lingerie way up high, revealing her sexy leg. He was having quite a great time there with this wax figure, indeed. Of course, this was a sight to behold! The man was a piece of work and seemed to be enjoying himself, unaware of who was watching.

The Keystone Kop said, "My God, Logan! Look. What in earth is this guy trying to do?" in a most exasperated voice. He turned to the drunk man and demanded, "Tell me, what in the hell do you think you're doing, sir?"

The drunk man replied, slurring his words terribly, "Oh, I'm just tryin' to have a lil' bit a fun here, sir…" not even realizing what he was *really* doing!

He was given a very harsh warning and immediately told to leave the set and the museum lest we should phone the police on him. The drunk guy resisted at first, and the Keystone Kop (who was much bigger than the drunk fellow) grabbed him firmly and made him get up off the figure and leave as I stayed with him to make sure there wasn't any trouble.

However, the Keystone Kop had to be extremely careful when getting this drunken fellow off of Gina's wax figure for fear of breaking it. He took great care and used his strength and savvy to gingerly unravel this man off of this attractive wax figure. Afterwards, I carefully placed the sexy lingerie back on the wax figure in its proper position the way it was originally meant to appear. It turned out that Gina was completely intact and unharmed… well, other than the fact that a drunken stranger had totally molested the poor wax figure!

I am not one hundred percent certain whether or not the Keystone Kop actually called the police on this man who had consumed way too much alcohol and crossed the line with a wax figure, but if he did, I know that he left the best part of the story off the record from the police because I never heard anything else about it. But we had quite a laugh from that one.

When Gina Lollobrigida came to Movieland to see her own set and to dedicate it, she came up with quite a cute and interesting idea. She wanted to put on lingerie just like her wax figure had on and get into the set, laying right down on the chaise lounge next to her wax figure. It was a beautiful set with lots of red velour.

So Gina got into the set and posed with her wax figure. It was very adorable and made for some great photo opportunities. Gina showed a huge interest in the set, how it was made and how everything worked in the entire museum. It was quite a compliment to see how fascinated she was with the set and the museum itself, and we were quite happy about that.

The lovely Gina Lollobrigida poses behind her wax likeness at Movieland.

# Chapter 14

## Dick Martin, "Come As You Are Dressed" Party

One morning in the museum, Lovetta came around and told us about two figures we needed to start working on next. We asked her who they were and she told us it was Dan Rowan (1922-1987) and Dick Martin (1922-2008) from the *Laugh-In* (1967-1973) bunch. We needed to get them set up, fitted and measured. We made our appointments and it was planned that we would first meet with Dick Martin at his home. Mr. Martin was the talented television comedian and director who achieved television immortality as the co-host in *Rowan & Martin's Laugh-In* comedy series.

We got the Rolls Royce out and Jack, myself and the whole gang headed out for Dick Martin's home. Upon arriving I noticed one of the cars in his garage had a girl's name on the license plate. A gorgeous woman opened the front door and I figured right away that she was Mr. Martin's girl. I asked her if that was her name on the license plate of that splendid car, and she confirmed that it was. She kindly offered us drinks. I had a lovely Manhattan while we waited for Mr. Martin.

Finally, Mr. Martin appeared in his bathrobe on the mezzanine floor up above us and said in a welcoming tone, "Hello! Hello! Hello! What is it you'd like me to wear?" I suggested to him that a tuxedo would be splendid, since he did so many of his appearances in tuxes. He said he would be back down in about five minutes.

Sure enough, he promptly came back down, ready to go. We got him set up on a swivel chair and it worked perfectly for taking photographs at all angles. He was extremely professional and cooperative. When I called him Mr. Martin he said to just call him "Dick."

I asked him what kind of expression he would like to be represented with in his wax figure. He told me that since he was always acting surprised, he would like me to portray him just that way, with a wide-eyed look. We thought it was perfect and very suitable for his personality. He was just the nicest fellow.

While we were packing up our things after the session was finished, I complimented him on the beautiful doors leading into his stunning dining room. His dining room was set up for an amazing dinner party that night, complete with a beautiful candelabra and tableware. We could smell the roast that his cook was working on in the kitchen. He told us that he was having a "Come as You are Dressed" dinner party that night.

I was curious as to what "Come as You are Dressed" meant for a dinner party. Dick went on to explain to me that the latest trend in Hollywood at the time was to call people up first thing in the morning, and tell them they are invited to a dinner party that night but they must come to the party wearing exactly what they are dressed in the moment they are called and invited. I thought that was a very fun and cute idea. He had about twenty five guests coming that night. The entire house was being fixed up for the event.

I looked out of the dining room windows and could see a lovely cabana and pool outside. Being on the top of a mountainous area, he had an amazing view from the dining room as well. All the lights below were stunning as was the view of all of Hollywood. I admired the doors once again and noticed they looked really old.

I asked Dick if the hinges were handmade. He admitted that the set of doors on either side of his dining room were two-hundred-years-old. He had bought them at an auction that was held after William Randolph Hearst passed away and Hearst Castle was vacated. They were attempting to sell surplus items that would not end up staying in Hearst Castle after it became open to the public. There were so many amazing things all over his home but many of these items were not labeled.

So the deal was that they had been put up at an auction called a "know nothing auction." You'd take a risk if you bid on an item because you would know nothing about it. It could be an amazing, authentic artifact from some part of the world, or it could be junk. But either way, if you wanted the item you would hope to be the high bidder. He thought it was fun and took his attorney there with him to bid.

When he saw this old, beat-up long box being put up for bid with no labels on it, he was intrigued. About two or three Hollywood people he knew were putting bids on it, mainly out of curiosity to see what was inside: trash or treasure. Well, after the final bid was made by his attorney, he ended up with this beat-up, old box. He said that he had paid about two thousand dollars for it.

When he opened the box later on, he found these gorgeous doors. They had been covered with many coats of paint, so he had to have them worked on to get stripped. The man who worked on the doors for him knew about the wood and how lovely it was. He also knew that the doors were over two hundred years old from the way they had been built.

They were lovingly cleaned up and restored to look almost like the original condition they had been in. They had handmade brass hinges on them and they were something very special. We were quite thankful for Dick taking the time to tell us the story of those lovely doors. We had such a fun time with him.

One last thing I remember about Dick Martin was the small bald spot on the back of his head. I had never noticed it before and he admitted that he never let it show on television. I asked him if he just used a simple little hairpiece and he replied (with a wink) that all he did was slap on a little shoe polish before they filmed and it worked out just fine! We laughed together about his little secret.

As he walked to the front door with me he said he had just come up with a great idea. He said when he had called everyone early in the morning to tell them to come as they were dressed before work, he was going to greet them at the door with his tuxedo on. It sounded like fun to me!

Dan Rowan (left) enjoys a moment with his co-host Dick Martin (right) and their wax likenesses that Logan Fleming created for Movieland from the TV show *Rowan & Martin's Laugh-In.*

# Chapter 15

## Dan Rowan

The following week we set up an appointment with Dick Martin's co-host of *Laugh-In,* Mr. Dan Rowan. Now this was also a very nice meeting, but entirely different from the one with Dick. Mr. Rowan was much straighter and a bit more serious. He was quite distinguished, a bit less comical, but extremely nice and classy.

As we entered Mr. Rowan's home, he was extremely courteous. He let me call him Mr. Rowan. We had some nice photographs taken of Mr. Rowan and talked with him about his wax figure and agreed upon his choice of expression.

I decided to go ahead and ask Mr. Rowan how he and Mr. Martin got into show business in the first place. I had heard they had been in a very popular, crowded bar and were so witty and clever with their jokes that the word had just gotten around. The owner was so impressed with their little "show" that he spread the word, and people would come in just to hear their jokes. It got to be such a big thing that the owner of the bar would almost advertise for them. That was the rumor I had heard, anyhow. Dan Rowan had always been known as the straight man and Dick Martin was the comedian. And Mr. Rowan confirmed this to be the truth about their start.

The *Rowan & Martin* Movieland dedication party for their wax figures went off swimmingly. They brought their wives and were just hilarious. At the dedication, they did a little bit where their wives were instructed to pick their favorite guy there. Dick Martin stood next to his wax figure and Dan Rowan stood next to his. Their wives immediately walked up to the wax figures instead of their actual husbands and put their arms around the wax figures! It was a hoot and a holler and everyone there had a great time. Their wives really helped make that party a ton of fun for the guests. There were some wonderful pictures taken from this event that were very entertaining. It was quite a tremendous dedication party, and their wax figures also turned out great.

# Chapter 16

## The
## Oldies
## but Goodies

One of the key reasons it was so fun to work at the wax museum was because of its owner and our boss, Mr. Allen Parkinson. He was very close personal friends with so many Hollywood people. One of his friends was Hal Roach (Harold Eugene "Hal" Roach, Sr; 1892-1992), the studio producer and director from the 1910's through the 1990's who knew all the classic stars of comedy, and the renowned Keystone Kops who made so many great movies at that time. This gave Mr. Parkinson an "in" to meet Laurel and Hardy, Charlie Chaplin, and many of the early greats.

Many of these early movie stars would come to the museum on a regular basis. They really had a lot of fun showing up, walking around and seeing all their counterparts from their time. One of the regular stars who showed up was the actress, Zasu Pitts (1894-1963). Sometimes her name was mispronounced but she would quickly correct whoever was mispronouncing it to say it like "Zay-Zoo" instead of "Zah-Zoo."

It turns out that Stan Laurel (1890-1965) of *Laurel and Hardy* (late 1920's – mid-1940's), co-star of one of the most popular comedy shows of the early-to-mid-Hollywood Classical Era, was a great friend of Mr. Parkinson's. He was the one who gave him permission to put the *Laurel and Hardy* set in the museum. This was shortly after Mr. Oliver Hardy (1892-1957) had passed away, sadly. In hopes of having a good memorial and recognition, Mr. Laurel had permitted this set to be created.

Ken Maynard (1895-1973), a former early cowboy movie superstar who had also performed with the Ringling Brothers Circus, could be seen regularly coming to the museum. Known for wearing a white cowboy hat and a very fancy shirt and having a pair of six-shooters, Ken Maynard appeared in more than ninety films from the 1920s to the mid-1940s. At first he was pointed out to me but after a while I could spot him every time he came to the museum. I never really got to know him, however.

Logan puts the wax head on his wax creation, a likeness of Stan Laurel, next to the wax figure of Oliver Hardy.

# Chapter 17

## Buster Keaton

Another great old-time comic was Mr. Buster Keaton (1895-1966). He was very close friends with Mr. Parkinson and would show up to so many of the dedications and events at the museum. It was always a treat to see him, and Mr. Parkinson loved to have him around. He added a lot of luster to the museum.

However, one thing that no one knew back then was that Buster Keaton was a very, very shy fellow. He had owned up to me privately about this fear. You would never have guessed this was the case after seeing some of his antics, especially some of the things he did during his old Civil War pictures. However, he was in fact painfully shy and intimidated by large crowds. In spite of his shyness, he was a very huge, popular star, one of the greatest comics of all time, and a great athlete.

When he confessed to me about this fear, I could tell that he was quite serious. When he came to the museum as a favor to Mr. Parkinson, he would oftentimes go directly into the men's room and kind of hide for a while, until he got up his nerve. It really took a lot out of him.

However, there was one time when Mr. Keaton actually could not leave the men's room and when he finally did, he just left the museum altogether. For some reason on that particular day, Buster Keaton just could not rack up the courage to face the people. But he sure did his best 99% of the time, and it was a delight to have him there at the museum when he was up to the task. I am truly honored to have met Mr. Buster Keaton, who was one of the nicest, most talented and memorable comics that ever graced the motion picture industry. He was truly a gem.

# Chapter 18

## Mary Pickford and the Museum Dedication

Mary Pickford (1892-1979) was also another star who came to the museum on a regular basis. In fact, she was among the stars that came out to dedicate the museum for Mr. Parkinson when it first opened its doors. In the year of 1909 alone, Mary Pickford appeared in fifty-one films! It was not unusual back in those days for stars to churn out several films per year, often even working on more than one picture at a time.

In fact, it was Ms. Mary Pickford who broke a bottle of champagne on the corner of the building for Movieland Wax Museum's initial dedication and grand opening. The actor Charles Buddy Rogers (1904-1999) was with her that night along with a host of other stars of the times. There were huge searchlights shining up into the night sky and the dedication of the museum was quite a major event. It attracted a very large number of people, and Mr. Parkinson was in his element.

Slim Summerville (1892-1946), the star who indirectly helped me get my job by proving I could improve his wax likeness, was best known for a series of feature-length comedy films that he did with Zasu Pitts. He came to the museum regularly and showed up to enjoy it as often as he could.

The well-known and lovely actress Sophia Loren (1934 to present) was there a lot, too. In fact, Ms. Loren dated Mr. Parkinson at one time and they were very close friends. He would visit her in her gorgeous Italian Villa (she was born in Rome) and she would come to the museum and to Los Angeles often to see him. They met through her agent, Bebe

Daniels, one of the biggest Hollywood agents of the time. I will mention more about Ms. Loren's set a bit later on.

Another star that Mr. Parkinson dated for a time and who also visited the museum was none other than the very talented and very beautiful Ms. Natalie Wood (1938 – 1981). The exquisite Ms. Wood had actually made fifty six films for television and the silver screen and received three Oscar nominations before turning twenty five years of age.

It made it quite interesting and fun for the museum guests when they would catch glimpses of these major Hollywood stars coming and going. Celebrity sightings were quite commonplace at Movieland back in those days.

# Chapter 19

## Vincent Price
## and
## his Antics

The famous actor, writer and gourmet, Mr. Vincent Leonard Price, Jr. (1911-1993) was one of the most interesting stars that we ever interviewed. He did something for the museum that no one else would have thought of ever doing. Mr. Price was a very unusual man. He not only had one of the finest private art collections in all of Hollywood, but in the world. He was not only interested in art, having been educated in art history and fine art at Yale, but he was also very much into having fun. In the 1950's he began doing horror films, with a role in *House of Wax* (1953).

One of the main reasons Vincent Price was interested in being in scary, horror films was because he had so much fun scaring people. This was one of his true passions, although he really was an extremely nice man. Mr. Price showed up at the museum one time while I was there doing some work on another project for Mr. Parkinson.

Mr. Price was talking to Mona Poe (our Girl Friday) and he was looking all around the museum, taking it all in. He loved the whole place. So Mona took him to see his set. There he saw himself portrayed as the evil wax sculptor, Professor Henry Jarrod, injecting fluid into the body of a girl that he is making into a wax figure (from *The House of Wax, 1953*). We had a wax body of a girl strapped down on a table, still breathing. It was a pretty gruesome set with all the gory details. He was really pleased with what he saw.

Vincent Price had a thought, suddenly. Being the type to have fun scaring people, it would be an amazingly fun opportunity for him if he could "impersonate" his own wax figure in the set.

Mona was with him at the time and told him that if he really wanted to do that, she could probably have it arranged. He was so excited and thrilled with the idea of this actually being possible. He thought it would be so very much fun. She told him if he wanted to do it he just needed to let her know and she could have it set up for him.

He decided he wanted to do it that very day. He had nothing else on his schedule and he was there, so why not? She told him it would be no problem. He had already figured it all out. "Alright, I have it all set. Do you have a dolly that I can borrow to transport these figures around?" Mr. Price asked. She said that indeed, they did.

Mr. Price instructed Mona to have one of the guys who worked at the museum go over to his set with the dolly right amidst all the guests at the museum, take out his wax figure and wheel it into the back room as if it needed to be worked on. He said he would then put on the same smock that was on his wax figure, and then they would wheel him back out on the dolly, while he pretended to be the actual wax figure. Mona alerted me to what Mr. Price was doing and I quickly got into the prank.

He told Mona that once I put the "figure" back on the set, he'd have me adjust his head, and hands and arms any way I wanted as if I were working on the actual wax figure, right on the set, so as not to arouse suspicion. He told us he would have no problem acting like a dummy. We all chuckled.

We decided to do it. We wheeled the wax figure into the back room. Vincent Price put on the dummy's smock and got back on the dolly. We arranged his arms in a somewhat rigid position so he could hold them steady as we wheeled him out. He was brought onto the set and two employees lifted him off the dolly and back on to the set, while he acted very stiff and wax-like. They took his arms and put the needle in one of his hands and posed him as the original wax figure. He told the workmen to get off the set and watch the fireworks.

As Mr. Price held himself very, very still, he waited patiently. When just the right amount of people would come by to look at his set, he would ever-so-slightly wiggle one of his fingers. Inevitably, one of the museum guests would see this slight movement and exclaim, "Oh! I swear I just saw Vincent Price's finger move!"

Everyone would stand still and watch closely. They would gather around and look for a while. Pretty soon, he would blink his eye. Someone else would notice that. But he would not do the same thing twice. However, soon enough there was a pretty big crowd standing in front of Vincent Price's set, waiting and watching.

Eventually, a little old elderly woman elbowed her way through the crowd and got up right next to Vincent Price's figure. She put her bifocals on and scrutinized his face, up close. She finally said very loudly, "Humph! That doesn't look a thing like Vincent Price!"

Well, Mr. Price couldn't stand it much longer. He finally broke his silence and said aloud, "Madame... I beg your pardon!"

This scared the old lady to death. She was startled and said, "Oh! Mr. Price! I am so sorry. So sorry! I-I-I did not mean to offend you!" He acted like he was very hurt, and she kind of wiggled out of the crowd and took off quickly. He then told the amused crowd standing around to hang out because the fun was just about to begin. Mr. Price was absolutely in his element. He'd wait until he had a large crowd in front of him and then he'd scare the devil out of them. He did this over and over all afternoon.

We finally had the real wax figure returned to the set after wheeling the real Vincent Price to the back room again. After this day, more people would come to this set in the museum after having heard of Mr. Price's antics. They would wait and wait and wait, hopeful and sure that at any moment Mr. Price would move or blink to scare them. But he never did.

I'd also like to say that Vincent Price was one of the most humble people you'd ever know. When he was older we had asked Mr. Price to come back to Movieland to do some voice-over sounds for our horror chambers area of the museum. In the middle of his dialogue, he was supposed to do a little menacing laugh with a chuckle. When we asked him to do this he told us that it would be a rather difficult thing to do, but he would try. And he did it perfectly for us! We now had his trademark voice to help us promote the dark and scary side of Movieland.

I will always remember what a nice man he was. His wife at that time was very ill, and he was planning on getting on a plane the very next day to head back to England to be with her. I recall him being very concerned for her health.

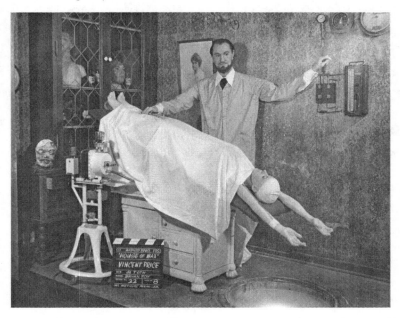

This picture is of the real Vincent Price, posing as a wax figure of himself in order to scare museum guests. He had a great time doing this! *Photography by Peter Klein, Movieland Wax Museum.*

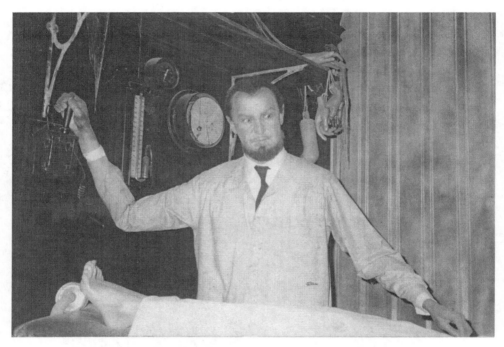

The wax figure of Vincent Price on his set for the movie *House of Wax* (1953).

# Chapter 20

## Burt Reynolds, Christopher Reeve

Shortly after sculpting Vincent Price and having one of the best times we ever had at Movieland, we began to work on a wax figure of Mr. Burt Reynolds (1936 to present). This was not too long after Mr. Reynolds did the movie *Deliverance* (1972), which was a huge hit.

However, after the movie was filmed, Mr. Reynolds had suffered from a severe case of mononucleosis, in part from exhaustion and partly due to eating unhealthy food during the long and rigorous filming process. Therefore, he was suffering quite a bit during his recovery from this illness, but still made arrangements with us to have his fitting and wax sculpture created for the museum. He was a real trooper.

For the measurements and photo sitting, we ended up going out to the studio where Mr. Reynolds was working at the time. He had his own business office on the studio lot. We arrived and our crew went directly upstairs to his office. I was the last one to come up the stairs. While ascending the steps, I could hear a conversation going on with the receptionist. She said, and quite loudly, "Logan Fleming? It couldn't be him! You can't mean that!"

I had no idea what was going on or why Burt Reynolds' office receptionist was so insistent that I could not be arriving at that moment, or what the big deal was about my arrival in the first place. I slowly entered the room, extremely puzzled. My crew was asking the receptionist why she was so surprised and what she was so shocked about. She said she could not believe there was a Logan Fleming with them. They pointed directly at me and said, "Yes, here he is. This is Logan Fleming and he's our wax sculptor at Movieland!"

The receptionist reeled around and, looking at me, stated, "Are *you* Logan Fleming?" I told her I was indeed Logan Fleming, and that I had heard her surprise.

In the meantime, Burt Reynolds had heard all the commotion. He walked into the office and looked right at me, saying, "What did you say your name was?" He and the receptionist seemed most intrigued.

Before I could answer, the receptionist answered Mr. Reynolds, "Logan Fleming is his name, apparently!" and she pointed right at me. Mr. Reynolds seemed very surprised, too.

However, Mr. Reynolds grinned and then explained that the reason they were so shocked to hear my name was Logan Fleming was because his ranch foreman down in Florida was also named Logan Fleming. Well, it was a funny coincidence, I had to agree. The odds of meeting your namesake, especially with a unique name such as mine, must have seemed very unlikely. Mr. Reynolds went on to ask me if I had only one "M" in my last name. I confirmed this to be true and he said, "Well, you must be Irish! Because if you had two "M's" in your last name it would indicate you were Scottish." And then he went on to ask me if I had sons, and how many, what were their names and ages. Amazingly, Burt's Logan Fleming also had three sons around the same age as my boys. We really hit it off because of these coincidences.

Now after the humorous beginning to this meeting we were told to call him "Burt" so that is what we did during the fitting. And he was fine with it. We proceeded to get started with the photo shoot. Burt was extremely friendly and nice. He looked much thinner than he had appeared in the film *Deliverance* due to his recent health issues. He had been consuming a steady diet of hamburgers, sodas, etc. during the shooting of the film and he was now paying the price. Burt spoke about wanting to start eating better again and getting back into a healthier state.

At any rate, Mr. Reynolds was on the road to recovery when we met with him. We had a very pleasant meeting and I mentioned having him come out to dedicate his wax figure and set when it was completed. I reminded him that it was an honor for him to be invited to have his wax figure at Movieland and that it was not something that he would be paid for. I told him that it would just involve about an hour or so of his time for a sitting and then a scheduled event at the museum for the dedication. He was well aware of the requirements and quite happy to oblige us.

He mentioned to me that he had lost thirty or more pounds since *Deliverance* was made, and that his biceps were a lot smaller than normal. I told him I'd beef up his arms a bit for his wax figure in that case. He was very happy about that. I told him I had pictures from *Deliverance* and could see how much larger he looked, normally. I told him I'd add enough "weight" to the figure for him.

When Burt came out to dedicate the set, he definitely looked heavier and more like his normal self. Burt's wax sculpture turned out great and he was thrilled with the results. He measured his biceps and he was impressed with how close I had come to his actual larger measurements. He was extremely courteous and kind to the fans, too. He was more than happy to talk with them and sign autographs for them.

The original *Superman* (1978) movie starred by Mr. Christopher Reeve (1952-2004) as Superman and Clark Kent, of course. He was such a phenomenal actor, star and human being and we had wanted him in the museum for some time. I'm not sure how it came to be, but the connection was finally made between Mr. Reeve and the museum. Movieland set a plan into action to try to have Mr. Reeve accept our offer for his wax figure to be made.

Mr. Reeve told our receptionist, Lovetta Kramer, that he had heard many great things about Movieland and the wax figures. He was very impressed with what he had heard. In fact and fortunately for us, Mr. Reeve just happened to be a good friend of Burt Reynolds. This helped Mr. Reeve decide to have his wax figure created because Mr. Reynolds told him how great he thought we were.

When Mr. Reeve accepted our offer, we got our gang together and went out to meet him for his interview and fitting/photography session at his private residence. Mr. Reeve was one of the stars who was fine with our calling him by his first name. He was exceptionally nice to us; however he seemed quite upset that day. I spoke with him about this, telling him I noticed that something was troubling him. I wanted to make sure it was nothing we had done.

He told me that there was a story that day in the *National Enquirer* that had really irritated him. The story had quipped that before they gave Mr. Reeve a trainer to buff him up for the *Superman* role, he did not look exceptionally muscular and well-built, and they gave the trainers too much credit for his powerful physique. He was also annoyed because he took much pride in being a very strong and fit person; he was quite large, in fact. It was obvious that they had "tuned him up" for his role in *Superman*, but it was not uncommon for stars to get into shape (or out of shape) to fit the needs of a particular character in a role they would be playing.

We told him we sympathized with his frustration over the tabloid article and he was happy about our understanding of his mood. We got some great shots and measurements of Mr. Reeve. The meeting went smoothly. He gave us the name of his tailor and told him we could probably get one of his original costumes from the *Superman* movie if we wanted one. For that opportunity, we were very grateful and decided to give this a try. That would be a huge bonus for us!

We were successful in getting an original costume from *Superman* for Mr. Reeve's Movieland wax figure. Since the costume was nylon and had to fit the figure like a glove, I had known that I had to take very exact measurements ahead of time. Luckily, the outcome was a success and it looked wonderful.

Later on, Mr. Reeve brought a friend of his to the Movieland set. She, too, really enjoyed this display and the museum. We had a huge space reserved for the *Superman* set. I made a small model of the set to show the set designers and builders what I wanted it to look like. I wanted to recreate the Fortress of Solitude, where *Superman* used to go, out in the Arctic wilderness. The Fortress was a massive crystalline repository for all knowledge of the universe that had been collected by the people of Krypton, including the destruction of their planet. It was also the place where Superman could go to communicate with his real Kryptonian father, Jor-El, for wisdom and advice.

The designers executed my idea splendidly. They made it out of fiberglass, down to molds being made for slabs of crystal. There was also a lot of plastic used in this set. It turned out just beautiful with a delicate blue hue. This was one of the most famous and fabulous sets that we had ever built and we ended up duplicating it for our sister museum in Florida, as well.

Burt Reynolds, standing next to his wax likeness from the film *Deliverance*.
He had lost a lot of weight from a poor diet while filming this movie,
but got himself back into shape quickly after.

Logan works on the wax figure for Christopher Reeve from his famous film *Superman*. *Superman* is a registered trademark of DC Comics. *Zelones & Associates Photography, Orlando, FL.*

# Chapter 21

## Cliff Robertson

**M**r. Cliff Robertson's (1923 to 2011) wax figure and set were created before I started working at Movieland and was one of the earliest that had been created for the museum. His wax figure was of him when he portrayed John F. Kennedy in *PT 109* (1963). During World War II, John F. Kennedy had been the captain of PT 109, a boat that carried extremely fast and dangerous torpedoes. This particular boat had been taken into battle and eventually sunk by a Japanese destroyer. Kennedy and the other survivors of this collision had actually made it to a nearby island.

They had come upon some shelter and had survived on food which they found on the island until they were able to create a signal, eventually being rescued by the Navy. This incredible, mid-ocean collision story was just too amazing to not be made into a movie. The *PT 109* became a cultural phenomenon after Kennedy was elected president. To assure historical accuracy, the White House had full approval of the script and casting. Kennedy personally selected Cliff Robertson after viewing many screen tests of other actors including Warren Beatty (Jackie O's choice), Peter Fonda, Edd Byrnes and Jeffrey Hunter. Ultimately, the film was finally produced in 1963.

One day, Cliff Robertson decided to come out unexpectedly to see his figure. As mentioned earlier, he was one of the first stars to be portrayed in the the museum and I wasn't involved in the sculpting of his figure. I never felt that Cliff Robertson's sculpture and set looked a whole lot like him, to be honest. The hair did not seem right, either. So Cliff came to visit the museum one day to really see his sculpture in detail, as he had only gotten a quick look at it when it was first installed. His set had been done before there were set dedications by the stars.

I was introduced to Mr. Robertson. He was a very nice gentleman and I was quite surprised by how much he actually resembled President Kennedy. He looked at the set where his wax sculpture was set up. It depicted a dramatic rescue scene from the *PT 109* movie, complete with water, machine guns and the destroyed hull of the PT 109 as it was sinking. He was pleased with the overall effect. But as Mr. Robertson was looking at his figure of Kennedy in the water helping other men, he turned to me and said, "They combed my hair to look like Kennedy's but it is just not right."

I told him to show me how he wanted the hair to look. He was thankful that I was willing to help him make his sculpture look more realistic. So Mr. Robertson took his comb out of his pocket and went to the restroom to style his hair appropriately.

I got a piece of wood while he was in the restroom and positioned it so I could stand on it to reach the figure, which was half submerged. Mr. Robertson came out and stood near me, next to the water on the set, with his hair appropriately styled, and posed for me. I took a comb and redid the hair on "Kennedy" until Mr. Robertson was happy with the way it looked. Finally, he said, "Now that's it! Much better." It definitely looked just like Kennedy after that. It was very nice to have him stop by and help us out like that. And it was well worth the effort because that little change made a huge difference.

After that day, Mr. Robertson came by a few more times to visit the museum. He was married to the American actress and socialite Dina Merrill (1925 to present), the daughter of Marjorie Merriweather Post (1887-1973), also known as Marjorie Merriweather Post Close Hutton Davies May. Ms. Post was a very well-known socialite. She had also founded General Foods, Inc. In addition, Ms. Post was also known for becoming the wealthiest woman in America after inheriting Postum Cereal Company when her father died. This company saw rapid growth in the 1970's and her fortune went up to two hundred and fifty million American dollars. Mr. Robertson brought his wife Dina with him to the museum on several occasions and it was really a pleasure to meet her as well.

# Chapter 22

## Stars Hall of Fame, Orlando, Florida

In the early 1970's when Movieland was at its peak, Allen Parkinson decided to sell the Museum to Six Flags Corporation and move on to other ventures. Not long after the acquisition, Six Flags decided to put a new wax museum down in Florida called the Stars Hall of Fame. It was not too far from Disney World. Our task was to figure out what needed to be done to get the museum set up. Six Flags wanted to have the same wax figures put up in this museum as we had at Movieland.

I used to take one set at a time from Movieland, sometimes two, and close them up for a period of time. I would take the wax figures, undress them, and send them on to a company we'd commissioned to make the molds of the figures. They would take separate molds of the head and the body. From the original wax figures, they would make a wax head and a fiberglass body. Then they would reattach the head to the body with hardware. The original wax figure would be reinstalled into its set in Movieland. I'd redress them, do any necessary touch-ups, and set the scene back up. Then it would reopen.

In the meantime, they would bring the recreated figures with the wax heads and fiberglass bodies to us. These figures had no eyeballs in the heads, and no hair. I had to add these touches and make them look exactly like the originals, duplicating each figure. It was a tremendous job, but it was fun to recreate them from the original figures.

After they were recreated, they would get fitted and costumed by our costume makers. Then they would be shipped to Florida. This was done for all of the major Movieland figures. I am guessing around one hundred thirty to one hundred forty figures were recreated and shipped to the new wax museum in Florida.

There were many costumes added for these wonderfully entertaining sets. If the original costumes could not be donated to the museum they were always made by a company called Western Costume, usually from the original patterns that were used for the movie costumes. The same or extremely similar materials were also used. Western Costume is one of the oldest businesses in Hollywood to work on motion picture costumes. They have been in business since 1912.

This was all done in a couple of years' time. It kept me extremely busy because not only did I have the major task of recreating over a hundred major celebrity wax figures for the museum in Florida, but I also had to keep up with all the new celebrity figures that were being created for Movieland, and maintain all the figures that already existed at Movieland. I had never been busier but it was a great and interesting job that I had, and I loved every moment of it.

Eventually, we had all the duplicates created for the museum in Florida and no one could really tell the difference whether they were the originals or not. This made all of us who collaborated in this effort very proud. In May of 1975, the Stars Hall of Fame in Orlando, Florida finally opened. It was quite a sensation and a huge success.

# Chapter 23

## Robert Stack, Frankenstein's Photo Booth

*T*he *Untouchables* (1959) was a very successful television series starring Robert Stack (1919-2003) who portrayed the famous Chicago Prohibition agent, Eliott Ness. His wax figure was posed with him holding a machine gun, ready to fire.

Robert Stack was more or less one of the earliest figures that was created for Movieland. I never did get to interview him because he was installed before I started at the museum. However, his original figure was not realistic at all, so I had to redo it with paint to make it look much better. The results were tremendous.

Right next to *The Untouchables* was a photography set for the film *Frankenstein* (1931) so that people could come in and have some fun photo opportunities. The person who had originally played Henry Frankenstein was the actor named Colin Clive (1900 to 1937). We employed a very nice gentleman named Mr. Klein who took pictures of the brave guests that were daring enough to get right next to Frankenstein for a photo. The monster looked pretty gruesome when you got close to its face and because of that, it was a popular thing for the guests to do. They sold a lot of pictures there.

Mr. Klein also enjoyed going around the museum and observing people and listening to their reactions and comments as they would stand and gaze upon the wax figures and sets. We liked to keep track of this activity so that we knew which figures and sets were a "hit"as well as those that were less popular for our guests. Every few months we'd get together and check the responses.

We had a funny experience one day, right in the middle of the museum at the *Frankenstein* set. Mr. Klein was waiting for some guests to come through; it had been a bit slow that day. Mr. Klein noticed a little elderly woman near the *Frankenstein* set. The lady had a camera with her and she was going around taking pictures of the stars and the different sets, enjoying herself.

From Mr. Klein's vantage point in the photography booth, he could see through to some of the other sets. He could clearly see the Robert Stack set very well from where he was. He noticed this little old lady looking at the Robert Stack figure but he did not think much of it. She was just viewing it.

Some time passed, and a few guests came by to have their photograph taken with *Frankenstein*. He noticed that this woman was still standing there, gazing at Robert Stack. A little more time went by and there she was, still seemingly mezmerized by Mr. Stack. He thought it was quite strange that the woman was not moving along.

Mr. Klein was just engrossed in watching this old lady. Finally, he could not stand the suspense any longer so he approached the woman and asked her, "Ma'am, could I ask you something? What is it that you are doing in front of this figure for at least the last forty-five minutes with your camera ready, doing nothing? Why are you not taking a picture when you keep holding the camera up as if you will take one?"

The woman replied to him, "What do you mean, Sir? You can't fool me! I know that this is Robert Stack! I saw his finger move about a half an hour ago. I am going to stay here until he moves again. He cannot stay still for very much longer." He tried to convince her that this was just a wax figure, but to no avail. He walked back to the *Frankenstein* set and took some more photographs for some of the people. He finally had a chance to look back at the old woman to see what she was up to.

Lo and behold, she was still standing there in front of the Stack figure! He could not believe his eyes, and was beginning to think this woman was crazy. Well, he decided once and for all to convince this poor woman that the figure was not a real human. He walked onto the set because, of course, he had special permission to do so. He walked up to the Robert Stack wax figure and thumped it on the chest a few times. You could clearly hear the sound of his fist bouncing off the figure, which made it very apparent that this was a wax figure after all. The woman waited a few more minutes, contemplating this fact. Finally, she shrugged her shoulders, put her camera down and turned to leave, convinced that Robert Stack would not move. However, she still looked disappointed and said aloud, "I could have sworn I saw his fingers move!" as she left. Finally!

Now, as funny as this story is, I took it as quite a compliment that my work on the Robert Stack wax figure looked so authentic if even to a very old lady that she'd believe he was a real person! This was a very comical event... one of many that happened in the museum.

Logan and Lt. Colonel John H. Tomlinson USMC (now retired)
with the *Frankenstein* figure that Logan created in the popular photo booth.

# Chapter 24

## The Poseidon Adventure
## and
## Special Effects

One of the best sets we had at the museum was the *The Poseidon Adventure* (1972). This was a rather long and large set, built like the boiler room inside of a ship, with the entire engine upside-down. It had Ernest Borgnine (1917 to present) in it as well as all the other actors positioned in their places. The only major actor from the movie that was not included in this set was Shelley Winters (1920-2006). She had been in an earlier sequence in the picture and while we would've loved to include her, she didn't appear in this particular scene depicted in the set. She did, however, play a very important role in the movie and was just as popular an actress as any of the top actors of the movie.

*The Poseidon Adventure* set was very realistic and the special effects were incredible for the time. It included fake fire with rags, a wind blower, and special, flashing lights. There was also water coming in along with steam flying up into the air. It was very dramatic and stirring.

Another set that was one of our best in my opinion was the *The Guns of Navarone* (1961). It was just such an authentic set, designed by our great set designer Gene White. He took great, detailed notes of the actual photographs and buildings from the film where this particular scene had taken place. The setting was a bombed-out old building where they had taken refuge. As you would walk through the set and through the building, we had many speakers strategically positioned and up very high on cables towards the three-story ceiling to create the realistic sound of bombs exploding. The speakers would descend down rapidly right above the guests, simulating the feeling of having bombs coming down on top of you as it got louder and louder above your head with a tremendous explosion.

Gia Scala (1934-1972) played a turncoat in the film. She was with a group who were trying to evade the Germans but all along she was on their side. This movie turned out to be one of the top pictures for that year, with the tag line, "Still! The Greatest High Adventure Ever Filmed!"

Gia Scala was not at the opening for *The Guns of Navarone* set at Movieland, but she did come in to the museum to visit some time later. However, at that time she looked a bit lost and I felt sorry for her. I was honored to take her through the museum and show her the set for the movie in which she was so splendid. She just looked at it in amazement and knelt down next to her figure, touching it. It was very moving for her. She revealed to me that it was quite challenging to look so innocent in so many scenes when all the while she was actually working for the other side to obtain information. Gia spent quite a bit of time that day hanging around her set, mostly in solitude. There was not much of a crowd in the museum that day, and she rather enjoyed her own company. I left her for a while and told her to say goodbye before she departed. Sure enough, Ms. Scala came to find me later on near the front of the museum and thanked me. She told me how many great memories the set and its figures had brought her, and she was quite gracious. But still there seemed to be something going on inside and I could see the sadness in her eyes that day.

After she left the museum, I never saw her again. And I heard not two months later that she had tragically committed suicide. She was on her last straw when she visited the museum, and I had sensed it that day. This left me with a very sad feeling for some time.

# Chapter 25

## Keystone Pranks

As mentioned earlier, we had a crew of Keystone Kops whose primary job was to provide security but they were also around to entertain the people. They would pose themselves up to look "fake" like a wax figure throughout the museum. The Kops would often scare the guests, but it was all in good fun.

The biggest scare I can recall was on an extremely busy day. Out in front, at the first turn that one would take after entering the museum, we would always station a Keystone Kop. So this day, it was an extremely hot, weekend day. People were just coming inside in droves, quickly. Maybe they were rushing inside to partly escape the heat while being entertained, but regardless of the reason, it was packed.

Jack Collins, who I've spoken of earlier was our chauffeur and head Keystone Kop. Because he was in charge he usually left the "pranks" to be carried out by his staff. However, occasionally they would need added security inside the museum and he would have the chance to pull off some of his own pranks on unsuspecting guests. He was particularly good at making himself look like a wax figure and scaring people. He was also a former firefighter and was very good at providing security.

On this day, as people were flooding into the museum, Jack was standing in one corner near the main entrance. He spotted this one older couple who had a lovely daughter with them. She was just a knock-out, about twenty years old or so. She could have been a model and looked very confident in herself. Her parents walked in behind her.

Jack noticed that this young stunner had a pencil in her hand. Just before they approached, he got into position and stuck his hand out before she saw him. He had placed his hand in a relaxed fist position with just enough room to stick an object like a pencil inside his loose grip. It was almost as if he was asking for this young girl to stick something in his hand.

Sure enough, she took the bait and stuck the pencil in his hand. She was quite cocky and commented on how funny this wax Keystone Kop looked as she and her parents walked around past him. Jack was brimming with excitement, waiting for the opportunity to strike. Finally, she decided enough was enough and it was time to take her pencil back out of the wax Keystone Kop's hand.

Well, Jack was a very strong man. Unbeknownst to this young lady, he gave the pencil she had stuck in his hand a very strong, tight grip. She came up to him and tried to pull the pencil out of his hand. She pulled and tugged and still could not retrieve her pencil. She was becoming quite puzzled and exasperated. Finally, she gave a big yelp as he let go of the pencil for her! He suddenly said, "Madam, what IS it you are trying to do?"

This obviously scared the living daylights out of this doll, and she jumped back, startled beyond belief. She had no inkling that Jack was real and so the joke was on her. Poor girl, she actually lost her bladder control right there, in front of everyone, creating a mess on the carpet. She was mortified, and covered her face, running out of the museum.

Surprisingly, her parents thought this was the funniest thing ever. They knew their daughter needed a little humility and this was the perfect moment for it. Her father laughed so hard at this event that he tripped over some of the molding around the carpet and fell to the floor. He laughed so hard he could not get up for quite a few moments. His wife was in hysterics, too.

In spite of the parents not being angry, Jack was extremely apologetic to the parents about scaring this young lady so severely. He assured them that he would refund their tickets, as his antics meant no harmful intention. They said they would not even think of asking for a refund. They wanted to continue through the museum and see the entire show. Their daughter had been so high-and-mighty lately that they knew it would actually be a little lesson in humility for her. While there were many innocent victims startled and surprised by the Keystone Kops posing as dummies, this one goes down as the most memorable.

Now, I had also created an actual wax figure of a Keystone Kop made to look exactly like one of our real Keystone Kops. His real name was Walter and he had his routine that he did in the museum to look somewhat like a mechanical man. So when Walter was out in front, he would do his mechanical man bit. Then it would appear that he had moved over to the *Laurel and Hardy* set where we had positioned his wax likeness.

When the guests came upon the *Laurel and Hardy* set and saw this wax Keystone Kop in the set, they thought he was the real gentleman that they had seen at the front entrance behind the car and expected that he would be doing his funny little mechanical bit right there again. They would laugh and talk to "Wax Walter" as if he were real, waiting for him to begin his gig. Yet, he never answered back to them because of course he was a wax figure! Some of the guests waited around quite a while before they figured it out. It was a lot of fun.

Then, the guests would come back to the front after seeing the wax Keystone Kop at the *Laurel and Hardy* figure, and see the real one again. They were so confused, and could never figure out how he got back to the front through all the mirrors so quickly, and if he was real or not unless he did his mechanical routine. It was quite a hoot!

# Chapter 26

## Nancy Sinatra
## and
## Authenticity in the Museum

Mr. Parkinson always made it a top priority to have authentic props of the highest quality inside the sets…only the very best. He had purchased exquisite cobalt glass vases for the John Drew Barrymore (1932-2004) set, standing two to three feet high. Those were worth thousands of dollars each but he would not put imitation cobalt vases in his museum. Other examples of authenticity included expensive antique furniture, crystal, Carrera marble from Italy, donated costumes worn in an actual film by the star or genuine collectible guns. This was especially pleasing to those who were knowledgeable or who collected antiques or other fine objects. People could tell that all the sets harbored real, high-quality items and not fake ones. Perhaps because his museum was all about imitating famous people, he wanted to make up for it by having the very best, authentic décor that money could buy throughout the entire museum. This added an amazing amount of class to the museum.

During the Museum's heyday, we had several big stars who had made extremely successful careers and motion pictures that everyone was after. One of the most well-respected and sought after stars that everyone wanted to see get into Movieland Wax Museum was the very beautiful Nancy Sinatra (1940 to present).

Word was put out to ask Miss Sinatra if she would like to be in the museum for an edgy action/drama movie she had done titled *The Wild Angels* (1966). She was in fact quite happy and honored to be extended this invitation to have her wax likeness in the museum. On the Movieland set for *The Wild Angels*, there was a motorcycle that was an exact duplicate of the one in the film. Nancy Sinatra's wax likeness astride this custom-made motorcycle was reflected from all possible angles by a completely mirrored set.

Miss Sinatra had also just recorded a wonderfully fun song called *"These Boots are Made for Walkin'"* (1966) that had been quite a hit and her popularity was gaining rapidly. We went to her for a sitting and measurement session and it went very smoothly. She would be wearing a very short dress in the set so, in particular, I had to take very accurate measurements of her entire legs. I had no trouble with this as she wore panty hose and was very cooperative.

After it was completed, we had her wax figure posed for us on the motorbike and she looked just beautiful. The wax figure turned out lovely.

However, eventually when the set had been created there was a mirrored floor underneath the motorcycle. So Nancy Sinatra's wax figure was posed on top of the motorcycle over this mirrored floor. It was very beautiful and effective with special lights on the set. This all created a wonderful effect and image.

The challenge came when it was noticed that you could see way up her leg from the mirror's reflection underneath her. She (her wax figure, that is) was wearing a pair of long, flesh-toned stockings that went up over her hips. So she was completely covered. But due to the color of the stockings it appeared as if she had nothing on underneath her skirt.

You would be surprised by the amount of people, especially those who were very conservative or religious, who took offense at this. They felt she should be wearing obvious undergarments underneath her skirt so as to not give off the wrong and improper impression.

We asked Nancy about this and she did not like the idea. She never wore separate underwear because she wore stockings with built-in undergarments and that was how she wanted to be portrayed: just as she was. Those who objected raised quite a scene so it was finally determined that we put a white, fancy panty over her wax figure's stockings and that ended the dilemma right there. Apparently, Nancy Sinatra's wax figure was finally deemed appropriate to all the public.

Nancy Sinatra's wax figure at Movieland from the movie *The Wild Angels*.

# Chapter 27

## Smothers Brothers

After Nancy Sinatra's figure was completed we got a call telling us that we would be doing wax figures for Tom Smothers (1937 to present) and Dick Smothers (1939 to present), aka The Smothers Brothers for *The Smothers Brothers Comedy Hour* (1967). Tom and Dick Smothers were an all-American double act who usually performed folk songs, which would eventually lead to them having arguments with each other. Tommy Smothers' shtick was, "Mom always liked you best!" Tommy, who was the older brother, usually acted somewhat slow, and Dick, who was the straighter-laced brother, would act as if he were more superior to his brother. They would eventually become one of the longest-lived comedy teams in history.

At that time the Smothers Brothers were very popular. The interest was mutual to have them in the wax museum. They were very helpful to us in getting their measurements, photographs and such. We had a great set figured out for them. It would consist of a large musical guitar with them standing inside it. After the figures were completed, it all was set up well and lots of publicity ensured.

Unfortunately, Tom and Dick Smothers got into politics at that time. They made a few comments in their comedy routines that were not received well by some people and their popularity waned a bit after that. Later on, they pulled themselves back into mediocre success but never the sensation they originally had been.

# Chapter 28

## The Clampett Clan Takes a Trip

We did a set and wax figures for the "Clampett Clan" up on the old clunky car of theirs from *The Beverly Hillbillies* television series (1962-1971). The set featured Buddy Ebsen (1908-2003) as Jed Clampett seated on the front seat with his son Jethro Bodine, portrayed by Max Baer Jr. (1937 to present). Then in the back seat were the gals including Daisy May "Granny" Moses played by Irene Ryan (1902-1973) and the lovely little blonde Donna Douglas (1933 to present) who played Elly May Clampett. The old car was specially made for this set as an exact replica of the car in the television series, and later on there was another identical car made for the Florida museum. The resemblance was uncanny.

Irene Ryan who played Daisy Moses and was affectionately called Granny, was very delightful and fun. The museum got a big kick out of Irene one day. Irene was scheduled to go on the *This is Your Life* (1952-1961) TV program. She had also agreed to dedicate her *Beverly Hillbillies* set at Movieland.

Unbeknownst to Irene Ryan, we arranged to have the *This is Your Life* program that was airing on TV actually in Movieland Wax Museum. They moved the entire program that was airing on TV to their set inside the museum. So we surprised Irene tremendously that day when she showed up at Movieland, ready to dedicate her *Beverly Hillbillies* set, and we ended up shocking her with the filming of the actual *This is Your Life* TV show! She ended up being the main subject of the *This is Your Life* program for that night. Ralph Edwards did the hosting of this program. He asked her a bunch of questions about *The Beverly Hillbillies*.

She was such a great sport and did a wonderful job for the show. It also did not hurt to get the additional publicity for the museum by having set up this ingenious marketing event.

Another interesting fact about *The Beverly Hillbillies* revolves around their pet hound dog. We needed an actual taxidermy hound dog to sit in the car with the Clan or it would not have looked authentic. The hound dogs that the Clampett Clan had as a pet in the show came from an area in the country where dogs were considered to be a part of the family, so much so that these dogs are absolutely loved and revered as much as any other family member and they never part with them, even after they have deceased. So it would be virtually impossible to convince these owners to turn over their deceased dogs to be a prop in a set at a wax museum.

To make matters worse, we needed not one but two full-grown hound dogs that looked like the dog on the TV show. One in time for the opening of our Stars Hall of Fame Museum in Orlando, Florida and the other for our Movieland set. Not only that, but these dogs were in great demand to begin with in this southern part of the country because they were used largely for hunting and guarding homes and such. And the dog in the TV show was an exceptionally large, beautiful hound dog. So we had quite a tall order to fill. We started to worry that we would never be able to get our dog for the set on time for the opening of our new museum in Orlando. We were getting resigned to the fact that we'd have to have one made, knowing that it would never look the same as an authentic dog.

Our only hope was that maybe one of several southern taxidermists we contracted might locate the right dogs for us; ones that had been in an accident or unfortunately died in some manner of natural causes.

Finally, after a good long while, we found a taxidermist who brought us the word that a full grown hound dog had died. This poor hound dog had been dealt the misfortune of dying on the highway after being struck by a fast-moving vehicle. This in itself was very sad news, but it was how we got our dog. He was not too badly destroyed on the outside so that the taxidermist would be able to preserve his poor body permanently for our set, and he became a blessing to us for that purpose, poor fellow. He looked just like the original dog as well, so he served a great purpose after his life ended. This was just in time for the new museum's opening. We will forever be thankful to this dog. We also had as difficult a time finding a dog for the Movieland set, but we eventually found one.

We had more extremely interesting times with *The Beverly Hillbillies*. As we were working on the promotions and the set at Movieland in Buena Park, we were also doing a set for this show for The Stars Hall of Fame in Orlando. It was going to cost a pretty penny to ship all of these wax figures down to Florida, so I had to try to come up with some creative ideas on how to transport them. There were numerous figures to ship for *The Beverly Hillbillies*. After some collaborative brainstorming, the idea was brought up that we would put the wax figures on an airplane and they would fly on down to Florida. I thought this was a superb idea, because the cost of the airplane tickets would be much less than shipping costs due to the size and weight and quantity of all the figures.

Therefore, we got some approvals for this and it was full throttle ahead. Since the figures for the Hillbillies were already created in the sitting position for placement in their old truck on the set, they would fit perfectly on the airplane seats with their seatbelts on. It was a perfect plan! The additional bonus to this plan was that we saved even more money by not having to order these guys any food. Back then, you paid extra to get meals on planes and of course the wax figures did not have much of an appetite. This was a very fun journey for us.

We arranged ahead of time with our travel agent to let us go onto the plane at the Los Angeles International Airport with a forklift and put the figures in their seats, all strapped in, before the real passengers boarded the plane.

We were able to get them onto the fork lift and ride it up to the rear emergency exit of the plane, board them through the emergency doors, carry the figures into the plane and seat the figures in the rear of the plane. We had the entire Clampett Clan strapped into their plane seats. I rode along with them to Florida to make sure they were not damaged. I sat down near them and buckled myself in, the rear emergency doors were closed, and then the passengers were allowed onto the plane from the front. This would have never been possible now with the stringent security standards we have in place because of 9/11.

It was quite interesting to watch the scene unfold. People slowly began filing into the front of the plane, gradually making their way to the rear. The people were doing their thing, putting their luggage into the top racks and eventually ending up towards the rear where the Clampett Clan and I were already seated and strapped into our seats. One lady had a little boy with her who was about eight years old. Their seats were close enough to our seats for them to see our faces. I was curious to see how long it would take any of the passengers to notice *The Beverly Hillbillies*.

Quite a few passengers got in and were so busy getting themselves situated that they did not take the time to notice us. After quite a few people were in the plane near us, still no one had noticed. Except the little boy; he was something else. After he got into his seat and buckled up, he turned around and saw Jed Clampett sitting there. His eyes got as big as saucers. He kept tapping his mother's arm and she kept flaking him off, not wanting to be bothered. She was too busy reading her magazine. But the little boy kept nagging at her. Finally, he whispered something to her.

When his mother turned around to look at us, she was horrorstruck. There in front of her eyes was the entire Clampett Clan from *The Beverly Hillbillies*. They were all seated neatly in their places, buckled in. The little boy scrutinized them and kept whispering. Eventually, I could see the whispers on the plane take off like a wildfire, turning into frantic conversations as the noise grew. I saw more and more sets of eyes turning back at us as the word spread. Everyone thought the Clampett Clan was in the back of the airplane.

As the flight attendants made the passengers sit down just before take-off, they could not all keep gazing in our direction. Many of them thought these were the real actors! The captain and crew of course had been notified ahead of time. The flight attendants were going to have a ball with this.

As the plane's engines started up and began readying for take-off, the little boy would try to get up but his mother wouldn't allow it. He tried a few times, but to no avail. Eventually the plane taxied out and went down the runway, taking off smoothly and without event.

Since we were near the rear of the airplane there was a restroom close by. Once we were at altitude, the "Fasten Your Seatbelt" signs came off and word kept spreading, there began a constant, steady flow of passengers to the rear of the plane "going to the bathroom." The entire large group of this airplane's passengers evidently got word of *The Beverly Hillbillies* sitting at the rear of the plane. Thus, it seemed that every passenger suddenly needed to go to the bathroom and to the back bathroom in particular. One of the flight attendants told me she had never seen anything like it.

It was fun and I was having quite a tremendous time telling all the passengers about the wax figures and how we were making our way to the new wax museum in Orlando. In fact, I got many people so interested they were promising that they would definitely come by once it opened up. This conversation and constant stream of people to the rear of the plane kept up during the entire flight. It was definitely an eventful, interesting and exhausting flight because I don't think I had more than a few minutes except during my meal, to have a break from talking to people. But I thoroughly enjoyed meeting so many wonderful folks. One of the flight attendants joked with me that the airplane was not getting any business in the other bathrooms!

Finally, the plane was getting ready to land in Florida. As we were positioning ourselves for a landing, who would you think showed up back at the rear of the plane but the co-pilot. Well, the co-pilot told me he had to come back to the rear of the plane to see for himself what was going on. He said the news had spread clear to the cockpit that Jed Clampett and his family was sitting at the rear of the plane. This young man took a good, careful look at the entire Clampett clan. He told me he was very impressed with their likenesses to the real people. He excused himself to the cockpit so the pilot himself could come back to see the clan. The pilot got his look at the wax family and talked with me for a few minutes as well.

The plane finally landed and even then, more people made their way to the back to get a quick look at the Clampetts before they disembarked. Eventually, after the plane got entirely cleared out, we were able to get all the wax figures unbuckled and down the forklift and off the airplane into a proper carrier. They were taken to the museum in Orlando to be installed for the grand opening.

Logan Fleming helps lift the wax figure of Jethro Bodine aka Max Baer Jr., onto an airplane to transport it and the entire Clampet Clan aka *The Beverly Hillbillies* from Los Angeles to the Stars Hall of Fame in Orlando, Florida. *Photography by Norton.*

A photo of *The Beverly Hillbillies* set at Movieland.

# Chapter 29

## The Gift
## of Having
## Original Costumes

A s the museum grew, many of the new sets actually had authentic movie costumes contributed by the stars directly. This was always a great honor for us to preserve a scene from a classic movie loved by the public, and to do so using the very same garments that were worn by these talented movie stars.

Sophia Loren (1934 to present) contributed her costume for the set from the film *Two Women* (1960) aka *La Ciociara* (Italian) for her role as Cesira. Ms. Loren gave Mr. Parkinson one of the dresses she wore in this incredibly moving film about a mother and daughter who are fleeing from allied bombs in Rome during World War II and the circumstances that befall them. For her role in *Two Women* Sophia Loren won the Academy Award for Best Actress. This was the first time an acting Oscar had been given for a non-English-speaking performance. Sophia Loren also won the award for Best Actress at the 1961 Cannes Film Festival for this same movie role.

Marlo Thomas (1937 to present) contributed an original Cardinali design with beautiful black boots for her set from the television comedy series *That Girl* (1966–1971). That costume was quite a gift to us, and we were always a huge fan of Marlo Thomas.

We also had Ward Bond's (1903–1960) wax figure wear a complete uniform costume that the famous actor and "wagon master" wore in the famous television series *Wagon Train* (1957-1965). For this set, the costume was a gift to Movieland from Mr. Bond's widow, a costume which was used in the actual filming of the series.

When original costumes were not obtainable by the stars or the studios, then duplicates were made to fit the wax figures. Many times these duplicate costumes were created from the original costume patterns for authenticity. If the fabrics were not available they would have to be specially made or woven.

For example, it cost $2,500 to recreate the bejeweled robe fabric for the Charles Laughton (1899-1962) wax figure. That was a lot of money back in 1970. This was done by Western Costume and became one of the costliest costumes in the museum. Mr. Laughton wore this robe in his Oscar-winning performance for playing King Henry VIII in *The Private Life of Henry VIII* (1933). This was one of the nicest sets in the museum.

Also, in many cases we had special lighting and side effects including some of the original soundtrack recordings added to the sets at Movieland. The rewards for all these efforts were tremendous in the reception by the general public who visited the museum.

The wax likeness of Marlo Thomas from *That Girl*.

# Chapter 30

## Chuck Connors, The Rifleman

We had a wonderful set in the museum for *The Rifleman* (1958-1963) television series. This Western adventure series starred Mr. Chuck Connors (1921-1992). Prior to his acting career, Chuck had played professional sports both in the NBA and Major League Baseball. In 1946 he joined the newly formed Boston Celtics and played for a short time.

He then switched to baseball and joined the Brooklyn Dodgers where he played in only one game. He then played with the Chicago Cubs as a first baseman for part of the 1951 season. He is only one of twelve athletes to ever play in both the NBA and Major League Baseball. After his stint with the Cubs his professional athletic career came to an end when he was sent to the minor leagues where he played with the Los Angeles Angels. He realized that sustaining a career in professional sports was probably not in the cards for him.

However, playing minor league ball near Hollywood would prove fortuitous when he was discovered by an MGM casting director. This led to roles in quite a few movies and his trademark role of Lucas McCain in *The Rifleman* television series which ran for four seasons. On *The Rifleman* set we created a very authentic-looking cave complete with stalactites and stalagmites. It was like a mine shaft inside with a small railroad track going through it. Up on a ledge was *The Rifleman* with his rifle in hand, cocked and ready to defend. There was also a bad guy placed off to the right just inside a coal flight that was hiding from him. Chuck was coming after the bad guy.

One particular summer I was just returning from a long trip with my family. I stopped by the museum to check in and noticed that one of the ladies who did the evening cleaning for the set was acting somewhat sad. I asked her what was wrong. She said she had some bad news to tell me. She proceeded to tell me that when people came in the museum to see this set, they were a bit elevated and could look down into the railroad tracks where they could see Chuck Connor's likeness holding his rifle.

Apparently, one of the museum guests had gotten a stick and stood along the barrel's edge, trying to get the rifle. They tried to break the figure's fingers so they could get to the rifle. Instead, they caused the wax figure to accidentally fall all the way forward flat onto the railroad tracks. His face hit the track directly and it just shattered into hundreds of bits. The darling cleaning lady was quite upset about this, but she had saved and picked up every little single piece she could find of Chuck Connor's face. That effort on her part just warmed my heart.

In addition to the damage done to Mr. Connor's face, they had broken one of the hands of his figure. The rifle and body were still intact. It was mostly the head and face that had been annihilated.

I had decided I would try to glue the head and face back together. I put it all on a table and spent about a week trying to put it all back together with carpenter glue. With a little bit of touch-up, wax work and repainting, I finally got the face all intact, amazingly enough. In the end, his face looked surprisingly as good as new and his figure was saved.

These types of vandalisms happen occasionally in museums. The person who had messed with Chuck Connor's face had used a long stick that went around the camera so he was never identified. Most of the time, however, our security worked.

Movieland set of *The Rifleman* with Chuck Connors.

# Chapter 31

## Finding the Right Horses for Ben-Hur

Right after I first got to Movieland and started working there in 1964, Mr. Parkinson had arranged for a wonderful set to be put into the museum. This would be the largest set at Movieland: the chariot scene from *Ben-Hur: A Tale of the Christ* (1959), starring Charlton Heston (1923-2008). Mr. Parkinson wanted the exact type of horses pulling the chariot as in the days of chariot racing in Italy. Remember, he liked authenticity in every way possible.

One of the greatest taxidermists in the world was known as Mr. Bishop. He was responsible for finding the exact type of horses  previously mentioned and making these horses come back to life by mounting them in a galloping position to recreate the famous chariot racing scene.

Amazingly, Mr. Bishop was able to get hold of three of these specific, strong horses for the *Ben-Hur* set, but he just could not get a fourth horse. He could not and would not use the wrong type of horse. Therefore, it took some time but he finally found the fourth horse and got it mounted in position. Right as I began my career at the museum, the fourth horse was being mounted for the *Ben-Hur* set.

I also had some very good friends named Mr. and Mrs. Jan Snoey at that time and Jan was in the Foreign Press. He would cover stories for Belgian magazines. Through our friendship with the Snoeys, we met a woman named Hilda Uloa who was in charge of seating and table selection for the Golden Globes award ceremonies. As a result, my wife and our family sat at some very fine tables at the Golden Globes during those days.

At one of these particular Golden Globes shows, I recall seeing Charlton Heston after his successful filming of the Academy Award-winning movie *Ben-Hur*. I could never forget how large and powerful Mr. Heston was. And it was a good thing because his role in *Ben-Hur* had been quite a rigorous part.

Jan Snoey introduced us to Mr. Heston, who had just come back from filming the final chariot scene for the movie with the real horses. I remember how large and strong Charlton Heston's hands were when I shook them. He laughed about his hands due to the calluses he had built up from the chariot race scenes he had filmed over and over. He had mentioned that the chariot scenes were some of the most difficult and dangerous scenes he had ever shot for a movie. Mr. Heston went on to explain that they had to film these scenes over and over while trying to avoid getting injured. There had been one bad injury on the set, unfortunately. But overall, it had been very successful. He then said to me, "I hope the next time I shake your hand, Mr. Fleming, that my hands will be much softer, like yours." We all had a good laugh at that. I will speak much more about our times at the Golden Globes later.

Movieland set of *Ben Hur* with Charlton Heston and the hard-to-find taxidermy horses.

# Chapter 32

## Slim Summerville
## and
## Zasu Pitts

R ight near the Gene Kelley (1912-1996) set for *Singin' in the Rain* (1952) was a set that Mr. Parkinson wanted me to finish. It included the head of Slim Summerville (1892-1946), which I had originally done at the beginning of my career with the museum in efforts to get my job. I was so very proud of that head; it was the reason I was working for the wax museum in the first place.

I had never had the time to finish this head, however, because I had happily gotten extremely busy with many other high-profile wax figures and projects upon my employment with the museum. Mr. Parkinson finally wanted Slim to be finished up and he also wanted me to put Ms. Zasu Pitts (1894-1963) in there with him.

The two of them had been in a very funny picture together called *Miss Polly* (1941) that had been quite successful. Zasu was very funny and quite a popular star back in that time, and she and Slim Summerville made a fabulous comedic team.

I finally got the set with Slim and Zasu finished. It turned out fantastic. Sadly, I was not at the museum when Mr. Summerville came to visit his set. But Ms. Pitts told me she loved the way the set had turned out.

Several years after I finished this set, both Mr. Summerville and Ms. Pitts came to the museum to visit their set and see all the other wax figures and sets, many of the wax figures' subjects whom they had met in the past. They really liked the museum, and their set in particular. I was honored by their feedback. It also brought back some great memories as to how I got started in the first place.

# Chapter 33

## Danny Thomas Day

One of the biggest days we had at the wax museum was the Danny Thomas (1914-1991) set dedication for the film titled *The Jazz Singer* (1953). We had their entire family at the museum for "Danny Thomas Day" and he brought his beautiful daughter Marlo with him. Danny Thomas had been kind enough to provide the original suit that he wore from *The Jazz Singer*.

Many other stars had been invited and showed up to see this set dedication. Jack Haley Jr. (1933-2001) showed up and posed next to the Tin Man who he portrayed in *The Wizard of Oz* (1939). His wax figure was there in the museum along with Judy Garland (1922-1969), who of course played the legendary character of Dorothy. The famous comedian and Academy Award-winning actor Red Buttons (1919-2006) was also in attendance. There was a huge luncheon and celebration which turned out to be exquisite. It was quite a day.

In fact, when they opened up the new museum in Florida, Danny Thomas also showed up there and came to his duplicate set dedication at that location. I had the pleasure of being introduced there and getting on the stage with Danny Thomas. I'll talk more about this later.

Danny Thomas was a marvelous man to know and gave a lot of his time to Mr. Parkinson. He was also extremely fun to be around.

I should also mention at this time that Jack Haley's daughter Gloria was involved in helping us shoot a commercial for the museum with him in it. Gloria was posed next to the Tin Man (her father) and it was one of the best commercial ads for the museum that was ever made. *The Wizard of Oz* set was one of the greatest sets we ever built at Movieland, even complete with the little dog Toto and the "Yellow Brick Road."

# Chapter 34

## Laurel
## &
## Hardy

Another set that was one of the first ones ever made as well as a focal point in the museum was the *Laurel & Hardy* set. I spoke a little about Laurel & Hardy earlier but there is much more to tell. Originally, this set was right in the center of the museum. Immediately in front of it was the turntable with the wax figure of the director D.W. Griffith standing on it, revolving around and appearing to direct the various stars in their big movies that were represented in the museum in that time.

By the time the museum was opened, Oliver Hardy (1892-1957) from the *Laurel & Hardy* series had passed away. Stan Laurel (1890-1965) was living alone at this time, in somewhat obscurity. As he had gotten older, Mr. Laurel seemed to live a simpler, humbler lifestyle, out of the spotlight after enjoying all the major successes in his earlier career. I don't think he was very happy at that time. Mr. Parkinson liked him a lot and Mr. Laurel was very respectful of him.

However, Laurel was not very happy that Mr. Parkinson wanted to put their wax figures on the set in the wax museum with normal skin coloring. The reason is as follows: I found out later on after working for the museum that in the earlier pictures back in the days of the Keystone Kops and classic comedy pictures like those of *Laurel & Hardy*, the characters' faces were painted with white makeup, resembling clowns. Therefore, when black-and-white pictures were taken of them in the early days, it made them appear much more comical. So Laurel preferred that their wax figures should resemble them with very white complexions, just the way they were photographed back in the day of black-and-white movies. He wanted to keep the authenticity.

Although Mr. Parkinson wanted to stay authentic every chance he could get, he also knew that people would be confused or puzzled about their faces being painted clown white. Therefore, for the sake of the museum he decided to give them normal complexions and not yield to Mr. Laurel's requests. Stan Laurel was quite unhappy about this decision and thus did not show up for his set opening and dedication.

The *Laurel and Hardy* set in the museum was one of the most popular ever. And this was because they were one of the greatest comedy teams of all time, and loved by so many fans.

And as time went on, I believe that Mr. Laurel realized Mr. Parkinson was right and ended up quite pleased by the success of the set and of the museum as well. The set had an actual, old-time 1923 Ford automobile in it complete with steam coming out of the radiator. It looked great, all cracked up as if *Laurel & Hardy* had crashed into the front of the Bijou Theatre. That is the way the set was created. There in front of the car were *Laurel & Hardy*, looking a bit giddy since they had just foolishly wrecked the car.

Later on, we moved things around when we put all the mirrors into the museum to create a labyrinth out of the show instead of one huge showroom. When this happened, we had to move the *Laurel & Hardy* set over to the side and put it in a place that would be less central.

Logan clowning around as he puts the Laurel & Hardy set together.

# Chapter 35

## The Great Sophia Loren

Another one of the earliest sets that Mr. Parkinson put in the museum was the one I mentioned before in which Sophia Loren got the Academy Award for the great film *Two Women* (1960).

The *Two Women* set was one of the sets that I chose to remake because, quite frankly, it was not a good enough representation of Ms. Loren, initially. This bothered me because of her amazing beauty, and also because of the close relationship she had with Mr. Parkinson.

Before I had a chance to get this figure of her redone, she had seen it. I wanted her to see that I had made her wax figure into a beautiful woman just like she was. The initial figure just did not look like her. But she never complained about it. Ms. Loren was a first-class woman.

Upon seeing the initial wax figure of her, Ms. Loren said, "Oh Alan. How beautiful. What a nice thing." She even kneeled down next to the figure and was so extremely gracious, it just touched your heart.

I just wish that she had come later and could have seen the way her wax figure looked after I redid it. While she never showed her dislike of the original, I think she would have been so much happier if she had seen the final figure.

# Chapter 36

## Newer Set Additions and Collaboration

It was now May 4, 1972, ten years to the day since the Movieland Wax Museum first opened its doors to the public. In ten exciting and busy years at Movieland, so much had changed. The museum was now entertaining at least one million enthusiastic visitors a year. It was hugely successful at this point in time. This success led to an ambitious expansion with eight or nine brand new elaborate sets with top-quality wax figures dedicated within the past two years.

By far, one of the most spectacular, newer sets that we ever added to the museum later on was the *Ben-Hur: A Tale of the Christ* (1959) set. We discussed it earlier, but we need to talk about it in a little more detail because it was a significant addition to the museum at that time.

The *Ben-Hur* set depicted the famous chariot race in all its glory. In the foreground you saw the handsome and extremely talented Charlton Heston and his four beautiful white horses winning the race while his vanquished friend-turned-enemy named Messala played by actor Steven Boyd (1931-1977) lay badly wounded on the ground. In the background there were hundreds of spectators watching as the events unfolded.

Creating a set on such a grand scale involved huge challenges. I like to mention these challenges so the public will appreciate just exactly how many different talents and efforts were part of each set's collaboration. There was my wax artistry involved, of course, but so many other highly talented individuals were involved. There were a large number of people helping to build the sets, the original visionaries, the actors themselves, the talented costume designers, hair artists, electricians and machinists, other artists, and many others.

Everything had to come together for each set within the museum with the proper timing, elements, individuals and foresight or it just would not work.

To sum it all up, interestingly enough each individual Movieland Wax Museum set was like a mini-movie production all its own. I feel that this is a significant fact about the dynamics of set building at Movieland which really tied it into the world of making movies and Hollywood productions.

With regards to *The Wizard of Oz* (1939) set, this was another very important later addition to the museum, and one that drew a great many people in on its own. An entire new section of the museum was added that consisted mainly of foliage as if you were walking through a gorgeous, green forest. *The Wizard of Oz* set was in that section of the museum surrounded by lovely trees and lush greenery where you would suddenly find yourself walking on the Yellow Brick Road. It was definitely a sight to see.

Another spectacular later addition was the *Spartacus* aka *Spartacus: Rebel Against Rome* (1960) set. Kirk Douglas and his fellow gladiator named Drode, played by actor and athlete Woody Strode (1914-1994), battled it out to the death as Sir Lawrence Olivier (1907-1989) who played Marcus Licinius Crassus, the Emperor, gave a thumbs down. The "thumbs down" signal meant that one of them was to be killed. Actress Jean Simmons (1929-2010) who played Virginia was standing up above them, looking down into the arena. The realistic quality of this set was quite dramatic.

Then there was another newer addition which included a scene with the lovely Marlo Thomas from the *That Girl* (1966-1971) TV Series. This was a charming set for the museum. Marlo had a huge following and her TV show was extremely entertaining. She was a fan of the museum and we were a fan of hers.

Also mentioned previously was the *Beverly Hillbillies* (1962) set with the Clampett Clan, riding along in their outlandish old truck. They drove that old jalopy into the hearts of television viewers everywhere. That set was also on the edge of the foliage area.

Another set added to the museum was the set where Debbie Reynolds (1932 to present) who played Sister Ann in *The Singing Nun* (1966) rode her motor bike down a quiet forest path lined with real trees, also in the foliage area.

Will Rogers (1879-1935) was in the foliage area on his set for the Western film *Limb Shot* (1931) sitting on an old, dusty wagon apparently ready to sport some of his down-to-earth philosophies from the wagon top. Lasso in hand, Will Rogers gazed out at the Movieland visitors. The realistic quality and western feel of this set was stunning.

Tony Orlando (1944 to present) was one of the people we created a wax figure for around this same time frame. They wanted his set to be about the 1970's comedy and variety television series titled *Tony Orlando & Dawn* (1974-1976). There were Tony Orlando and the girls Joyce Vincent Wilson (1946 to present) and Telma Hopkins (1948 to present). They were very lovely ladies known as "the Dawn girls" and were always dressed in tremendously fashionable attire. Tony Orlando normally appeared in a tux on the show and it went over quite well.

We had a sitting with Tony Orlando and then later on with the Dawn girls. The sittings went seamlessly. Mr. Orlando had promised that he would donate a pair of the special costume shoes that he always wore on the program. Also, he helped us get the perfect outfit for his figure with his tailor's help, which really helped enhance this set. The Dawn girls' wax figures wore matching costumes just like the original television show characters wore.

Everything seemed to go extremely well with the *Tony Orlando & Dawn* set. But I noticed that Mr. Orlando had lifts on his shoes. The lifts seemed strangely high and I did not recall anything like that on his shoes before, but they said these were the original shoes from the show. It turned out that after we got all the figures dressed and all the costumes were in our hands and everything set up, we learned something we had not known beforehand.

Mr. Orlando had always wanted to look at least one full inch taller than the Dawn girls on the TV show. Therefore, he had always worn lifts on the show. The shoes he donated to us also had lifts, so it seemed apparent that he wanted to make sure that the wax figure was also taller. One day we got a call from the producers of the *Tony Orlando & Dawn* show, and they requested that the wax figures appear on the show. We were delighted of course, and it was arranged. But when Mr. Orlando stood next to his wax figure, he looked to be at least an inch shorter than the figure. I was not exactly pleased about this and never understood it. He had given us the original costume shoes with lifts, so we could not complain to him about it. As it turned out, no one had any complaints. I suppose if he had worn lifts while standing next to his wax figure, then it may not have been as noticeable, but we will never know.

Movieland set of *The Wizard of Oz*.

# Chapter 37

## More on Spartacus, The Douglas Boys

We mentioned that Kirk Douglas was in the museum along with Woody Strode in one of the *Spartacus* scenes. To give you some background and as mentioned previously, before the revised, bigger *Spartacus* set was finished we had Kirk Douglas as *Spartacus* on a turntable fighting Woody Strode out in the middle of the museum, revolving around continually near D.W. Griffith's position.

I had some exceedingly wonderful photographs to work from for Kirk Douglas. I had many photographs of him in brief costumes so I could see his entire body, all his muscles and veins and such. I made up my mind that I would put every detail that I could see in the photographs in his final wax figure, including specific moles and veins in his arms and legs that showed up in the photographs. I did everything I could to make his body look authentic. He was not a giant man but he had a beautiful physique from a lot of working out. He was in superb shape.

I used to know some of the old makeup artists back from the *Spartacus* set. One of them was named Wally Westmore. He was a good friend of mine and he loved to come out to the museum. Sometimes he brought his family and friends to the museum and he greatly enjoyed coming to see the wax figures. And this interest he had kind of went along with his industry of being a makeup artist.

Wally was looking over the set of *Spartacus* one day. They had made the original motion picture overseas, sometimes having their movie sets in the desert. There were many movie sets that had been built out in the desert. Many of the extras for the movie that played the gladiators were the very muscular "Muscle Beach" type of men. In fact, many of these extras were actually found at the one and only Muscle Beach in Venice, California. These screen extras had to look exceptionally buff in order to depict the gladiators who worked very hard at becoming muscular and strong to give themselves the best chance possible at survival as they fought to the death in the arena.

Wally told me one of the funniest things that ever happened during the filming of *Spartacus* was when they were on the set and played a practical joke on Mr. Kirk Douglas. As I mentioned before, Mr. Douglas was not as tall as he seemed and not quite as large as all the gladiators that were found at Muscle Beach, but he had a very well-built, strong physique. Apparently, he felt that he needed some cushioning for his body for one particular scene that he had to film.

In this scene, Kirk Douglas and the gladiators were practicing their calisthenics and training to become very successful gladiators in the best of shape. They had this one bar that they had to run up to where they would do many chin-ups for one short scene in the movie. After a bunch of these buff gladiators run up to the bar and do their chin-ups, Kirk Douglas has his turn.

Mr. Douglas knew he was a bit smaller than these other gladiators, so when the scene was being filmed, he requested that a gladiator who was not quite as big as he was go to the chin-up bar right before him. This would make him look larger than that gladiator before him and more comparable in size with the larger and more muscular men. So they got a smaller fellow ready to go right before Mr. Douglas, and this assured the actor that he would look as large as possible.

The day finally came when this one scene was to be filmed out in the hot desert. Generally, there were not too many actors or extras out on any given set at any one time, so as to keep things under control and less costly. They did not need a huge entourage out there as it made things more complicated and slower to film.

In this one scene, however, they had quite a few Muscle Beach fellows preceding Kirk Douglas and running up a hill and directly to the chin-up bar. Then, as mentioned before, the slightly smaller gladiator would take his turn running up to the bar, and then Mr. Douglas would come looking just a bit larger than his predecessor. The word eventually got around about the plan to have this smaller guy in the mix for this scene.

A practical joke began taking on its own life. Someone had arranged to get the one and only, World Famous One-Armed Chin-Up Artist to show up. This fellow was quite tall and very thin. He could do one-armed pull-ups or chin-ups to no end, as he was the world champion. So in good fun, they thought this would be a funny joke. Only the movie extras knew about this plan. They would have this one-armed champion do his part right before Kirk Douglas would go on.

On the day of this particular scene's film shoot, it seemed that every single soul who had been working on this movie within range showed up to this set to watch it being filmed. Kirk Douglas was wondering why there were so many extras and people buzzing around to watch this scene. He was puzzled. However, the director Stanley Kubrick convinced Mr. Douglas that it really was quite an interesting scene to watch with all these muscular men and Kirk Douglas himself doing these chin-ups. Mr. Douglas could not really understand why everyone would be quite so intrigued by this particular scene, but he went with it.

So when it was time for everyone to shoot their scene and the cameraman shouted, "Roll 'em!" all the big guys started running up the hill, covered in sweat. They ran up to this chin-up bar on queue and began to do their chin-ups as rehearsed. So after the large bulk of these muscular men finished their chin-ups, Kirk Douglas was getting ready to run up and do his part. Right before Kirk Douglas was just about to do his part, there came this very tall, skinny World Champion One-Armed Chin-Up Artist who ran straight up to the bar right ahead of Mr. Douglas. This guy ran right up to the chin-up bar and did about five or six one-armed chin-ups, better than any of the muscular bunch could do with their two-armed chin-ups. Well, that just set off the entire group of actors and spectators alike. Everyone just busted up laughing as hard as could be, tearing up in the eyes. Right away, Mr. Douglas could see that this was all a set-up, a practical joke, and at his expense! People were just losing it, cracking up with laughter.

When Mr. Douglas realized what was going on, he just threw everything on the ground and simply stormed off, stomping hard. He was visibly upset and just walked right off the set. He took his role very seriously as an actor and wanted this scene to look the best it could. It was somewhat of an unkind joke, but everyone thought it was just the funniest thing ever. They did not expect Mr. Douglas' reaction, to be certain. People felt bad about that.

Mr. Douglas did not feel real good about showing up for the next couple of days, because he was still quite taken aback by this joke at his expense. But after a few days, they coaxed him back out and they finished the scene and it all went off without a hitch. It seems that my friend Wally Westmore thought that was a pretty funny story, as did most of the people who witnessed it, but unfortunately the recipient of the joke did not take it quite as well as everyone had hoped. But he got over it in time. And Wally Westmore thought the wax figure and all the details of Kirk Douglas had turned out very authentic, having witnessed the actual filming himself.

When the time was right, Jack drove Mr. Douglas over to Movieland and then went over with him to join me while he looked at his wax figure. Mr. Douglas just could not get over the amazing detail, especially on his body, with every mark and vein in just the right place that I tried to replicate. He was obviously just impressed beyond belief. Mr. Douglas said to me, "This is just unbelievable. You've got every mole and vein of mine in the exact spot!"

He was also very impressed with how the figures were on the turntable, rotating. I told him that we were planning on having a full-blown set for *Spartacus* in the future. Mr. Douglas was very happy to hear this news and said he would be thrilled to come out when that set was finished to see it later on. Jack took Mr. Douglas back home, and he was more than gracious, thanking him very much for the ride.

# Chapter 38

## Bonanza

lso in the green forest section of the museum mentioned earlier, there was the beautiful *Bonanza* (1959-1973) TV Series set. It had the full front of the farmhouse and real trees around it. Our set designer and builder also built some simulated tree trunks out of fiberglass and then affixed real bark to them to look authentic. Even the branches had been fabricated to look real. The artificial foliage, along with the real trees, which had been preserved professionally, made the entire set look very impressive. There was a beautiful old, red wagon sitting in front of the farmhouse to complete the effect.

All three of the main characters from the *Bonanza* TV series were in front of this whole scene. Dan Blocker (1928-1972) was on the right side, Lorne Greene (1915-1987) was in the middle and Michael Landon (1936-1991) was off to the left. It looked very realistic and fit in beautifully with the museum.

There was one thing about Dan Blocker that I noticed when I was making his wax figure. This was that unless he smiled quite widely, it looked as if he did not have any upper front teeth when he smiled. I had a hard time figuring this out but I made the figure just like I saw the photographs, and in the photographs Dan Blocker did not seem to have any main front teeth. So that is the way I created him and he looked very natural.

One day, Mrs. Blocker (Dan Blocker's mother) came in to see the set because she had heard about it and was very interested in seeing it first-hand. She asked for me and of course I was very happy to take her over to the set so she could see it. We had a rail-type of fence around the set. When Mrs. Blocker looked at the figure of her son, she thought it looked very nice. But she asked me if I wouldn't mind if she went over the fence to look at her son closely. I told her I did not mind at all.

So I helped her over the low fence and she walked right up to her son Dan's character named Eric "Hoss" Cartwright. She was a little tiny thing and Hoss was six feet four inches tall. She looked right up at him and said, "Yep! You got him!"

I asked her what she meant by that. She said that I had accurately depicted how it looks like his front teeth are not there when he smiles. I told her that I had simply gone by what I saw in the photographs. She told me that I had done it just right. The reason that he had these issues with his teeth, according to his mother, was because he was terribly afraid of the dentist. She called him a "baby" about it. Apparently, old Dan had been told by his dentist that they would need to move his two side teeth near the front of his mouth out forward more because they were blocking his front teeth somewhat. It was going to be a pretty involved procedure to do this and he refused to go in and do it. He was apparently told by his mother on many weekends to go to his dentist and allow them to do the work.

Eventually, he had waited too long and there was no room for the other front teeth to come down. The procedure would be even more involved at this point and that is why his teeth looked the way they did. He had not listened to his mother or his dentist out of fear. His mother ended the story by saying that her son was a big, old "scaredy cat" and that she just could not get him to ever go to the dentist.

With regards to costumes, as mentioned before we would always try to get the original, authentic costumes for the sets. When that was not possible we got the next best thing by going to Western Costume, who would make most of our costumes from the original patterns because they had almost all of them. They monopolized the TV series costumes and they were the best.

Each costume would be created according to the measurements of the figures I made. For the authenticity of the look and fit of the costume on the wax figure, we would send the entire wax figure to Western Costume so they had all the precise measurements and exact size for the costumes. It was quite an incredible feat: they would build a costume directly onto the wax figure, made to look exactly like the original costume from the movie or television show, usually with the exact pattern and fabric that was used. This way, they had very few alterations to make.

Getting back to the *Bonanza* set and costumes on this set's figures, the authenticity of the look of the entire production made this one of the most popular sets we ever had in the museum. It did not hurt that *Bonanza* was one of the most popular television series of this time, either.

# Chapter 39

## Paul Newman, Robert Redford and Gene Kelly

aul Newman and Robert Redford as *Butch Cassidy and the Sundance Kid* had always been one of our most beloved sets. They were, of course, two of the most popular leading men in Hollywood. Unfortunately, I did not get a chance to have a sitting with them at all. What I did, however, was to get many good pictures and their measurements to work from. I always tried to get movie stills and photographs of the front, back, three-quarters view and side views of the stars. I also liked to have several full body shots.

I always gathered as much material as possible to work with for each wax figure that I created. I even had to make sure I had all the colors correct and accurate, from skin tones, eyes and hair, to clothing and backgrounds. After all the paraphernalia and pictures were gathered and ready for use, the next and most important step was to begin creating the actual figure. Also, I could sometimes get very recent and accurate body measurements from some of the star's costume designers or seamstresses, which would make it possible for me to make their full body wax figure as close as possible to the real thing. So with the photographs and measurements, I made each figure. They actually turned out to be as good a pair of figures as any others I did in the museum with sittings. People loved them.

However, I had a lot of trouble creating the Paul Newman, Butch Cassidy figure at the beginning. This is because I did not have a perfect, full face shot of him dead-on from the front. I had some three-quarter shots and side shots, but no full frontal view. So after I created the figure, it was well received but nobody really said, "Wow!" I had to create the figure the best I could with the pictures I had because Mr. Parkinson wanted it finished.

I thought that as popular as Paul Newman was, it would have created much more of a stir from the museum guests and his fans. I could tell that people did not think that the original figure looked exactly like Butch Cassidy; they thought it looked pretty darn close, but not exact enough to cause a sensation.

I looked high and low and finally after several weeks, I found a pretty decent picture of Paul Newman as Butch Cassidy from the front, straight on. I took the Butch Cassidy figure back into my museum studio, temporarily.

I studied this photograph, remeasured everything and I found out that his upper lip needed to be a little less long, and there was just a little too much space between the nose and the mouth. He needed a bit less of a "horsey" look. So I carefully changed it by making his upper lip slightly shorter. This meant reworking almost the entire face from the nose down.

Once this "little" change was made to Mr. Newman's figure, there was a tremendous difference in how he looked and how the people reacted. In fact, this change made the whole set come alive. And this exercise really showed how the slightest change in one of my wax figures could make or break its success. It also showed how important it was to have a full frontal photograph to work from. Some of these figures became a bit of a work in progress until they were just right. After reworking this one, the *Butch Cassidy and the Sundance Kid* set became one of our most popular sets and caused many female hearts to flutter at the museum, I have been told. I take this as a huge compliment.

Mr. Newman was going to come out on many occasions to look at the set, but it seemed that something just always came up. In fact, he was going to come out with Mr. Redford one time. However, when Mr. Newman could not make it, Mr. Redford decided to wait until they could come together. And this went on and on and on. They never did get out but they gave their approval of the set based on all the pictures they saw. They told us how much they appreciated and were honored to be in Movieland Wax Museum.

We had an interesting opening at the museum one time. Mr. Gene Kelly came out to the museum to open his set from his greatest picture ever, and one of the greatest scenes in this picture, *Singin' in the Rain* (1952).

Mr. Kelly was escorted to Movieland at the request of Mr. Parkinson in our Rolls Royce for what was called "Gene Kelly Day." There were lots of people there due to Gene Kelly's popularity. Mr. Parkinson ushered him in and up to his set where he checked it out. Gene Kelly just loved the set. It was so attractive with Gene Kelly wearing a yellow rain coat and hanging on a lamppost while rain was pouring down, leaning and singing his heart out. We were thrilled with his satisfaction.

Picture of the wax figures Logan created of Paul Newman and Robert Redford
from the movie *Butch Cassidy and the Sundance Kid*.

# Chapter 40

## Lawrence Welk

The museum was always very crowded during the summertime, averaging eight thousand or more visitors a day. This prompted us to take our family vacations during the summer because I could not get much work done on the sets when so many people were constantly filing through the museum. This time off allowed us to travel extensively. During the 70s & 80s we travelled over almost all of the United States, showing our children so many things that Liz and I had never experienced as children. We both grew up in the era of the Great Depression and it was such a pleasure and a blessing to be able to show our children Kevin, Miles, Craig and our niece Sara so many amazing and educational places and historical sights. We both felt that travel was a privilege and an education in itself.

Anyhow, we received a last-minute notice that Lawrence Welk (1903-1992) was going to be doing a sitting with us one late spring day, right before the busy summer season kicked in. I was told that we would be creating two figures for Mr. Welk; one for the new museum in Orlando, and one for Movieland in Buena Park. This was a tall order, so we had to quickly do this sitting with Mr. Welk before I went on vacation.

We met him in his office. Mr. Welk had a large building that he owned in Santa Monica. His offices were up on one entire floor with a huge banquet table, crystal chandeliers and other ornate furnishings. It was quite lavish and a very inviting setup, complete with a full bar for entertaining. He undoubtedly used this office to entertain people.

When we met Mr. Welk and his agent in his office building, we had all of our people with us, including our photographer, our publicist, the driver and of course, we had our swivel chair. Mr. Welk was a very nice, interesting man. I took measurements from him and he was very cooperative. In addition, he gave me some paperwork with all his measurements and clothing sizes.

During this meeting, Mr. Welk told me he had some new music that he was going to use on his program. It happened to be a waltz. Our publicist Lovetta was very cute, and Mr. Welk noticed her and thought that he would like to try out this new music with her doing the polka with him. Lovetta was a good sport and said she would try. They had a blast dancing around the room to the polka. It was a fun moment for Lovetta.

After they danced for several minutes, Mr. Welk sat down to take a rest. As he was sitting down, he mentioned that one of his greatest thrills ever had been giving Arnold Palmer three shots in the PGA Tour the day before. I asked him more about this, knowing that outside of music, golf was his favorite pastime. As Mr. Welk was telling us about his thrilling day of golf, I noticed a beautiful diamond ring that he was wearing and complimented him on it. He proceeded to tell me that his ring had quite a story behind it.

The ring on his finger had kept his band going on more than one occasion. I asked him what he meant by that. He told me that things were very tough back during the Great Depression, especially in the Midwest. Money was very tight, and times were hard. His band was as loyal as any band could be. They were blowing into these little Midwestern towns all the time and they would find gigs here and there, but they never knew when they would get their next one. Sometimes they had to wait four, five or even more days until their next paid gig came up. They would often simply run out of money.

Mr. Welk's ring had saved their necks several times. It had become such a regular occurrence to use the ring for survival that it had actually become a laughing stock amongst the band members. They would hock the ring any time they had to, just to keep themselves eating and alive until the next gig. They would have a nice big meal, keep themselves going a bit longer, and then they would find their next job. Suddenly, they would go back and purchase back their ring once they made enough money back as things started to look up again. And the cycle continued for quite some time.

The usual way they would transfer from one place to another back then was by riding the freight trains. They had it down to a science and it was a way to get a free ride to the next job. They'd wait until the train would pull into the little town and get all loaded up. When the conductor was all set and ready to move ahead, and at just the right moment, they'd run like bats out of hell, the entire band and all of their instruments, and hop onto the trains at lightning speed. It was a dangerous thing to do, but back then in those difficult times it was also much more commonplace than you would think.

One of the biggest challenges was getting the large double bass instruments (also known as bass viols) loaded onto the trains with them. He said they had ruined more of these large instruments than he cared to admit. Finally, they figured out that it would take four men, two up on the car and two down below, to gently put the bass viols onto the flat car without wrecking them. Of course, whenever they lost a bass viol, the ring came into play again as collateral to purchase a new one.

This is how Lawrence Welk's band got started back in the Midwestern cow towns. Of course, eventually they became a major success with their wonderful band and long running television show. In the past, they had definitely paid their dues, though. This is what made Lawrence Welk's ring much more sentimental.

With all the great photographs and measurements of Mr. Welk I was able to make one very high quality, duplicate wax figure of Mr. Welk, with his baton high in the air. That is how he always used to pose. As an aside, Mr. Welk had also asked me if I could make his wax figures look just a few years younger than he actually was, and I had no problem trying to do my best at fulfilling his wish.

We were given word after those two figures were completed that we were to transfer them to Hollywood where they would be on *The Lawrence Welk Show*. One would be for the Stars Hall of Fame in Florida and one would be for Movieland Wax Museum. Mr. Welk would pose with both figures on the show.

The figures were delivered to the studio. I brought my family with me to see the show and we were really looking forward to this. One of the figures of Mr. Welk was wheeled right into the studio where the program would happen. Another one was on a wheeled cart and left on the back stage temporarily. As Welk's cast began to drift in for the show backstage, my family was already seated with the audience in the front so they did not see how the cast reacted to Mr. Welk's figure. But they could see how the audience was going to view this wax figure of Lawrence Welk. I was standing directly behind the figure so I saw and heard the reactions of the cast as they saw it for the first time. I heard many positive comments about how great the figure looked.

The little girl who used to do the polka for the show came in early and looked at the wax figure of Mr. Welk sitting on a four-wheeled dolly back stage. She approached it and said, "You know, Lawrence, I've got a few things on my chest that I'd like to discuss with you right now. I have wanted to tell you this for some time but just haven't had the courage to do it until now." Everyone who was in the show was standing around and listening, realizing that there was some fun in store. The little girl continued, "You know the polkas that we do on the show? I just detest them because you are *always* stepping on my feet! They are always so very sore after the program. I just hate to tell you this but it is really bothering me..." and she continued on and on while the cast chuckled. The little girl continued pointing her chubby little fingers at him and telling him a thing or two as the real Lawrence Welk walked up behind her and stood there, listening to her with a twinkle in his eye.

She finally finished her bickering and told Mr. Welk's figure that she felt much better now, having gotten all of that off of her chest. Finally, she turned around and there stood Lawrence Welk, grinning from ear-to-ear! She gave Mr. Welk a huge hug, wrapping her arms around him as he said, "Oh, is that how you *really* feel?" And the stars of the show just laughed at this very fun little number before the actual show started.

Soon it was time to place the actual wax figures in their proper places behind the curtain. Then when the curtains were ready to be drawn, everything would be ready for the audience. At this time, they were advertising the old Geritol product. During the advertisement, the spokesperson would step into a little booth and talk about the product and how Geritol could make you feel much better and so forth. That was how the "commercials" were done during the show back then.

The show started off perfectly with the two figures set up in their places on stage. We left Mr. Welk to get up onto a dolly in between the two figures. He assumed the same, precise pose as the wax figures. There were then three "figures" all set up and ready on the stage for the show to begin. The show was pulled off without a hitch, and was great fun for all. I have to say that it was probably one of the most enjoyable, entertaining nights for one of these openings and it was special that my whole family was with me.

All of the stars and those associated with Mr. Lawrence Welk's band including Mr. Welk himself were some of the very nicest people I have ever had the pleasure to meet and to work with. They gave me some of the best memories I have ever had while working for the wax museum.

Later on after the sitting for Mr. Welk, his two wax figures were taken to Movieland and the Stars Hall of Fame. We had openings and dedications for both sets at each location, with Lawrence Welk present. He was so very much loved by his fans, and it was apparent and quite nice to see that he was delighted with his career. It is always so refreshing to see someone who loves what they do for a living.

Logan meets with Lawrence Welk to discuss his wax figure. *Norton Photography.*

Lawrence Welk (left) standing next to his wax likeness created by Logan.

The hand of Lawrence Welk with the all-important ring he would pawn again and again to keep his band going.

# Chapter 41

## Gone with the Wind

Another poignant event was when an airplane hostess offered mint juleps to Scarlett O'Hara (Vivien Leigh; 1913-1967) and Rhett Butler (Clark Gable; 1901-1960) from the wonderful American classic film titled *Gone With the Wind* on their Eastern Airlines flight to Atlanta. They were on their way to the Stars Hall of Fame. The only wrench in her hospitality was that she was offering the beverages to the wax figures, not the actual stars! The figures were seated in the airplane with all the other guests, looking as real as anyone else buckled in with their seat belts. It was an honest mistake, but suffice it to say that the $20,000 wax figures looked real enough to be offered a popular southern drink by an unsuspecting airline hostess. This was another delightful compliment.

Behind them, one of our managers and a friend of mine to this day named Colonel John Tomlinson rode along with our figures on the airplane to protect them. However, wax figures obviously do not need to order airplane meals, so we got a very good deal back then on their air fares. They were buckled in their seats like all of the other passengers. In a photograph I saw, it is clear that John and the passengers were all having a good time and that they caused quite an enjoyable commotion on the airplane. The "stars" were all dressed up in their *Gone with the Wind* attire.

The lovely *Gone With the Wind* set with Scarlett O'Hara and Rhett Butler
(Vivien Leigh and Clark Gable).

# Chapter 42

## Western Sets

Another set that had tremendous popularity was the John Wayne (1907-1979) set that was based on the movie he made called *Hondo* (1953). We had the backdrop of the western wilderness painted by one of the most talented movie set painters in Hollywood. I've seen pictures of this set in publications and books all over the world. Many people who have seen this photograph think it is really a picture of the real John Wayne and not of his wax figure.

While John Wayne had not come to Movieland for his own set dedication, he had always been very enthusiastic, respectful and supportive about having his wax figure and set in the museum. He also had a strange aversion to coming in and attending a huge dedication event for his set. This may have been partly due to the fact that his best friend Ward Bond's wax figure was just a few sets away from his set. The actual reason for Mr. Wayne's aversion was never quite clear, but he just was not really comfortable coming in and making a big deal out of anything.

The talented actor Ward Bond's (1903-1960) wax figure was another one of our very best figures. Mr. Bond appeared to be exiting the set and looked just as real as he could ever look. As a matter of fact, as mentioned earlier, his wife gave us one of his complete costumes that he actually wore on the set of the *Wagon Train* (1957-1965) TV series. This show was about different experiences during the long trek of some people in their wagon train as it traveled from post-Civil War Missouri toward California through the plains, deserts and Rocky Mountains. The first journey was led by a gruff but good-at-heart Major Seth Adams played by Ward Bond. He traveled along with his very helpful frontier scout named Flint McCullough, who was played by the actor Robert Horton (1924 to present).

Having Mr. Bond's authentic costume from the TV series really helped finish off this set and made it look top-notch. I worked very hard and put in quite a bit of extra time and effort to make him look extremely authentic, and the results were spectacular.

Anyhow, Mr. John Wayne got word of how authentic Ward Bond's wax figure looked on the set for *Wagon Train* in the museum. He admitted to us that he just was not very comfortable being in the museum so very close to his best friend's authentic-looking wax figure for some reason only known to himself.

John Wayne was a very large man at six feet four inches tall, and wore a size ten-and-a-half shoe. He had a careful gait to the way he walked in his high-heeled cowboy boots. It gave Mr. Wayne a very deliberate and distinctive walk that was all John Wayne, which made him more invincible than others.

In the film *Hondo*, there was a sheepdog that was equally as big a star as Mr. Wayne himself and both were portrayed in the Movieland set. One day I was on the *Hondo* (1953) set working on some minor details around where the little plants and bushes were in the foreground. All of a sudden, the cutest little girl burst through the bushes and onto the set very quickly. This little girl was with her mother, a very high-society type of lady, dressed to the nines. The young girl was dressed as cute as a bug's ear herself. However, she had just shot onto the set inappropriately of course and burst out, "Lookie lookie lookie here, Momma!! It's Lassie!"

The little girl was of course pointing to the dog, not to John Wayne's figure. The little girl's mother said, "Oh, no, my goodness! That's not Lassie! My goodness dear, that Lassie was a very beautiful dog. This is just an old sheepdog! This could not be Lassie!"

Well, I had to correct this lady right away. I told her that her little daughter was absolutely correct and that this dog was Lassie. She said, "Well, I saw the actual motion picture and the dog in it was an old, beat-up sheepdog!" So I explained to this woman that the makeup artists were due some major credit, for they had transformed the beautiful dog that played Lassie into an old, haggard-looking sheepdog for the film *Hondo*. I explained to her that it took over five hours to transform Lassie into a beaten-down looking dog.

I went on to explain that they used Lassie for the films because no other dog could do what was needed to shoot the scene. I had a friend who was on location for the film that had seen director John Ford go through several real sheepdogs but none could "act." After five days of trials and tribulations they called in Lassie to shoot the scenes.

Lassie helped make that movie one of Mr. Wayne's most successful pictures ever. The little girl's mother did not know what to say. Her little girl said, "See Mommy! Mommy! Mommy! I told you so!" and her mother grabbed her hand and guided her right out of there. Her mother was irritated that she had been incorrect and her little daughter had pointed it out.

Continuing on in our Western section was country singer, Mr. Roy Clark (1933 to present). He had been invited to have his figure in the museum and to come down for his measurement and interview appointment. Mr. Clark was very popular back then. Down in Nashville he was (and is) a regular legend. He was also extremely popular in Branson, Missouri, where he had his own big entertainment club.

At the time Mr. Clark came in for his sitting, he was carrying around quite a bit of extra weight. He was a big man, very full through the face. He had a very pleasant look though, and spoke with almost a chuckle. We did Mr. Clark's measurements and took careful attention to accuracy to get all the details and photographs of his complete persona and appearance.

He gave us one of his great western outfits with a very beautiful coat to use for the set. When everything was done, I dressed his wax figure with the beautiful western costume he had presented to us for use in the museum. Since I was very careful to get his exact body measurements, the clothes fit beautifully.

When Roy Clark came to the museum to dedicate the set I was completely astonished, initially. Mr. Clark did not look at all close in size to his wax figure. He was much, much thinner and appeared to have lost up to fifty pounds. It just shook me up. I was obviously concerned because we had to take pictures of him with his wax figure. This was not going to be the opening night but just a preliminary visit by Mr. Clark to take some photographs. He apologized to us profusely but explained that his doctor had ordered him to lose weight and he had taken heed to his doctor's advice. But it sure made him look much smaller, and of course the costume he had provided fit his wax figure just fine like it had fit him in the past. He even seemed a bit shorter when standing next to his figure.

So Mr. Parkinson noticed the discrepancy between Roy Clark's appearance in person and the wax figure that I had created and worked so hard on. He commented that I normally was so accurate and wondered why the measurements were so off in this case. He thought Mr. Clark looked like just "a little bitty guy" and not like himself in the wax figure. This comment from my boss upset me, of course.

I went to Allen Parkinson's office and explained to him what had happened. I told him about Mr. Clark's medical advice and how he had followed it, not mentioning anything to me in the process and surprising me on this day as much as Mr. Parkinson was surprised. I told him that it bothered me as well because it made me look like I was off. I had hoped the final pictures to be taken later would be a bit better and that maybe Mr. Clark would have put on a little more weight again by that time. Of course we could not count on that, but I had hopes. I also told Allen that I would see to it that Mr. Clark would look to be the same height, even if I had to give him a slight rise or platform to stand on during the final photograph session. This seemed to appease Mr. Parkinson.

Well, Mr. Clark did return and we had a marvelous reception and opening for him. The public just loved him and everyone seemed extremely pleased with the entire production and set. When he stood on a very discreet platform he looked to be the same height as his wax figure and he had luckily gained just a little bit of weight back.

Mr. Parkinson left me a note commenting that he was perplexed as to how things turned out so well at the opening reception and that Roy Clark had looked just fine next to his wax figure. He was quite pleased with the final results, as I was. He congratulated me and told me that Mr. Clark was very happy with his wax figure, too.

One other point of interest to mention was that when the museum personnel and I had originally arranged for Mr. Clark to have his first measurement appointment, our driver had picked him up in the limousine. When the driver arrived at his hotel, Mr. Clark's entire entourage was there with him; they consisted mostly of local hometown "mountain boys." Thus, our driver picked up Mr. Clark's entire group and the chauffeur had been instructed to take Mr. Clark out to a nice meal at the restaurant of his choice. Of course, since Mr. Clark's entire entourage was with him it meant that they would be treated with the same respect and graciousness.

Interestingly enough, Mr. Clark had picked out a little hamburger stand in the middle of Watts in Los Angeles that he had heard great things about. His neighbors had raved about this hamburger place, so Roy wanted to try it. They were all very excited to try the burgers. Our driver Jack Collins sought out this rather well-known hamburger joint in Watts and took them to it.

Everyone had a wonderful time, and many customers gathered around them when they discovered Roy Clark was in their midst. It made for quite a buzz around town. Everyone had gotten a kick watching Roy Clark enjoy his delectable hamburger.

Another noteworthy thing to mention about Roy Clark is that he was absolutely a family man. Roy was very close to his father, whom he loved dearly. His father had been extremely instrumental in helping Roy get his career going, with a lot of support and encouragement. He had even brought his father out with him to one of his measurement sessions. When the museum had arranged one time to put Mr. Clark up in a nice hotel nearby as a matter of convenience, Roy had also taken it upon himself to arrange to have another hotel room right next door to his room reserved for his father so that his father could be there at the meeting and share in the experience. Mr. Clark was truly a very wonderful man, through and through.

The wax likeness of John Wayne from the set for the film *Hondo*, one of the most famous wax figures that was ever made by Logan Fleming for Movieland.

Logan's wax figure of Roy Clark, with the actor himself standing proudly next to it.

# Chapter 43

## Sanford and Son

Another very popular set at Movieland Wax Museum was *Sanford and Son* (1972-1977), the popular TV series that had quite a long run. The two principal characters from the show were Redd Foxx (1922-1991) and LaWanda Page (1920-2002) and both were portrayed in the Movieland set. LaWanda was always mad at Redd and chased him around with her heavy handbag.

When I went to Redd Foxx's home to do his measurement and photo session, we brought our swivel chair to get precise views of every angle of his face and body as we usually did. Jack Collins, our chauffeur, the publicity lady and photographer all went with me to help get this done. We were lucky to get extremely fantastic pictures of him. During this meeting, Mr. Foxx admitted that he had so much fun working on his show. Although he always appeared to be fighting with LaWanda on the TV show, in real life they had become very close friends and had just a wonderful, fun time working together on *Sanford and Son*.

Mr. Foxx was also a very interesting man with an interesting background. I noticed that Mr. Foxx had a picture of the artist Grant Wood's famous piece titled "American Gothic" hanging in his front room. Everything about it was authentic except that he had somehow had the picture changed to depict himself and his wife in place of the farmer and his wife from the original piece of art. It made for quite a funny, interesting conversation piece of art in his home. He had an extremely amazing sense of humor, and this picture somewhat portrayed it even more so. I told him I thought it was quite a picture with the changes he had made. He called it his "American Portrait" and he was very fond of it. He told me in jest that his farm was not doing so well but that he was putting up his game face in the picture. It was cute.

I noticed he was quite well-built, solid and muscular, but not too large. I asked Mr. Foxx if he had ever done any really serious athletics and he mentioned that he had done some boxing in the past. He had quite a few fights and was somewhat successful at it until he got into the movie industry.

We also had a very nice sitting with LaWanda Page at a later date for this set. LaWanda lived in Watts at that time and we went to her house. She met us at the door. LaWanda was a very sweet lady. We had the Rolls Royce sitting in front of her house and we all went inside and set everything up so we could take some nice pictures and get some great measurements for her wax figure. It was a successful meeting and she was very fun and joked a lot with us. There was a huge dog in her backyard that growled and barked the entire time due to all the fuss going on inside. LaWanda told us that she would not dare let that dog inside for our sake! It was obviously there to protect her.

After the meeting with LaWanda, I asked her if she had a seamstress that she could refer us to for her costume measurements. She told us that she did not have a seamstress and asked if I could just take all of her measurements myself. Well, from time to time it became a tad embarrassing for me while measuring some of the stars, especially the women. To get an accurate measurement of her entire body, I had to measure her upper legs and thighs. If a woman is wearing slacks it is not such a big deal, but LaWanda was wearing a pure white dress. She had very dark, flawless skin, and it was quite a contrast.

So I started at her ankles, then her knees, and made the measurements that were needed. Her dress was just above her knee and I was not sure how I would take her upper thigh measurements. I contemplated this for a moment, not sure how to proceed. LaWanda could tell from my expression and hesitation exactly what was going through my mind right then. I looked up at LaWanda finally and she looked down at me. She said aloud, "I know now, you need to measure my thighs!" and I was a little flushed but I agreed and told her I needed these measurements to make an accurate wax figure of her.

She reassured me that it was okay to proceed and said, "Go ahead Mr. Fleming, go ahead and measure away!" and with that she suddenly took her white dress and pulled it way up. I proceeded to complete her thigh measurements as quickly and precisely as I could. I told her as soon as I was finished and she dropped the dress right back down in place and then we all chuckled. As we were laughing about the whole situation she told us she used to be a burlesque queen so she didn't have modesty issues and we laughed some more. She kissed us all goodbye. She was really the sweetest thing ever. We had a great time with LaWanda Page. We told her that when we were ready for her set opening, we would be in touch.

Movieland set of *Sanford and Son* created by Logan Fleming.

# Chapter 44

## Touching Moments

As I mentioned once before, Mr. Parkinson was quite a collector of cars. He loved Rolls Royces in particular. Mr. Parkinson had decided that he wanted a very special touch added for an extremely endearing star's set in the museum. This star was none other than the gorgeous Ms. Gloria Swanson (1899-1983). The "special touch" was a custom, gold Cabriolet Rolls Royce shipped all the way from England. It was an extremely rare car as there were only five ever made, and it was in mint condition. Ms. Swanson had been a huge star and he wanted her to have that gorgeous car in her set.

This set depicted a scene from the last picture that Gloria Swanson ever made. In this film, Gloria Swanson played the character Norma Desmond in *Sunset Blvd.* (1950). Her character was a washed-up silent screen actress whose golden days were behind her, yet her sad and pathetic delusions of being invincible turn her into a demented, lonely recluse.

William Holden (1918-1981) played opposite Gloria Swanson in *Sunset Blvd.*, and thus he was on the set standing at attention with her as she stepped out of this striking car. Eric Von Stroheim is also depicted in the set and was her chauffeur in the movie.

When Gloria Swanson came out for her set opening she was dressed to the nines. As she stood next to her wax figure, Mr. Parkinson presented her with a beautiful red carnation. He explained to her that he had a habit of walking through the museum daily to this set, and the lady who was standing closest to it would be given a red carnation, which was quite an honor. Ms. Swanson was just delighted by this! She accepted the carnation from Mr. Parkinson and told him that she would save it for many, many years because it meant something to her.

In the museum, the figure of Cantinflas aka Mario Moreno Cantinflas (1911-1993) from the movie *Si Yo Fuera Diputado* (1952) was very close to the Gina Lollobrigida (1927 to present) set. In this movie, Cantinflas plays a young, local shoeshine boy who is elected by his local community to run for a public office because they are tired of the same old politicians who never make any changes for them. Cantinflas was one of the most popular comedic actors in Mexico. Mr. Parkinson felt that Cantinflas should be represented in the museum because he was connected with so many of the movies and stars that we represented.

Cantinflas was a marvelous fellow. He came down to Los Angeles quite often. Almost every time he came here he wanted to visit Movieland Wax Museum. He became very good friends with Mr. Parkinson. He was very friendly to all of us and one of the nicest fellows you would ever want to meet. He told me that it was a real pleasure and an honor for Mr. Parkinson to include him in our museum.

We used to have a number of the stars' parents come in to visit the museum. It seems to have given them comfort and pride in seeing their children's wax likenesses dressed in beautiful costumes and from familiar, younger times. One of the most regular visitors from the group of parents was Gary Cooper's (1901-1961) folks. His mother came to the set quite regularly.

Another person who came quite often was Mario Lanza's (1921-1959) father to see his son in *The Great Caruso* (1951) set. Mario Lanza was dressed up in opera garb just like he was in the film. For his set, we simulated the feel of a small opera house, complete with theater seats and a stage. People could sit down, listen to music and watch Mario Lanza perform. His figure rotated from side to side as if he was singing to the audience. When Mario Lanza died prematurely, his father took it extremely hard. He was heartbroken beyond words. Something like that was never supposed to happen to this man, his son.

After this tragedy, Mr. Lanza's father would come to Movieland quite often to pay tribute to his son and to visit his set. This was quite a moving and emotional sight to behold. This poor man would sit in one of the opera seats, bring out his handkerchief and just weep his heart out, spending about a half an hour or so listening to the haunting opera music and watching the wax figure likeness of his beloved son.

As sad a spectacle as this was, it was very important for his father to come. The set we built actually became somewhat of a shrine, and it helped this father get through his mourning process. It helped release him from the despair that he was feeling over having lost one of the great loves of his life. This turn of events truly gave a deeper meaning to *The Great Caruso* set and it moved so many of us more than he would ever know.

Another big star that we had in the museum was Edward G. Robinson (1893-1973). On his set for *Little Caesar* (1931), Robinson was moving on a turntable with a gun in his hand, supposedly in a pawn shop. As he turned, the gun would be pointed at the person watching the set. Edward G. Robinson was all dressed up in his overcoat and hat and it looked very authentic.

One day I was walking through the museum. I had no idea that Mr. Robinson came into the museum quite often or even that he was a good friend of Allen Parkinson. But I spotted him in there one day with Mr. Parkinson and he wanted to see his set. As I walked by, Mr. Parkinson stopped and introduced me to Mr. Edward G. Robinson. Allen went on to tell me that Mr. Robinson really liked his wax figure and the set itself. Mr. Robinson confirmed this himself, telling me that it was a great representation of how he would have looked in the movie. He liked the gun and the rotating effect and the way everything worked together. I told him how much time we put into the set and how we decided to plan it out, and he was impressed. I was glad to have met Mr. Robinson as his pictures had been taken before I started working at the museum and we'd not had a sitting with him.

# Chapter 45

## "The Great Sexpot,"
## Mae West

W e had heard some rumors for several days that the striking blonde bombshell Mae West (1893-1980) was possibly going to be coming to Movieland to have her measurements taken for her wax figure. Mae West (whom I feel was "The Great Sexpot") was the sexy, witty and bold actress of many movies and shows who coined dozens of flirtatious quotes and double entendre in order to bypass many of the old Hollywood rules of etiquette, yet she was still able to completely captivate the hearts of many men (and women, too!). She was the first woman to really bring sex out of the closet (or bedroom, for that matter) and not only did she sing and dance with extremely sexy and suggestive moves, but she really epitomized "sexy" with her voluptuous figure, sassy humor and sensual voice.

When we finally got the call to go out and interview Mae West we were extremely excited. Mae West had been such a huge star prior to this time, and although she was much older now, she was still exceedingly beautiful and had quite a colorful and fascinating history. The gentleman who handled Ms. West's photography and fitting appointment was her agent, the popular Ty Jurras.

Generally we had our own publicity lady, Lovetta, to accompany us to all the sittings. However in the case of Mae West, our publicity lady was politely instructed not to attend the actual sitting, so of course it was handled instead by Ms. West's agent. This is because, as we soon found out, Mae West *never* invited other women into her private life or personal affairs. She always wanted men surrounding her, even as an older woman.

We had Ty Jurras, her agent (which Lovetta spoke with to make the arrangements), the photographers, the driver Jack, and I, all in our limousine. Mae West owned the

Ravenswood apartment building in Los Angeles. This is where we had arranged to meet her, in front of her apartment (although she owned the entire building). When we got there in the limousine we knocked on the door, and she answered it in person to greet and invite us inside.

Her apartment was very beautiful, exquisitely furnished, extremely feminine and decorated with lots of white, pink, silver and gold. She had many lovely things in her apartment, including a white, nude statue of herself on top of the piano. The entire apartment "felt" pink. We took the swivel chair with us and as we set everything up with the lighting and all, the sitting began.

Mae West was wearing a sexy negligee with a corset underneath. She looked stunning, especially for her age, as she was quite older by this time. Mae West was very interested in everything that was going on, now and throughout her career. She was used to handling her own business affairs all her life and had quite a lot of business savvy. She always had the last say in everything. She also had a very distinctive way of speaking with a lot of growl-like sounds, like "Arrrrh!" which gave her a touch of an edge to what she said. Needless to say, she had her own way about everything.

Ms. West asked a lot of intelligent questions on how everything operated, and how the wax figure was created. While taking in all of our answers, she was doing a great job of staying posed with the same expression on the swivel chair so we could get shots of all the important angles. About halfway through the sitting the photographer had to change film and we had to stop for a moment. Ms. West was sitting upright in the swivel chair at this time and during this long pause. I could see that she was really working hard to keep herself in the same position while the film was being changed. She would sag slightly and then pull up straight, showing her great will power. She had great pride in what she did, but due to her age it was a bit of a struggle for her to stay comfortable in one position without moving. Somehow she managed to do it. She was always such a strong-willed woman.

Mae West told us the figure that she envisioned for herself was to be six feet tall, even though in fact she was a little woman. She was nowhere close to being six feet tall and was probably barely five feet tall in real life. However she insisted that when on stage she measure exactly six feet tall from the bottom of her shoes to the top of her hair. It was a rule she lived by for many, many years.

If you look back to old clips or watch her films, she almost always looked quite tall, but she wore long, flowing gowns or clothing that covered her feet. No one knew that she had lifts on, or platforms that were many inches tall. Her walk was always kind of a shuffle, a sexy swagger, and this was probably due to the outrageously high shoes she had hidden underneath her clothing. She said she would wear lifts on her shoes for us, too, so she would appear six feet tall in person at the dedication of her set.

She had very, very dark blue eyes. They were stunning. Although Mae West was by no means a natural, gorgeous beauty, she made herself up to look extremely striking and beautiful in her own way. The entire "package" of Mae West was indeed beautiful. And she was looking great for her age, with very few wrinkles, although I could tell up close that she had had a little work done. She looked exceedingly good except for a little bit of extra skin at the bottom of her chin. In fact, she brought it to my attention. She pointed to it and said, "Arrrh, I forgot this." She was annoyed with herself because she normally had a little strap that pulled the skin from under her chin upward toward her ears and clipped into her hair, to make it look tighter. She had forgotten to wear it that day, so I reassured her that I'd take care of it and make her neck and chin look tighter for her wax figure. She was relieved with what I told her. It was like I was giving her wax figure a bit of plastic surgery! But it would look just like Mae West, all done up and prettied for the world to see.

The appointment went very smoothly. Ty Jurras decided to inform us that Mae West had special muscle control, and the ability to move many of her muscles independently from each other. I was instantly curious as to exactly what he meant, since I was not completely familiar with this fact about her. It never struck me initially how unusual of a thing this was until I saw it for myself. Ty asked her to show us this muscle control. She made a comment that it would be kind of difficult to do with her girdle on, but he egged her on. So she said, "Arrrrh! I've got my girdle on, but I'll do my best." Mae West was always such a good sport about things when it came to entertaining men.

She started by undulating one of her breasts in a circle, rotating it towards the center of her body. Then, Mae West started rotating the other breast in the opposite direction! She kept both breasts rotating around and around in opposite directions, even with a girdle on. They were really moving! It was an unbelievable sight. I could only imagine how that looked on stage, in full costume. Then she said, "I usually get the guys going pretty wild in the front rows at about this time! Then when I get the top moving, I start undulating my entire lower body which really wows them." When she finished, we thanked her for the "show" and all of us were genuinely quite impressed with the unique talent we had just witnessed. It was incredible.

I asked Mae West how she learned to do this. I was fascinated with what she told us. She informed us that it was her dear father who had taught her how to do it when she was much younger, but it was never intended to be a sensual move. It was just supposed to be an exercise that they did to keep their bodies in shape and their muscles toned.

Her father had been a former pugilist who fought with his fists for sport. Her father had been very close to performing at the world class level fights. So this muscle control was meant to help condition his body. Mae West didn't know it then but this muscle control would play a big part in her future success as a performer of burlesque. Then, years later as she was trying to make a name for herself she happened to see a new dance that was gaining popularity called the Shim-Sham-Shimmy, also known as the Shim Sham.

She thought that if she integrated the moves of this dance with her burlesque routine that her audiences would go wild. Her instincts were right but in fact they reacted far more wildly than she had ever anticipated. Mae found out later that in doing what she thought were Shim Sham moves, she was in fact unintentionally and unconsciously throwing in a lot of moves from her controlled muscle workout that she had learned from her father years before. After seeing the reaction it caused, she of course started regularly including the extra muscle control in her routine.

No one had ever seen dance moves like this on stage before and thus her shows were enthusiastically received. With each performance she kept adding more of her own moves and personality to her dance routine which caused her shows to gain even more attention. Soon Mae West became the latest craze, first in New York and then across the United States. The Shim Sham ultimately became Mae West's trademark dance move and was so popular it was renamed the Shimmy.

Mae West was certainly an independent spirit and was always in full control of her career. While she enjoyed immense popularity she radically challenged the moral code of the day, knowing she was controversial. However it just didn't seem to phase her. She was surely ahead of her time, and one of the first people to commercialize sexuality. In fact, history can credit Mae West's brand of suggestive one-liners, sexual antics and controversial performances with starting a firestorm that was responsible for the formation of the religious Hayes Office (which controlled the movie industry for years).

Anyhow, getting back to our sitting with Mae West, after she showed us in person her "Shimmy" performance we thanked her again. Ty asked her one more favor as we were walking out of her apartment. He asked if she would take just a quick moment to show us her bedroom because he thought it was just so unbelievably spectacular, and therefore we boys just had to see it. Flattery from a man usually won Mae over, and in this instance it did.

Mae West thought about it for a moment. Finally, she said, "Ahhhrrr, alright fellas. Alright." She led us into her bedroom. I could only think, "My word, does this woman have a bed!" It was the largest, most oversized, and high-canopied, round bed with four posts that I had ever seen or imagined. To top it off literally, there was an enormous, custom cut oval mirror, the full size of her bed, directly over the bed itself. I turned to Mae West and said, "What is the mirror for, Miss West?" in full earnest.

She turned to me, leaning forward against me, winking her eye. She said to me, "I likes to sees what I'm doin'!" and we all laughed.

I said to her, "Yeah, you can sure see with that mirror!"

She replied, "Well, it's a good thing if you can see what you're doing, because you do a better job!" and everyone laughed again. She was very witty and sexual, even in her older age. As we left her amazing bedroom I could not help but notice how pink, white, silver and gold everything was in there, not to mention in her entire apartment.

I had always been interested in the picture she made with W.C. Fields (1880-1946) called *My Little Chickadee* (1940) which was one of her biggest, most popular pictures.

When asked, Mae recalled working with W.C. and she admitted that she never smoked or drank her entire life. She told everyone that she had only one vice during her life, and we all knew what she was referring to. When she spoke about W.C. Fields, she told us that he had gotten under her skin quite a bit when they filmed and worked together, mostly due to his drinking.

Apparently, W.C. Fields always had a flask of whiskey around somewhere near or on him. Mae finally told him that she would not work with him any more if he continued his drinking because it was against her principals. She even had it written into her movie contract that he would not drink or be drunk while filming with her. W.C. told Mae West that he would acquiesce and she thought they had the problem licked after that.

Sooner or later, however, W.C. had continued to hide his whiskey all around the sets, here and there. The funny thing about this is that according to the people who saw the shows that he was in claimed that W.C. Fields did his best and funniest work when he had tipped back a few drinks. They said he was absolutely much more humorous when he was drinking. So Mae West had to mostly put up with W.C. Fields' drinking antics but she really did not like it at all. It really infuriated her and she stated that she would never do another picture with Mr. Fields again. However, the picture they did together ended up being a huge, popular film. In fact, it was her biggest movie hit ever at that time.

What I learned from Mae West was that despite the drinking, W.C. Fields had become a huge hit and had an incredible career which had taken him to great heights and he had at one time been one of the biggest stars in all of Hollywood. But sadly, he had a terrible, ungainly attitude on life. He had also had a terrible beginning, poor fellow.

W.C. Fields had a very hard upbringing early in life. He had never gotten along with his father, and had eventually ran off and left his home as a young child. He bounced around a lot, sometimes going hungry for a while here and there. His life was very hard and he suffered a lot until he finally got a break with show business. First, he got a job juggling at an amusement park. From there, he ended up in vaudeville through his amazing juggling talent. He could juggle six, seven or more cigar boxes up in the air, all at once. It was an unbelievable routine to watch.

W.C. ended up on Broadway doing several shows, and then he had a huge hit with the movie titled *Poppy* (1936). This put him in a different category of success. *Poppy* brought him a big contract with the studio. After making many other films, he got extremely successful very fast. However, the sad truth was that W.C. Fields never really seemed to achieve true happiness. When W.C. was busy working, he hated everything and everybody around him. And yet, he always came out looking funny and even hilarious. Somehow he just blossomed as a comedian and made big, big money even though he was very unhappy.

When Movieland finally opened up, W.C. Fields had been dead for quite some time. We were never able to give him a sitting. But when I got there, Mr. Parkinson wanted W.C. Fields in the show at the museum. One of the reasons he decided to put W.C. Fields in

Movieland was because Ben Turpin (1869-1940), who had also been a very funny comedian, was in the museum. He had passed away earlier on, as well.

Ben Turpin was in show business as a serious man for some time and was not ever considered funny at all. This went on for some time and he was doing alright as a straight actor. But eventually, Mr. Turpin was in an accident during a vaudeville act which caused him to become cross-eyed. It was a great misfortune that worked to his advantage. This made him look so ridiculous, that people started laughing at him whenever they saw him. Instead of getting his eyes fixed or taking it to heart, he saw it as an opportunity to take advantage of becoming a comedian and trying something different with his career. I admired him very much for that. He decided he had something worth saving. And he eventually became one of the top comedians during the time of the silent films, Keystone Kops and all. This goes to show you, that you just never know what will influence your career.

Once we were finished with Mae West's sitting we picked up some of her photographs. I often would go pick up some movie stills of the stars I was about to sculpt, in addition to the pictures our photographer would take of the stars. The interview and sitting with the celebrity was always just the first step of many in the entire process to create a wax figure.

I thought Mae West's wax figure looked fantastic when I was finished creating it. Everyone else thought it looked great, too. My next step was a very important one, and that was to get the costume for the wax figure. We had Mae West in a set from her first picture with Cary Grant from the film *She Done Him Wrong* (1933). The costume designer for the film was the head designer in Hollywood at the time of this film. Her name was Edith Head. After finding this out, we asked if Western Costume still had the original patterns for the gown we wanted for the movie *She Done Him Wrong*. Western Costume found the patterns for the gown and although Edith Head was retired at the time, she had a big hand in reproducing the original costume for Mae West's wax figure. It was a dead ringer for the original costume.

I left word at Western Costume saying that we were coming over and that we were bringing the figure with us. We wanted everything to turn out perfectly. Everyone knew Mae West was known for being quite a bold, headstrong and take-charge woman. As mentioned before, Ms. West liked to surround herself with men. In fact, her entourage included some big Muscle Beach fellows from Venice Beach who acted almost like her personal bodyguards or escorts. She had gotten to know quite a few of these large, buff men and had befriended them. Ms. West was used to going anywhere she wanted, whenever she wanted, and sometimes just barging in with these boys in tow.

I had told Western Costume beforehand to make sure that no one was to see the wax figure undressed and they assured me that they would see to this. We just did not want anyone to see it that way because it would not look good and would invade Mae West's privacy. But unfortunately, while the costume was being finished, the figure was left lying down on its back in the direct sunlight, looking just terrible. Much of our concern over the figure's handling and privacy was that perhaps Ms. West would come in at any time to check out the progress of her wax figure or see the costume.

Well, a few days went by and all of a sudden we heard from Western Costume. Apparently, Mae West had decided she wanted to come see the figure before it was costumed. So, with two of her largest muscle boys by her side, she proceeded to go down to Western Costume. When she arrived, she simply demanded to see her wax figure. The people at Western Costume had told her that Movieland had given them specific instructions not to show anyone her wax figure before it was costumed and ready to go. Mae West just growled at them and demanded to see the figure right then and there. The boys with her said they would check with the gentleman in charge. While a Western employee went to find someone, Mae West just walked right in through the doors and started looking for her figure. A few people tried to stop her, but the big boys with her made it quite difficult. They all just bulldozed their way into Western Costume. Mae knew her way around Western Costume because she had been there before for previous projects. She owned the place as she owned any place she went, and made her way to the main room where she knew the figure would be and yelled out, "I want to see my figure, and I want to see it *now!*"

Everyone who worked at Western Costume and who was around at that precise moment was quite intimidated when this happened. They told her that her figure was without a costume, but she did not care at all. Unfortunately, the not-quite-completed wax figure for Mae West was still laying directly on its back in the sunlight. With the lighting and positioning of it there in that room, her figure just looked terrible. It practically looked like the devil. You can't put a wax figure, undressed, in that position and have it look any good. The direct sunlight flattens the detail all out of it, particularly without any painting. When the powerful and elegant Mae West finally laid her experienced eyes upon her unfinished, undressed wax figure, lying there stark naked on its back in the harsh California sunlight, she just blew up. She snarled, "I've never been *so* insulted in my arrrrhhh entire life! I simply will *not* stand for this! I will sue you all! I feel like cutting the artist's fingers off!"

They tried to reason with her, telling her as calmly as possible that the beautiful costume her figure would be fitted with and the final, proper finishing touches and paint would make her wax likeness look like a million bucks, even if it would never look quite as lovely as the real Mae West looked. On this day, no one could calm her down. She commented that she thought her wax likeness looked like a pig. There was absolutely no chance in hell to talk any sense into Mae West at that moment. They tried their best to placate her but there was no stopping her. She was on a good, old-fashioned diva's tirade that included pounding her fists on counter tops and tables throughout Western Costume. She threatened to sue all of us: Movieland, Western Costume, and anyone else involved. She was there all day long on her amazing rant.

By a stroke of luck, Mae West happened to like the gentleman who was in charge of Movieland. Ms. West continued to tell Joe, "I will show you guys what good is! I'm going to find my own guy to make my wax figure and he is going to make the real deal!" Ms. West made it clear that she wanted "a good figure" and not the "crap" she had seen that day. By this time, Allen Parkinson had sold the museum and a new man named Joe Prevatil was in charge. Joe was quite handsome and had caught her eye, because as mentioned before, Mae West was all about good-looking men. She called him up and read him the riot act. He was able to calm her down somewhat and told her that she needed to just wait until she saw the finished product, all dressed and touched up. He tried to assure her that she would be nothing but pleased with the end result, and that no one was supposed to see it until the product was one hundred percent complete. It did not matter what he said, she did not want to wait to see what it would look like. She told him that she would get her own guy to make a real Mae West wax figure.

Ms. West continued to tell Joe, "I will show you guys what *good* is! I'm going to find my own guy to make my wax figure and he is going to make the real deal!" because she wanted "A good figure" and not the "crap" she had seen that day. She made it clear that it would be this way; and of course, with Mae West it was always her way or the highway. Joe Prevatil knew that Ms. West would absolutely never find anyone else other than me who could make a good wax figure for her, but at the moment of her rant he just played along with her. There was nothing else Joe could do right then and there. So he simply appeased her, and told her to go ahead and get another figure made if she so pleased. He assured her that Movieland would continue their process and complete her figure and that she would be pleased.

Then as Joe spoke he came up with a perfect plan. He told Mae West that after Movieland finished her wax figure, and after she had one made on her end, would it so please her if she would decide which one was the best one? Then, whichever figure she chose as the best wax likeness of her would end up being the one on display at Movieland. This was a brilliant idea because it gave her all the power while he knew that no one could top what Movieland would produce. She thought a moment and said, "Ahhrrrr, I suppose that would be alright. I'll have one made of me that will show you guys up!"

So Joe told her to go ahead and get started so she would have two wax figures to compare with each other. Ms. West finally quieted down and that was the end of her tirade. The folks over at Western Costume were quite rattled by the events of the day. They called Movieland and they were told about the decision that had been made. They were assured that they would not be sued. He told them to go ahead and complete the costume and finish working on Mae West's wax figure. In fact, they told him that Edith Head was already completing the costume for Western.

Everyone agreed that Mae West's wax figure by Movieland with Western Costume would be just beautiful and extremely lifelike when it was completed. There was not a shadow of a doubt. But with the bullying appearance of those muscular boys and the brazen demeanor and threats presented to them by Mae West herself that day, they were still a bit diminished in their confidence. We tried to pump them back up and were quite successful, because the bottom line was that the costume designers at Western knew from experience how great the figures looked when positioned properly on set with costumes. It had just been a shame that the stubborn star had bombarded them and spotted the unfinished figure in the stark sunlight, undressed, unpainted, and very unflattering. They knew in the end that Movieland's Mae West adorned with their beautiful costume would ultimately be a knockout. They also learned not to lay a wax figure in the direct sunlight like that again, should another stubborn star decide to come take a peek.

Apparently, Mae West went ahead and found her own wax artist straight from Europe. Amazingly, she called up and insisted that our Movieland driver Jack Collins go pick up her wax artist and bring him to her. That was Mae West's bold style. This man was a pretty notable artist in Europe but had never made a wax figure before. He was a bit intimidated by her, and uncertain of the final result, but it was a great opportunity for him. Further, he knew full well that it was useless to say no to Mae West.

So Mr. Collins picked up this artist from his local residence in the limousine and brought him to the museum. He checked out the set and we gave him all the measurements and pictures and everything he needed to get started. He also had several of his own photographs. In my opinion, Movieland's management showed a lot of class and professional courtesy by making sure that this poor artist had everything he needed to help get him started on Mae's wax figure. So as Jack Collins was driving the European artist back to his apartment he asked the artist if he had a really good studio where he could work. Jack was feeling sorry for him but the artist assured Jack that Mae West had promised him that she would get him a place where he could create the wax figure.

Jack went on to ask him if he had ever made a wax figure before. The artist replied that he had never made a wax figure, but he had made all kinds of art before. Jack was very surprised and wondered why Mae West had chosen this gentleman to make her wax figure. He shrugged and said, "You know that when Ms. West makes her mind up to something, there is no way you can say no to her. It's pretty hard to buck her. She has liked my previous artwork and so she thought she'd give me the opportunity to make her wax figure."

Jack was astonished by the artist's admission that he'd never made a wax figure and said, "Oh my gosh, you know it is not an easy task to make a wax figure of a person, let alone of a very high profile star." To this, the artist agreed and asked Jack how he should do it and how he should proceed. The poor guy was clueless. He hadn't the faintest idea. Jack tried to share as much knowledge as he could with the artist, but it was not a lot because Jack was not a wax artist. The poor fellow was as nervous as anyone could be. He made Jack promise that if he called the museum he could ask Jack for advice or run questions by him as needed. He did not know who else to turn to. Jack promised to be there for assistance in any way he could. The poor guy was reaching out desperately for help.

We did not hear from the artist for quite some time. Occasionally, Mae West would call up the museum and quip that her artist was working diligently on her wax figure and that it would put us all to shame. We told her that ours was coming along fine as well and she showed no interest whatsoever in seeing our wax figure.

Well, a bit later on Mae West called us up. The poor artist she had hired had been just scrambling like mad to learn how to create a wax figure. He finally got the general information from someone, but we at Movieland definitely felt it was not in our place to teach him since he had been hired by Mae West. Therefore, we had left it primarily up to her to handle getting him the tools and resources he needed to make her happy. Finally, Mae West called up Movieland and told us that she had her wax figure all ready and she went so far as to say, "My wax figure looks so good, I don't need any damn costume on it to show you how good it looks! Boy, when you see this, you're going to see a *real* wax figure of me." So the gentleman in charge of Movieland told her that when it was totally ready, she should bring her figure and her wax artist to us and they could show it off.

Mae told him, "Aaarrrhhh, oh I won't let you see it until I'm ready to unveil it! I really want to surprise you!" She often dragged her words out for effect, and it was quite unique to hear her speak. They agreed that she could bring it over all covered up and as soon as Movieland's wax figure was ready, they would unveil both of them together to see which one looked better. She agreed.

A few days later, Mae West called up Joe Prevatil at Movieland. Mae told him that she was having some of her big muscle boy companions come along with her to bring the wax figure out to his office. When she arrived she was greeted by Joe. They went back to his office. She instructed the big boys to put her figure right over in the corner with her sultry drawl, adding, "When you guys get your wax figure finished, you bring it in here and put it right next to mine, and I'll go ahead and show you the difference!"

She was told that Movieland could do better than that and when their figure was ready, it would already be dressed in costume and over in the set, all ready to go. He told her that she could take a look then and tell them what she thought. She said, "Ahhhrrr, fine. But wait until you see mine. You'll see a *real* Mae West!"

So they kept her wrapped-up figure in the corner of Joe Prevatil's office while we added the final touches to our Mae West wax figure. We put a hair piece on it that had been given to us directly by Mae West so she could not complain that we did not get her hair just right. Eventually, the beautiful set was completed. It had a lovely staircase, beautiful wallpaper, and Mae West's figure, when finally placed in the set, looked as if it could take a breath, it was so realistic. She was standing at the foot of the stairs on the set, with a gorgeous costume wrapped around her body, standing the full six feet from the bottom of her shoes to the top of her head, just as she wished.

We could not wait for her to show up with her entourage of big muscle men, to see our figure and hers, and to compare the two. It was like a final showdown in a Hollywood western movie.

The day of reckoning finally came. Mae West had made all the arrangements with Joe Prevatil to come and show us all what a real wax figure of her was supposed to look like. She sashayed into the office and was prepared to be lifted over a step or two by her boys. Her clothes were so tight to add to her overall sex appeal that she could not always take a big enough step. In those instances, her muscle men would lift her over the steps to get her to her destination. It was quite a spectacle. Joe met them and brought them to his office. He asked some of the Movieland folks to unwrap the wax figure that she had brought. They unwrapped it while she again boasted how she was about to show us all what a real wax figure looked like. As the last piece of wrap came off of it, she practically jumped backwards in complete horror. Mae looked at the wax figure her artist had made, not making a sound. Finally, she exclaimed, "Why, that does not look a bit like me!"

It was just a horrible wax figure. There was absolutely no resemblance at all to Mae West. Flabbergasted, angry and embarrassed, she kept saying over and over how that did not look a thing like her. She eventually stormed out of the office and was on her way out of the museum with all the employees and the people at Movieland watching her. She was stomping mad, her big boys following her. Joe let her go, huffing her way out. Mr. Prevatil wanted her to have a little down time, a couple days to get over it. She did not even take a glance at our wax figure as she left the museum.

About two or three days later, Joe Prevatil got a call from Mae West. For once in her life, she sounded a bit apologetic in the tone of her voice, although she never did come out and apologize. She pensively asked Joe if she could come out and take a look at her wax figure. He told her he'd be delighted to have her come see it and the entire wax museum. She had never seen it. It was clear to us that Mae West was now very anxious to see her Movieland wax figure. She had anticipated this moment very much, after having been so dumbfounded about the wax figure she had commissioned. So when she got to the museum, Mae showed up with a swarm of male escorts. When she met with Mr. Prevatil, she requested that she have a moment before touring the museum to go view her own wax figure and set by herself so she could really take it all in without any distractions.

There was no problem with that, so she went on ahead of me and Joe towards her set. When she got to it, Mae West looked it over without saying a single word. She checked the wax figure and the entire set out from every angle very quietly, taking her time. As the anxious crowd of museum guests started backing up at her figure, she seemed oblivious to it. Mae West had absolutely no sense of urgency whatsoever about the large group of people slowly accumulating near her set, waiting to walk towards it and check it out for themselves.

Some of them had recognized her and were chomping at the bit to get in there and see her up close and personal.

Finally, Joe Prevatil had to say something because she was really holding up the museum guests. He walked up to Mae and gently told her that she needed to move along pretty quickly because a huge crowd was waiting to get through to see her set and to finish their tour of the museum. She agreed and went on along with him but still hadn't uttered one word about her figure. Mae really seemed to enjoy herself as Mr. Prevatil gave her a private tour of the rest of the museum explaining a bit about each set, star and movie. She remembered many of the stars who had sets there, people she had known from back in her heyday. Perhaps she even found some of it a bit sentimental.

After her tour she asked Joe if she could go back to her set and look over her wax figure some more, just by herself for a little bit longer. He told her he was fine with that, and he would hold off the people for a little while, and direct the people around the back of her set to give her some privacy. She thanked Joe and went back over to her set. She stood there and just looked at the figure and set again. She moved a little to one side and stood. She continued to check out her figure, the face, dress, clothing, hair, and background for quite some time and from each and every angle possible. As people went around the back of her set, they got very excited when they saw Mae West herself, in the flesh, standing near her actual wax figure. They were delighted, throwing her compliments left and right, telling her how gorgeous she was, how amazing and beautiful her "lifelike" figure was, and on and on. The guests couldn't get over it!

Mae stayed there for about a half an hour in silence the entire time. Finally, she came back out and went over to Mr. Prevatil. She made a comment about the color of the hair. Right away, Mona (who worked at Movieland) reminded Mae West that the hair on her wax figure was the hair she had given them to use. She kind of made her little sound, "Aaarrrhhh" and nothing more. She went outside and Joe Prevatil followed her. He asked her earnestly what she thought about her figure, after all that time she spent checking it out closely. Finally, she said to him, "Aaarrrhhh… okay." And that was all she said before she left. That was it. That was our time and experience with Mae West.

Now a little while later, we got another phone call from Mae West. She was inquiring about when her set opening and dedication would take place. We were delighted when she told us she wanted to be there to dedicate her set. We knew there would be a lot of people showing up to see Mae West when this happened. We set up a date and gave it to her. There were hundreds and hundreds of people who showed up that day. We had set up a temporary platform out in front of the museum for Mae West to stand on so she could address the crowd during her opening.

Mae was wearing an extremely tight dress that day, and she had to ascend several steps to get to the platform we had built for her speech. As I watched closely, I saw how beautifully the Muscle Beach boys helped her up the steps. They ever-so-delicately and discreetly lifted her up just under her arms and glided her up the stairs. You would never have known that she did not walk up the stairs herself if you hadn't watched very closely.

She got up on the platform and looked around at everyone. She cheered back to the crowd and said, "Yeah! Ladies and gentleman... I've still got 'em!" With that said, she pulled back her bolero-style dress and showed a bit of her bosom. Everyone cheered and went wild. After her little speech she went inside and dedicated her set and the event concluded. Her opening had been a huge hit, and she had fun in her moment of glory. Before she left that day she finally expressed to Mr. Prevratil that she thought her figure was beautiful. After all the drama leading up to this moment, it was satisfying to us that she admitted this, finally.

I am pleased that Mae West's experience ended on a positive note. I was particularly happy that I would be keeping my fingers as she had threatened to cut them off for doing such a terrible job!

Logan's wax creation of the legendary sexpot, Mae West, from the film *She Done Him Wrong*.

# Chapter 46

## Ann-Margret

nn-Margret (1941 to present) was another star that we called out for a sitting and interview. We went to her house with our entourage. She had started out doing a lot of beautiful stunt work and then landed some stage roles early in her career. I had seen her in Las Vegas doing a wonderful show with motorcycles. She ultimately became a huge star and appeared in many pictures. Some of her most popular movies were those she co-starred in with Elvis Presley (1935-1977).

When we were told to meet her in her home, Ann-Margret had been healing for some time from a terrible tragedy. She had been in a near-fatal accident that had happened to her while she was on stage performing in Lake Tahoe. She had been doing an act where she was suspended quite high above the stage. There was a technical problem with the equipment and she had fallen straight down, landing flat onto her face on the floor of the stage. It must have been a horrible sight for the audience to see her fall. Ann-Margret had been hurt very badly, landing on the left side of her face. Several bones including her cheekbones and temple were shattered to pieces.

She had many plastic surgeries after this to try to save her face. She had been a very beautiful woman and fortunately the surgeries proved extremely successful. It was hard to notice that anything had happened after that! When we were ushered into Ann-Margret's home, she had been out of show business for a while due to this accident. She appeared to us to be a little bit shy and somewhat worried about her face. But I took pictures from all angles and all sides, and it was hard to tell any difference. She was still considerably worried about the left side of her face. She kept asking me if I thought one side of her face looked "off" or flatter than the other side. I thought she looked very beautiful and I told her so. She just needed more time to build up her confidence.

Ann-Margret was measured all around from every angle and her wax figure ended up just lovely. She went on with her career to star in many other great roles and has had much continued success to this day. Overall, our experience with her was very pleasant. She was sweet, cooperative and polite.

# Chapter 47

## Opening
## the
## Stars Hall of Fame

I'd like to share a little more about the Stars Hall of Fame in Orlando, Florida and when it opened to the public. The grand opening was a few days out, and everyone was busy doing last-minute preparations, getting details on the sets completed, and I had been down there for about three weeks working on the lighting for each set. All of the wax figures had been delivered to their sets and final touches were being attended to.

On the opening day, we found out that there were quite a few celebrities who had been invited. Many of them were planning on showing up, so we were looking forward to a very big opening. My wife Liz was scheduled to fly down and meet me for the opening. I had not seen Liz for close to three weeks because I had been busily working on getting ready for the big opening. It was very exciting.

On the final opening night, I met my wife Liz at the airport in Orlando. We had a very nice reunion and headed to the museum. We were a tad late in getting to the opening, but they had an extremely great turnout. Mr. Parkinson showed up with the *Sunset Blvd.* star, Gloria Swanson (1899-1983) who played Norma Desmond in the movie. We had put in another big Rolls Royce on her set in Orlando. Mr. Parkinson brought Gloria Swanson a red carnation to the opening as he did for her at Movieland, for old time's sake. She was touched by this gesture and very excited about the whole event. Ms. Swanson toured the new museum with Mr. Parkinson. She looked over all of the other sets and thought it was going to be a very beautiful show for everyone. She was one of the biggest celebrities there that night.

Also on the guest list was Danny Thomas (1914-1991). As part of the opening events, they had created a dedication for his set at the new museum which I briefly mentioned earlier. When Danny Thomas showed up he brought his daughter Marlo Thomas (1937 to present). There were several of his friends there including Red Buttons (1919-2006) and Jack Haley (1898-1979), who had played The Tin Man from *The Wizard of Oz*, amongst others.

Speaking of Mr. Haley, he told me quite a story. When they started filming *The Wizard of Oz*, the studio had actually cast a different actor for the role of The Tin Man. His name was Buddy Ebsen (1908-2003), the great character actor who of course was most famous for playing Jed Clampett in *The Beverly Hillbillies*. When they made Mr. Ebsen up for The Tin Man part during rehearsals after only a couple of days this poor guy was overcome with a severe allergic reaction to the metal powder in the makeup that they used to cover his face and other parts of his body. This really threw a monkey wrench into the production and film progression of *The Wizard of Oz*. Everything was put on hold.

They absolutely had to find a replacement for this role because they did not have an alternative type of makeup to use back then. Jack Haley took a screen test and did well and was thankfully not allergic to the makeup. So that was how Jack got the famous role of The Tin Man. He never forgot how much fun he had making *The Wizard of Oz*. He also talked about what a great dancer Ray Bolger (1904-1987) was. He used his amazing athletic and dance abilities in his role as The Scarecrow. It had also been a joy for him to work with Judy Garland (1922-1969) as Dorothy Gale, Bert Lahr (1895-1967) as The Cowardly Lion, Margaret Hamilton (1902-1985) as The Wicked Witch of the West and Billie Burke (1884-1970) as Glinda, the Good Witch, and all the other cast members. He recalled working with the beautiful Billie Burke and talked about her story.

Billie Burke had started out in the Goldwyn's Follies on Broadway. She had been so beautiful and such an outstanding dancer that Samuel Goldwyn went crazy about her and made her one of the Goldwyn Girls. She would partake in many of the Goldwyn Girls' bigger extravaganzas on Broadway. All this led to her role as The Good Witch in *The Wizard of Oz*, which was a career-changing role for her.

My wife Liz and I saw Judy Garland at the Golden Globes once and I went up to her and congratulated her on the beautiful job she did in *The Wizard of Oz*. She told me that filming that movie was one of the happiest times in her life. She went on to say that everyone who was part of that movie was very dear to her, including the super cute Munchkins.

Speaking of the Munchkins, I want to mention that most of the actors were little people but there were a few children. It recently came out that there were only three surviving people who played the original Munchkins in *The Wizard of Oz*. They deserve many accolades because they were very talented and were a very important factor in why this movie was so special and original. It is probably not too difficult to tell that I am a huge fan of *The Wizard of Oz*.

Getting back to Danny Thomas, the plan was for him to stand on a stage during the opening and view his figure of the character Jerry Golding from his movie set for *The Jazz Singer* (1952). When the time was right, they ushered him up the stairs and onto the stage to see his figure. He checked out his wax figure quite thoroughly and proclaimed that he thought it was pretty darn good. The crowd just loved him. Then I was told to walk up to the stage next to him, since I had created his wax figure. So I went up, and he recognized me from Movieland in Buena Park. He greeted me cordially, since we had met before this moment. It was like seeing an old friend again, and I was introduced as "Logan Fleming, the wax artist."

At one point on stage, Danny Thomas got a really solid side view of my face. We were pretending that we were going to kiss the figure, and when I turned sideways, Danny Thomas said for everyone present to hear, "My God, he's got as big of a nose as I have!" and everyone in the crowd laughed (including me) at that remark. The funny thing is, in the photograph of this moment we really do look like we have somewhat similar noses, almost like brothers.

It was a real class act, the opening at the Stars Hall of Fame in Orlando. They had quite a spread, with really impressive food, appetizers, a full bar, and just about everything you would need to make it a special event. It was all set out in the open spaces in the front of the museum. The place was decorated just beautifully. Other celebrities that attended included Redd Foxx, the entire cast of *The Beverly Hillbillies* and the very famous actor, Glenn Ford (1916-2006). Mr. Ford also dedicated his set for *Teahouse of the August Moon* (1956) that evening. He was one of my wife's favorite actors.

I am sure I missed several of the movie stars that came earlier in the evening because as I mentioned, we got there a little late. I had been there earlier working on the lighting of the sets down to the very last minute that day. Then I had left to pick up my wife Liz, and I felt bad because she had waited for a while at the airport before I showed up. But I was literally working feverishly up until the very last minute.

The wonderful people who were hired to run the Orlando museum did a great job and were just marvelous folks, including Mr. John Tomlinson and Duffy Meyer. John Tomlinson was a manager in Buena Park, but he resettled in Orlando to help Mr. Parkinson run the Orlando museum. He was a former Marine Colonel and was just a wonderful man. Duffy Meyer was Lovetta's counterpart as the museum's agent down in Orlando. We had a wonderful time at the party and it was a grand event.

Logan puts the finishing touches on Danny Thomas' wax likeness
for the grand opening of The Stars Hall of Fame in Orlando, Florida.
In this photo they do look as if they could be brothers.
*Photo by Norton Photography, Anaheim, California.*

# Chapter 48

## Hair Today, Gone Tomorrow

Upon returning to Movieland in Buena Park, California, we were getting ready to interview another popular star named Mike Connors (1925 to present) who played the character *Mannix* (1967-1975) in this television series. We were in his home for a measurement sitting, and our photographer, publicity agent and I attended. I told Mr. Connors that he needed to give me the proper expression that he wanted his wax figure to have, and we used the swivel chair for all angles. We were just about ready to start taking pictures.

Right before we started taking photographs, Mr. Connors asked us if we would excuse him for a few moments and abruptly went into his bedroom. It had double doors that remained open, so we could somewhat see what he was doing. He went over to a rather large, decorative mirror in his bedroom and stood before it. Then he started to fuss a bit with his hair or so it appeared this is what he was doing from our standpoint. I wasn't sure why because I thought his hair already looked great, but he was pushing, patting it and working it with a bit of trouble, almost hurriedly.

Mike Connors always had very thick, black hair that looked very nice, and I was wondering why he stopped to fuss over it so much. A few minutes later Mr. Connors came back to where we were and finished the photo shoot. His hair looked really great, so whatever he had done to it had worked. We thanked him and then we all headed back to Movieland after the photo shoot to resume our business for the day.

I was in the break room at Movieland the next morning having a cup of coffee to start my day. It was a very nice break room with a relaxing atmosphere, and I was having a very pleasant conversation with one of the employees who worked for the museum. It was common for employees to meet for coffee and conversation on their breaks and I always thought it was great that everyone at Movieland was friendly, no matter what job they held.

As we sat there in the break room visiting, a couple of the Keystone Kops joined us. I was talking about my meeting with *Mannix* (Mike Connors) and how the meeting went. I was still trying to figure out why Mr. Connors had gone into his room and fussed with his hair so much right before the sitting.

One of the cleaning ladies who had come into the break room by this time joined our conversation and said, "I know what he was doing." We turned to her and were all quite curious by now. So we asked her what she thought. "Well, he was undoubtedly fixing his wig!" she proclaimed. "He has a hairpiece."

I was really surprised and would never, ever have guessed this by looking at him. Even up close I had not noticed and I have a trained eye for these things. But I was sure that she was right and then thought he probably had the best darned hairpiece I had ever seen! She mentioned that he had been on a program recently and how handsome she thought he was. He was quite a heartthrob with the ladies. While they interviewed him, someone had asked how difficult it was to balance his personal life with being a big star and sex symbol. They went on to ask him if he had any problems with women coming on to him, especially being a married man and all.

Mr. Connors had responded to this question by saying, "Oh, I have an easy answer to that!" Everyone looked at him, wondering what he would say next. Then he replied, "If I'm in a bar or someplace and a woman starts to make advances to me, I just take a hold of my hair and raise it up above my head and put it right back down again!" And as he did just that, he was also admitting to the world that he had a hairpiece. He had finished the interview by saying, "Most of the time, doing that kind of cools things down and takes care of the problem." The cleaning lady told us what a surprise that was for her to find out that the sexy Mike Connors was bald as a billiard ball. Well, after our little conversation in the break room, it was back to work for everyone but I had gotten the answer to the mystery and I found it quite interesting and amusing at the time.

# Chapter 49

## The Little Rascals

One of the Movieland sets that brought back childhood memories with many of our older patrons was from the *Our Gang* comedies also known as *The Little Rascals* (1922). The child actors were very famous due to the popularity of the shows. The main stars were Darla Jean Hood (1931–1979), Carl Dean "Alfalfa" Switzer (1927-1959), Billie Thomas, originally William Thomas, Jr. (1931-1980) and Elaine "Spanky" McFarlane (1942 to present). There was also Pete the Dog with his trademark circle painted around one of his eyes. These shows went on for several years and when some of the child actors outgrew their parts, they were replaced by new, younger actors. These shows were actually made up of several series of short comedy films. They were about a group of poor, young children and the many different mischievous adventures that they encountered in their day-to-day lives. These children were very funny and they got into trouble in so many different ways!

The set for the *Our Gang* comedies was that of a dentist office. The dentist was getting ready to pull one of the principal's teeth while the rest of the kids and even their dog were there in the same room. Mr. Parkinson had gotten hold of an old dental office after it had been vacated. It was brought in from a small town in the Midwest. All the dental equipment from this old office was used in the set to make it look very realistic. This included the medicinal items and dental tools. In the set, the kids looked frightened as they watched their friend having his tooth pulled.

These talented and witty child actors stopped by to visit the museum from time to time as adults. Darla was the one actor who came back several times. Her visits to Movieland made her reflect upon her days acting in the *Our Gang* comedies of *The Little Rascals*. She also mentioned to me that filming those funny stories with all their antics were some of the happiest times in her life.

# Chapter 50

## A
## Great
## Daredevil

One of the sets that we spoke briefly about previously was the actor Harold Lloyd (1893-1971), where he stood out on the ledge of a building. He made a lot of his pictures on building ledges and was quite a daredevil. They made it look like it was quite a long drop down in the film, as if he was in danger of falling a great distance. However, it was only in reality a few feet down because they used special camera tricks and angles. But he came off as quite an acrobat and stunt person.

In one of his great films called *Safety Last* (1923), he grabbed the giant hands from a huge clock on the side of a great big building and hung onto them, seemingly suspended in the air, up quite high. Mr. Lloyd became quite a hero in the comedies he was in. He brought some people with him to the museum one day to see his set. When they got there, it was the first time he had seen it himself because his set had been created before they did most of the set dedications. I had redone his figure to look much more realistic by this time.

In the movie for his set for *Mad Wednesday* (1947), there was a lion that was chasing him. He had done a dive onto a window ledge to get away from him. Mr. Lloyd appeared to be quite in fear for his life in this scene and had crawled clear out to the very end of the ledge to escape the lion's paws. He was wearing a very garish, brightly colored suit with a large orange and white checkerboard pattern. So when Harold Lloyd and his friends approached his set and he saw it, he said, "Oh, boy. Of all the movies I was in, and of all the suits I ever wore in them, this was the one suit that I hated the most!" whereas everyone roared with laughter. They all had a great time enjoying his set.

# Chapter 51

## Bob Hope

Our figure of Bob Hope (1903 – 2003) had been in the museum before I started working there, so sadly I never got a chance to meet or have a fitting with him. However, I did work extensively on Bob Hope's figure and his likeness turned out very realistic.

A very humorous thing happened at Movieland one day that still makes me smile when I think about it. We had temporarily taken out the wax figure of Bob Hope from one of the sets that he was in for a film he did with Bing Crosby. It was a movie where they had gone on a road trip titled *The Road to Bali* (1952). We were working on this set at this particular time and making some renovations to it so we had to get the figure out of harm's way. We temporarily paired Bob Hope up with Jack Benny instead of Bing Crosby.

Mrs. Hope thought it would be nice to come out and see his figure. Of course we welcomed her warmly, and Joe Prevatil arranged for a limousine to bring her out to Movieland.

Mrs. Dolores Hope enjoyed her tour of the museum very much. She told us that she had never seen such an array of realistic likenesses and many of the classic stars in the museum were people she knew very well. That was such a great compliment coming from Mrs. Hope.

Mrs. Hope finally got to the set and saw where we had placed Bob Hope's wax figure temporarily, right next to Jack Benny. While Mrs. Hope was admiring how nice her late husband's wax figure looked, a woman who was touring the museum walked up to where Mrs. Hope was. This woman seemed to be a bit forward and kind of walked right up and pushed her way in front of everyone. It put us off a bit but everyone slightly moved out of the lady's way and let her do her thing. When she walked up to the wax figures she commented, "I thought this place had good wax figures in it! This is the worst thing I've ever seen!"

Joe Prevatil was quite taken aback because Mr. Hope's wax figure looked very realistic. So he said to her, "Oh, for heaven's sakes!" and the lady made a comment that she thought Mr. Crosby's figure was terrible and it looked much more like Jack Benny than Bing Crosby! Well, Joe was quick to correct this woman when he told her, "Madam, excuse me but THAT IS Jack Benny!"

She did a double-take and said, "Oh…" and walked off in a huff, clearly embarrassed and possibly a bit puzzled. We all laughed our heads off and thought it was quite funny. The woman had really put her foot in her mouth. She had been quite surprised in her error and left quickly. Even Mrs. Hope thought this was funny. Of course, we put Bob Hope's wax figure back onto the correct movie set later on. Mrs. Hope enjoyed visiting the museum and was eventually able to see his wax likeness on the proper set.

We had so many stars and their family members come into the museum over the years to see their figures and also to see other friends of theirs who also happened to be memorialized in wax. They were almost always thoroughly delighted and impressed just as Dolores Hope had been. We took great pride in this, because the stars and their friends and family could be much harder judges than museum guests who did not know the stars up close and personal.

Mrs. Delores Hope visits her beloved husband Bob Hope's wax figure.

# Chapter 52

## Carol Burnett
## and the
## Slip-Up

Lovetta told me that the next project we were going out on was for the one and only Carol Burnett (1933 to present). Ms. Burnett was one of my favorite stars of all time, and I think one of the nicest people and greatest comedians who ever graced the stage. She is admired and greatly loved by so, so many people. I was quite thrilled when I found out that Ms. Burnett was happy and excited to be in the museum.

It was decided that we were not going to meet her in her home or in the studio, as we usually did with stars. Her agent thought it would be a lot easier for us to have the sitting at the Marquis Restaurant in Westwood, across from UCLA. On that particular day, they were not going to have any luncheons in their beautiful dining room so we had the entire room to ourselves. We really lucked out to have that space and privacy for Carol Burnett's fitting. We arrived at the restaurant and were met by Carol Burnett's publicity lady, who ushered us directly into the restaurant. The staff in the restaurant was waiting for us and ready when we arrived, so we went right in and got set up with our swivel chair and camera equipment. It was a great place for the meeting and very beautiful inside. We were all extremely excited that we were about to meet Carol Burnett.

After a short while, Ms. Burnett came walking in. She looked extremely approachable and friendly, and she was wearing a very slim-fitting, chic white dress. She greeted every single person who was there as nicely as anyone could ever be greeted. She finally got to me, and said hello in the sweetest way. She said, "Mr. Fleming, do you mind if I call you Logan?" and I told her of course, that I'd appreciate it very much. After that, Carol Burnett told me that I should call her "Carol."

Things started out very nicely and Carol told me she'd never been to a fitting like this so she was ready to do whatever we needed her to do. I explained to her about the swivel chair, looking directly at eye-level into the camera's lens, and coming up with a good pose or expression that she wanted her wax figure to have, while trying to remain still. I also went over the importance of all the different angles that I needed in the photographs of her in order to make the wax figure realistic and accurate from every viewpoint. She was not quite sure just yet about what type of expression she wanted her wax figure's face to have, so she requested that I give her a few moments to think this through.

While she was thinking I explained the rest of the process that we needed to complete that day. Finally Carol said to me, "I don't know, Logan. What do you think? I don't know what expression would be best for this." So I suggested to her that she could do a nice little smile, or a half-smile with a pleasant look. I also thought that a good laugh would be nice, too.

Carol thought that perhaps a big laugh would get old, but maybe just a nice, sweet expression would be good. She really wanted to please me as the wax artist and that really made me feel good because I could tell that she respected my opinion as a professional. I agreed with her and she got ready for the sitting and posing. I told her that whatever she felt comfortable with, she should just go for it.

We got started and began the different angles, measuring her face, her eyes, her color and all the different measurements and sizing details that were necessary. I measured from the top of her head to the widow's peak area, and from there down to her chin. After all of her facial and head measurements were complete, we went on to her body. Carol Burnett cooperated very well during all of this. I asked her if she had a seamstress who made all of her clothes who might already have all her measurements, because if she did then we could just have them send them over to us. She told me that it would probably just be easier for all of us if I just went ahead and took all of her body measurements right then and there so I'd have them and know that they were the most current and most accurate they could be. I agreed, and I started measuring Carol.

While I measured Carol Burnett for her wax figure, I happened to ask her about the significance of her pulling on her ear at the end of each little comedy bit that she did just before she signed off. She thought that was funny I had noticed, because it was somewhat of a secret gesture that she did for her own mother. This gesture was meant to say, "Goodnight, Mom." She went on to say that her mother would be devastated if she failed to do this, even one time, when signing off. She had been doing it so much and for so long that her own physician had mentioned that the ear she pulled on was actually a tiny bit longer or stretched out more so than the other ear. But this did not seem to bother her at all.

At one point, I had measured all the way down to her waist but I could not get her thigh measurements because of the dress she was wearing. I always needed the thigh measurements, especially for the women, because you want the figure to look smooth.

Anyhow, I went to the feet and measured her ankles, legs and calves. When I got to the top of her knees, I looked up at Carol Burnett and said, "Carol, you don't happen to have your thigh measurements, do you?" and I chuckled. She told me she did not happen to have them handy, and laughed along with me.

Suddenly, Carol Burnett simply suggested, "Oh Logan, why don't I just take this old dress off?" and with that, she just stood up and peeled off her thin, white dress over her head as if there were nothing to it! Of course what she revealed was less than you would see at the beach. Still, I was amazed at how comfortable Carol and other stars were in these situations. As a movie star you probably get so used to dealing with makeup artists, posing for photo shoots, having people help you in and out of costumes, etc. that you really don't have the luxury of being modest like most people. Anyhow, she was the consummate professional and told me go ahead and take all the measurements I needed…thighs included.

When I had everything I needed, I thanked her profusely for her help and cooperation. Her publicity lady was quite amused with the delicate situation I was in having to take all of Carol's measurements but also had been on hand the entire time and had helped make sure Ms. Burnett had everything she needed and was copasetic while they were there.

As they were ready to leave, Carol Burnett's driver pulled up to wait for them. We walked up to our Rolls Royce as well to load it up. As I was walking in front of the building towards our car, I spotted Carol Burnett leaving the restaurant in her car.

When she spotted me, she did something that really encapsulates just what type of a person Carol Burnett really is. She rolled down the window on her side of the car, and she stuck her head out of the window, waving quite wildly and enthusiastically, "Goodbye, Logan! Thank you. Goodbye, Logan! Bye!" and I got quite a chuckle out of this. So I bid her goodbye as well, and off this delightful lady went. What a great experience it was to work with Carol Burnett.

Carol Burnett's set dedication was also a treat. She loved her figure and the entire set. Although her wax figure had a friendly, tiny smile, Ms. Burnett could not help but give everyone a huge smile during the dedication, much bigger than her wax figure's smile. It was actually quite cute. She came to her event in a lovely gown made by Bob Mackey, the designer who did a lot of her television show costumes. She seemed to really enjoy her opening at the museum and even went through the process of giving the museum her handprints in cement as part of the dedication of her set.

Carol Burnett stands next to her completed wax figure,
doing her famous "ear tug" as a tribute to her mother.

Carol Burnett's
completed
Movieland wax
likeness in costume.

# Chapter 53

## Hulk Hogan, Tom Selleck

We created a wax figure of the wonderful and well-known wrestler, Mr. Hulk Hogan (1953 to present). Mr. Hogan was a huge man, standing six feet, six inches tall and over three hundred pounds, extremely strong and muscular. Hulk Hogan was very excited to see how his wax figure would come out when we were working on it. It took a lot of work on my part to create his wax figure with all the various bulky muscles, his large chest and whatnot.

In fact, when his wax figure was completed and Hulk Hogan came to see it, he just absolutely loved it and could not get enough of it. He visited it often and really checked it out up close, nose to nose, taking pictures and all. It was almost as if he was challenging another wrestler in the ring, eyeballing the wrestler very closely. We all enjoyed seeing how excited Hulk Hogan was over his wax figure. And this was always flattering for me.

Another figure we had at Movieland was that of Tom Selleck (1945 to present). He had a wonderful career and is a very handsome man. Mr. Selleck heard about his figure and he and his folks were invited out to the dedication of his set. It was located in a very prominent place in the museum, right near the main entrance. So he and his folks went to the opening for Tom Selleck's wax figure and they even helped him with his set dedication. We received many compliments from Tom Selleck's parents about how realistic his wax figure looked to them.

Hulk Hogan hams it up next to his wax likeness.

# Chapter 54

## Many More Stars, Golden Globes

I mentioned before that my wife Liz and I were very good friends with Mr. and Mrs. Snoey, who worked for a Belgian film magazine with the Foreign Press. Due to our association with them, we were invited to many events and awards dinners. At one particular Golden Globes event that took place at The Beverly Hilton Hotel, Liz and I had just walked across the red carpet and entered the bar inside the hotel. As we hung out in the bar area waiting for the festivities to begin in the main room, we could see many of the stars entering and walking the red carpet. While we waited in the bar area, I happened to notice a very tall man standing at the bar.

It was none other than Mr. Clint Eastwood (1930 to present). This was shortly after Clint Eastwood had made several of his successful Spaghetti Western films. Up until the time Clint Eastwood debuted in these Westerns filmed in Italy, he was not given much notoriety in Hollywood. But then everything changed after that and he became the iconic figure that he is today both as an actor and director.

So here at the Golden Globes we were standing near the wall in the bar waiting to be seated inside for the ceremony, and I decided then and there that I wanted to approach Mr. Eastwood just to tell him how much I admired his work in the Spaghetti Westerns.

At this point, he had barely done any American films and mostly bit parts at that. It was right before his huge rise to success as an actor. I approached Clint Eastwood sitting at the bar and said, "Pardon me, Mr. Eastwood, but I just wanted to let you know that I think your Spaghetti Westerns are just out of this world. I wanted to tell you how much I've enjoyed them. Everyone I've talked to in the U.S. who has also seen them very much appreciates and enjoys your work in these Westerns."

Mr. Clint Eastwood was so very nice and such a gentleman. He shook my hand and explained to this effect, "You know, I went over there to Italy because I just couldn't seem to build a momentum with my career here in America yet. I hadn't become very well known here but over there I had a chance for success and I always wanted to make Westerns. So once I started, one just followed another. You know, it has been a great experience and I sure appreciate your interest in my pictures over there. So thank you."

I went back to my wife Liz, who was standing near the wall, just kind of hanging out until it was our time to go into the auditorium and find our table for the dinner and program.

As we were standing there talking near the wall, I noticed that someone was standing right behind me rather closely. I seemed to have slowly backed myself against the wall near a corner and the shorter person behind me may have gotten trapped right behind me. I hadn't noticed until I felt them almost right against my back.

So I turned around and there stood the lovely Zsa Zsa Gabor (1917 to present), looking up at me with a slightly worried expression on her face. She was rather petite, and I stand six feet, two inches tall; I think she felt a little overwhelmed. As I looked at her, I said, "I'm sorry, I hope I'm not crowding you, Miss Gabor. I did not realize you were right behind me." She went on to tell me that she had been getting a tad concerned because she was getting crowded in closer to me, and I had unintentionally been backing her more and more closely towards the wall. We laughed about it, once she realized that I was harmless. So Liz and I said hello to Zsa Zsa and told her how much we enjoyed her pictures and this pleased her quite a bit. She was very friendly.

We thought this was somewhat funny because at a previous evening at the Golden Globes I had also somehow backed up into a star, standing near the bar's wall in the crowded room. This time it turned out to be Joan Collins (1933 to present) who was crowded up against the wall as I slowly, unintentionally had backed up to her while talking with Liz. I think it was because the room was so crowded that I was trying to get more space. When it happened that time, Joan Collins had been very polite and had just asked me to just give her a little breathing room because she was quite crowded near the wall. We had laughed at that moment with Joan Collins, too. It was like a déjà vu with Zsa Zsa.

At this particular Golden Globes event one of the stars who was being featured was the handsome and talented Mr. Robert Mitchum (1917-1997). He had quite a few of his family members there and several of them were also into acting or going into the business. This was right after Robert Mitchum had done a powerful and very successful acting job in a popular mini-series called *The Winds of War* (1983) on television. *The Winds of War* took place during World War II and Robert Mitchum had given a strong acting performance by playing a career naval officer named Victor "Pug" Henry, head of the Henry family.

When Mr. Mitchum was getting his award on stage, he had quite a lively reception from the crowd.

After the Golden Globes show that evening, we wanted to go back to the bar to have a nightcap before we headed home. There were many stars in the bar area at this time. Cyd Charisse (1922-2008) and her husband Tony Martin (1912 to present) were there. Cyd Charisse was beautiful and her career had been a great one, starting out in the Russian ballet and ending up with a contract at MGM for which she starred in many musicals, including *Singin' in the Rain* (1952) with Gene Kelly. She looked as lovely as ever in person, as I recall. So many beautiful stars were there mingling, laughing and having a great time that night. As a side note, Tony Martin is still performing in the San Francisco area as this book is written, after the death of his lovely wife in 2008.

I had watched the mini-series *The Winds of War* religiously and had found it quite interesting and stirring for I had been in the Air Corps of the Second World War myself. So I had watched it and marveled at the fine job that Robert Mitchum had done. I suddenly spotted Robert Mitchum across the room, standing near many of his family members. I walked up to Mr. Mitchum fearlessly and said, "Mr. Mitchum, can I give you a compliment please?" and he replied with a smile, "I'm always ready for one of those."

I told him how much I had enjoyed *The Winds of War* and how it had really transported me back in time while watching the mini-series, for I had been in World War II myself. He seemed so genuinely appreciative and really happy to hear this. Then Robert Mitchum introduced me to his family and everyone greeted me kindly.

As I thought back on this evening, I mentioned to Liz that I felt this was one of the best times we ever had at a Golden Globes Awards event. Our good fortune of having certain wonderful friends had also blessed us with the ability to attend these fun, glamourous affairs and mingle with the stars on a regular basis throughout my career. We both appreciated and cherished these opportunities. Liz reminded me that there had been several other times at the Golden Globes that were as fun as this evening, but that this one was definitely up there with the best of them. I was trying to remember the other Golden Globes after that and it really got me reminiscing.

One of the first Golden Globes we had ever attended was not even televised. It was before the Golden Globes became such a big and popular event like the Oscars. When they were not televised, the stars could be much more candid and say more colorful jokes than they could if they were being televised. It was quite entertaining to say the least.

At another one of the earlier Golden Globes events we had seats at a table that was raised up right next to the stage itself, just a tad higher than the stage. The curtains were within three or four feet from our table. As the stars came up to accept their awards they would breeze right by us within a couple of feet. We sure had the birds' eye view of everyone coming and going that evening. We were at a big, round table with several people and it was particularly special because two of our sons were with us this time.

Before we had been seated that evening, we had run into several of the stars as we were all getting ready to eat dinner. We had seen Jack Lemmon in particular, and my eleven year old named Miles noticed him right away. Miles was a wonderful piano player for his age and he had seen Mr. Lemmon (1925-2001) on the television playing piano. Miles had gone over to Jack Lemmon to congratulate him on what a wonderful piano player he was and what a fan he was. And Mr. Lemmon told Miles, "You know, this makes me feel very good that you complimented me on my piano playing because it really is not what I'm best known for but I really enjoy it. It really helps me relax after a long day at work."

My son Miles also mentioned that he played the piano as well and Mr. Lemmon spent quite a bit of time talking piano with him. They exchanged ideas and shared their favorite types of piano music with each other. I couldn't believe how very nice and gracious Jack Lemmon was with our son.

We had also run into Judy Garland (1922-1969) that night when we were all having dinner. We could see clearly that Ms. Garland was upset about something and felt very badly. Some of her friends were trying to comfort her but she was visibly upset. This made us sad but we obviously did not want to stare or intrude so we left them alone.

As we got ready for the main ceremony, it was likely that Shelley Winters (1920-2006) was getting an award that night. We had heard the buzz about her. She had received several awards in her time already. She was smiling just barely, a little quiet, standing there for a moment right next to our table before going on stage. I could tell that she was a little upset about something and just did not look quite like herself at that moment. She looked uncomfortable and probably sensed that we noticed it, too. She whispered to our table, "You know, I've had quite a few drinks tonight and I feel just a little bit worried that I'm not going to make a good impression. Would one of you mind giving me a sip of your drink so I can feel just a little bit more fortified before I go on stage?"

We told her certainly, and she went right around the table. Shelley Winters took a good swig out of each of our drinks! She really did a good job of drinking it up. We could all tell that she was extremely nervous, not really wanting to go out on the stage. But as soon as they announced Shelley Winters' name, the spotlight just went BAM! onto our table. She lit up just like a Christmas tree. As soon as the spotlight hit her, it was like Shelley Winters had been given a shot of adrenaline. She was just perfect standing there tall, like the Statue of Liberty. As she stood at the podium, Shelley Winters told a few jokes, and pulled off everything beautifully. As she walked off the stage, we could not believe what a wonderful job she had done, considering how nervous and upset she had appeared to be immediately before that spotlight had hit her. As she got to the other side of the stage, we could see behind the curtain. Shelley Winters rushed over to a gentleman standing behind that side of the curtain for support.

We saw so many incredible stars and talent that night. They were everywhere, and it was as if we had been submerged into the middle of their evening. They were right there, one by one passing our table which was so close to the stage. They laughed and joked a lot with us at our table for those few moments just before the spotlight would come upon them for their final few steps to the podium.

# Part Two
# The Palace of Living Art

We spoke a little earlier about the Palace of Living Art but I wanted to share a few more details about this very special part of the overall "Movieland experience." If you recall, the Palace was adjacent to Movieland Wax Museum and had been a dream of Mr. Parkinson's to build for many years. It took seven years to complete and opened in the late 1960's. Inside were some of the world's most famous paintings and artwork brought to life in wax along with faithfully reproduced copies of some of history's greatest sculptures carved by master craftsmen from around the world. Several of these sculptures were created out of exquisite Carrara marble which was actually taken from Michelangelo's own original private quarry near Pietrasanta, Italy. It took a huge team of people to create the Palace of Living Art and we all took great pride in bringing forth Mr. Parkinson's dream by applying exact, painstaking detail to the figures' likenesses, the set designs and the costumes throughout the entire building. Altogether, there were twenty five, three-dimensional sets at the Palace of Living Art featuring sixty life-size wax figures, plus the many marble and Plaster of Paris reproductions of famous statuettes.

I want to give special credit to Mr. Jim Mears, who did a masterful job in creating a palatial building that was worthy of these incredible masterpiece tributes. He personally saw to it that everything including all the beautiful paintings and sculptures from all around the world were presented in just the right manner.

Photography was not allowed in the Palace in order to preserve the integrity of these works of art. However when they were photographed, the wax figures looked so much like the original paintings that you could not always tell the difference. The Palace guests had the unique opportunity of seeing the subjects of famous paintings as they may have actually appeared when modeling for the artists.

The courtyard to the Palace faced the front of the building, which was beautiful in and of itself. There was a magnificent reproduction of *David* (created between 1501-1504) by Michelangelo as well, right in front of the building as you entered. This statue was carved out of a single piece of rare, flawless Carrara marble straight from Italy, and it stood in the Palace courtyard. It stood eighteen feet high, weighed ten tons, and took two full years to complete. It was stunningly beautiful, looking exactly like the original displayed in Florence, Italy.

*The Bronze Boar* was also in the Palace courtyard in another alcove. This bronze statue was created in 1612 and cast by the Baroque master Pietro Tacca. This was also an exact replica from the original which stands in a marketplace in Florence, Italy. It is supposed to give luck to those who rub its nose or put a coin in it. Another stone figure was of *Our Lady of the Sacred Heart* which stood near *The Bronze Boar*. This was created for the Palace of Living Art by Italian craftsmen.

*The Head of the Great Buddha* flanked by *Stone Figures* (artisans unknown) was also in the courtyard near the entryway to the Palace. These were authenticated from the Archeological Survey of India and were antiques. These pieces were completely unique and part of a tremendous art collection of Mr. Parkinson's which included pieces from all over the world.

The Palace of Living Art building had a Byzantine type of façade. It was very unusual and interesting. In the foyer as you entered the building, there was art replicated by Padre Andrea Pozzo (Italian, 1642-1709). He was a Jesuit Priest. The ceiling of the foyer was graced by a copy of a mural painted on the ceiling of the Church of Saint Ignatius in Rome by Padre Pozzo. The artist who replicated this wondrous mural by Pozzo was one of the best studio scenic artists that had been available. He did a magnificent job and it was meant to be viewed from a point in the center of the nave which created an illusion of a palace opening onto a sky filled with angels who seemed to hover and fly about happily.

Covering nearly one entire wall of the Palace foyer was a replica of one of the panels which decorate the inner temple of the shrine of Angkor-Vat in Cambodia, which was created by unknown Cambodian artisans in the Khmer Period (circa 1112-1153 A.D.). This panel was replicated for the Palace by the Louvre Museum in Paris. The panel was one of the greatest expanses of bas-relief that had been found in any existing monument at that time. It was believed that Angkor-Vat was likely one of the largest religious edifices ever built and it is the world's largest religious building.

No expense was spared in making the courtyard and foyer a truly grand entrance for the Palace and it gave the guests just a little taste of what was to come.

Rather than mention every single detail of the Palace, I would like to highlight just some of the artistic creations that were inside plus a little bit of information on each one.

I will also share some humorous and interesting stories that occurred within the Palace walls.

The first main room of the Palace of Living Art held copies of original artwork next to a set with our three-dimensional wax sculptures. This style is carried through the entire Palace where one could compare the original painting or sculpture with the 3D representation in wax including an authentic set to depict the background. *The Last Supper* by Leonardo di Vinci (Italian, 1452-1519) was reproduced on an entire wall in the Palace of Living Art. That room was made very large so this entire painting could be seen as you entered into the main room. The artist painted this original scene on the wall of a dining hall in a Dominican convent in Milan, Italy. It became pretty damaged over time but was refurbished and put back in the original building. All the sliding lines formed by the patterns of the ceiling walls drew the viewer's eyes directly to Jesus, who was silhouetted from the lights coming in from the window in the background. Looking at this masterpiece, you can imagine Jesus saying, "One of you shall betray me" and clearly see the apostles' individual reactions to His statement. This was quite powerful. As guests would continue walking along, on the other side of the *Last Supper* painting they would see the Palace's original three-dimensional *Last Supper* scene meticulously recreated to the smallest detail.

Moving along on the tour of the Palace, one would then view a multitude of amazing art masterpieces, some of which I will describe in this section. An El Greco piece that is called *Cardinal de Guevara* or Cardinal of the Inquisition (El Greco was also known as Domenico Teotocopulo). He was a Spanish painter born in Crete who lived from 1541-1614. There were amazing details from the three-dimensional figures including the distorted fingers of the left hand, the folds of the rope, and the penetrating gaze of the Cardinal of the Inquisition, all right there before your eyes looking just like the painting.

*Leda and the Swan* was created originally by Bartolomeo Ammannati (Italian, 1511-1592) and was originally carved by Ammannati from a design by Michelangelo, which is now lost. The beautiful copy of this work was carved out of pure white Carrara marble. As the Greek mythology goes, Leda was the wife of King Tyndareus but Zeus also dearly loved her. Zeus knew about Leda's strong love for animals and therefore transformed himself into a swan to gain her love and affection. This original statue has become a treasure of the Bargello National museum in Florence, Italy since 1872. Our copy of this statue became part of a very beautiful little fountain in the small, palace-like room.

Some larger sets were inset into the massive walls of one of the Palace's enormous rooms. One was a bust of Michelangelo. This famous sculpture was reproduced from the original that rests at the Louvre in Paris. It is believed that the original bust was created by one of Michelangelo's students and it is a beautiful job of the famed master.

Another inset held a *Bust of George Washington*. This was done by Jean Antoine Hudon (French, 1741-1828). This is the first bust done for one of the Presidents of the United States and was also reproduced for the Palace by the Louvre museum. The son of a servant, Jean

Antoine Hudon began winning fame for his talents at the young age of twelve. He sculpted over two hundred busts of prominent men and women throughout his career, including Napoleon Bonaparte and Benjamin Franklin, who in 1785 brought Hudon to the United States.

There was also a smaller, beautiful statue of a young boy pulling a thorn out of his foot called "*The Thorn Puller*" or "*The Boy Pulling the Thorn*" and the sculptor is unknown but the piece was sculpted during the Hellenistic Period (323 BC to 146 BC). The original bronze statue known as "*Spinario*" is now in the Capitoline Museum in Rome, Italy.

There was another section of wall that started out with a famous painting called "*Pinkie*" by the British artist Sir Thomas Lawrence (1769-1830). *Pinkie* exudes the radiance of a youthful girl and is very likely one of the most universally popular and most reproduced paintings of all time. The original is at the Huntington Library in San Marino, California. However, this painting bears a sad history. Shortly before *Pinkie* was supposed to be exhibited in May of 1795 at the Royal Academy of Arts, Lawrence received word that *Pinkie* (Sarah Barrett Moulton) had died at the age of twelve, the same year the painting was completed. She was eleven years old when she first posed for the artist. *Pinkie* hangs opposite "*Blue Boy*" by Thomas Gainsborough in the permanent collection at the Huntington Library. Had Sarah Barrett Moulton lived, she would have been the aunt for the great writer Elizabeth Barrett Browning.

*Mona Lisa* (also known as La Gioconda or La Joconde, or Portrait of Lisa Gherardini, wife of Francesco del Giocondo) is most certainly one of the most famed and prized of all paintings in history, created by Leonardo da Vinci (1452-1519). Leonardo da Vinci was in his fifties when he began this painting and it took four years to complete. It features the world-famous, enigmatic smile of Mona Lisa, who was the third wife of the Marquis del Gioconda. The Palace's representation of Mona Lisa shows how she may have appeared posing with the master, Leonardo da Vinci. She wears a dark dress and is wearing no rings, which is perhaps a sign of mourning for her child who had recently died. Many of these people who had paintings made for them so long ago had such sad happenings in their lives. There were many hardships to bear, and people died much younger.

On another wall was the Bust of Cardinal de Richelieu by Jean Varin, a French artist (1604-1672). This bust was also reproduced for the Palace by the Louvre Museum from the original piece that stands in the Library of Saint Germain-des Pres. Alongside this bust of Cardinal de Richelieu was a large painting originally done by Philippe De Champaigne, another French artist (1602-1674). After De Champaigne settled in Paris, he became one of the most important portrait painters of his time. His work was very honest, as he never sacrificed the character or personality of his subjects for sheer flattery. Next to this impressive painting was an exact copy represented in wax. As Minister of State to King Louis XIII of France, Richelieu succeeded in making the king absolute ruler and establishing France as Europe's first military power.

There was a portrait of King Louis the XIV by Hyacinthe Rigaud (French, 1659-1743). This portrait was made when the "Sun King" was 63. He was so pleased with it that he kept it for the Palace in Versailles and had a copy of it made and sent to Madrid. It also helped Rigaud win an appointment as a court painter. Because of his height and vanity, Louis the XIV invented the high-heeled shoe that he wore in this portrait. He wanted to look bigger, more prominent, and he felt he did not look important enough. He also came up with the style of French provincial furniture. He was quite artistic and doubled the size of the Louvre museum. He was also quite often known to ride horseback through the corridors of the galley. Due to the heavy weight of the clothing the king chose for the portrait, his servants posed for all but the figure proportions, facial features and hands. These details were completely finished before any background or accessories were added to the painting. It was such a terrific yet heavy costume that he did not want to go through the problem of holding it up for long periods of time. Parisian artists for the Palace all painstakingly recreated this figure, the set and the costume.

There was also *The Marriage of Giovanni Arnolfini* by Jan van Eyck (Flemish, 1385-1441). This is one of the most famous paintings in the National Gallery in London and known for its originality and complexity. The illusionism was incredible both in detail and for the way lighting was used to evoke an inside space. Looking closely, the artist, van Eyck can presumably be seen reflected in the mirror of the background of the painting. Van Eyck often involved himself in his paintings in reflections, windows or mirrors. Van Eyck and his brothers are also credited with the invention of oil paints. There has been debate about the subjects of the painting because the couple (Giovanni di Arrigo Arnolfini and his wife Giovanna Cenami) did not marry until thirteen years after the date of the painting titled after them. Also, the woman in the painting appears pregnant. However, most art scholars are now of the opinion that she was not expecting because they can point to numerous other paintings of female virgin saints similarly dressed; therefore they have concluded that this look was just a fashionable style for women's dresses during that period.

The statue titled *Lincoln* is modeled after our former President by Daniel Chester French (American, 1850-1931) at the Lincoln Memorial in Washington, DC. It is one of the greatest statues that has ever been made and depicts the Great Emancipator, deep in thought. It was scaled down to the normal size of a man instead of a giant statue and was created from his life mask. There was a lot of work put into reproducing it. Even the hands were done by being reproduced from a life mold taken just after Lincoln's inauguration in Springfield.

The set of Mona Lisa, wax figures and painting done by Logan Fleming,
at the Palace of Living Art. *Photo by Ian Schapel, Adelaide, South Australia.*

On the wall just past *Lincoln* and opposite the *Mona Lisa* set was a gorgeous statuette
figure of *Salome Receiving the Head of John the Baptist.* Alongside this sculpture is a very
famous painting by Guido Reni showing Salome's mother as she carries his head in on a
tray (Italian, 1575–1642). In the biblical story, Salome danced before King Herod and was
rewarded according to the wishes of her mother with the head of John the Baptist. Reni's
style, considered poetic and unrestrained by his earlier critics, is obvious in this painting.

There was also a beautiful display of *Aristotle Contemplating the Bust of Homer* by
Rembrandt van Rijn (Dutch, 1606-1669).  The original of this portrait is of two great
philosophers whose far-reaching influence still inspires all of civilization. It was purchased
by the Metropolitan Museum of Art for $2,300,000. Our Palace reproduction was stunning.
Working one's way around the museum in a circular direction, next there was a French scene
by the famous French Impressionist painter and lithographer Henri de Toulouse-Lautrec
(French, 1864-1901). It depicted Can-Can dancers and other characters of La Moulin
Rouge (The Red Mill). This was one of the artist's favorite haunts, seeing all the dancing
girls, costumes, people and just the gaiety of the atmosphere there. The colors expressed in
the dress and costumes of that time really impressed Mr. Lautrec. Permanently crippled as
a child from a fall that broke both of his legs, Toulouse-Lautrec was much smaller than he

The wax figure of President Abraham Lincoln, at the Palace of Living Art.
*Photo by Ian Schapel, Adelaide, South Australia.*

should have been. He preferred "slumming" it with the company of the citizens and artists of Montmartre to that of the aristocratic society of his family.

There were a few separate occasions when Jack Collins was watching over Movieland and the Palace when he walked to where *La Moulin Rouge* set was and came upon guests who were looking up the skirts of the French figures in this scene! This was a dishonor to the famous Toulouse-Lautrec. Seriously, there were quite a variety of folks who came to the museum including quite the mischief-maker from time to time. It sure kept us on our toes and really made us all want to keep the respect, professionalism and dignity of the stars' figures top-notch even more so.

Next to *La Moulin Rouge* piece we had a *Paris Street Scene* that was worked from photographs and paintings of that period. Artists flocked there to live, paint, experience and just be part of this Parisian lifestyle. In fact, today there are still artists from all over the world in Montmartre and it is still known as an artists' colony. In our display, painters showed off their works inviting Palace visitors to pose for portraits, purchase colorful shots, and sample sweet-smelling perfumes, jewelry, and souvenirs, much like it might have been in Montmartre over a century ago.

Further along the way there was a cave-like tunnel that took you out into a very unbelievable scene. This awe-inspiring scene was the representation of the *Crucifixion of Christ*. Included in the set was Jesus on the cross and the two thieves. Also depicted were the Virgin Mary, Mary Magdalene, John (the son of Zebedee), and several soldiers of the Roman legions, one of whom is holding the robe of Christ while casting lots for his clothes. This set was seventy to eighty feet in length and had a tremendous background showing dense clouds and terrible turbulence in the skies above. It made such a strong impact as the scene slowly revealed itself as you were coming out of the tunnel.

Walking a bit further, you would climb up to a raised vantage point and peer downward onto a tremendous landscape. Real rocks and scenery with rugged mountains in the distance helped create the extremely realistic feel of this set. There were also real trees, including a live Pepper tree. Extensive sound and lighting effects further added to realism of this set. While observing the scene unfold, Jesus dies on the Cross and the thunder and lightning begin, with colors changing and darkening dramatically. The skies begin to turn a blood-red with extremely desolate tones. The lighting on Jesus turns from blue to red as He breathes His last breath.

Painstaking effort was taken to recreate the Crucifixion as realistically as possible so that you would feel as if you were actually there in person experiencing this event for yourself. Many of the Palace visitors would stop and kneel down in front of the set, praying for what seemed like hours at times, moved in ways only they could understand. Some would weep unabashed, pouring their souls out toward the heart-wrenching and meaningful scene before them. It was truly a powerful experience, which I often felt honored to witness.

A photo of the set of the *Crucifixion of Christ* at the Palace of Living Art.
*Photo by Ian Schapel, Adelaide, South Australia.*

After another tunnel, you would re-enter the main Palace building. The first thing you saw was the *Statue of David,* the same one that stood in front of the Palace of Living Art, except this one was scaled down to human size and made of wax with natural flesh tones instead of the white Carrara marble. We also decided that it would be wise to cover this David's male genitals with a loincloth.

In fact, one rainy day when there were very few guests visiting the Palace, one of our Keystone Kops saw a middle-aged woman admiring the wax figure of David. She went on her way and he didn't think anything of it at the time until he noticed that she had returned to admire the figure again. This time she stayed quite a while and moved from one side and then to another as if she was checking out every angle of David. Our Keystone Kop was somewhat amused by all the attention she was giving to the figure. After all, Michelangelo had sculpted every toned muscle of his anatomy with such care and detail that David looked like an ancient poster boy with his chiseled jaw and perfect male physique. And the same details were applied to this wax figure of David. Again, she left and he thought that was the end of it. But when she returned a third and a fourth time, it piqued our Keystone Kop's interest and he decided he would stick around at a distance to observe her. Every once in a while, another guest or two would come and go but when she was alone again she would suspiciously turn her head to see if anyone was looking. Finally, she made her move! She gingerly crossed the barrier and walked into the set and gently peaked under the loincloth to see what was underneath! Our Keystone Kop came out of the shadows and caught her red-handed. In addition, a loud buzzer went off when she broke the barrier and entered the set. It is hard to imagine how embarrassed that poor woman was, but I had to laugh when I heard the story the next day.

Then there were three sets in a circular area. One of them was a replica of the *Laughing Cavalier*, a famous painting by the Dutch Baroque artist Frans Hals (1580-1666). In this picture the subject had a very mysterious smile on his face. Hals depicted a self-confident soldier with a suggestion of bravado in this painting. The captivating eyes in the original painting suggested a ripple of mirth which was said to follow the onlooker as he moved to view the painting from different angles. We had a perfect copy of this picture made from the original and it really did feel like his eyes followed you around, no matter where you stood. Our wax representation of the *Laughing Cavalier* had a terrific costume, and, true to form, the eyes seemed to move with you, the observer, just like the painting. It was captivating.

In addition to *Aristotle Contemplating the Bust of Homer*, we had several other Rembrandt displays. One of these was the *Portrait of the Artist's Son Titus* depicting Rembrandt's only surviving son when he was between four and seven years old. He was very close to his son and was dependent upon him during his declining years. The portrait was purchased in 1965 by the Norton Simon Foundation at an auction held at Christie's in London for $2,234,000. It now hangs at the Los Angeles County Museum of Art.

Rembrandt was a prodigious artist who had created nearly 650 paintings. Nearly sixty of these pieces were self portraits. Another Rembrandt display in the Palace was *Rembrandt, A Self-Portrait* which was completed in 1664, just a few years before his death. It revealed a dramatic self knowledge reflecting the tragedy of his decline into bankruptcy and disgrace.

We had a Palace original piece called *Don Quixote and Sancho Panza*. This piece was created in its entirety by artisans from Spain, inspired by the Miguel de Cervantes Spanish classical novel, *Don Quixote*. This original piece of work brought to life for the first time the legendary figures of the would-be knight and his squire as they were described in the book. It showed Don Quixote and Poncho together in the set with horses and a windmill. The wax figures and costumes were extremely authentic looking and beautiful.

*The Three Graces* portrayed some of the most beautiful forms of the human female body ever, by Hyacinthe Rigaud (French, 1659-1743). This was recreated by artisans in Paris as a three-dimensional reproduction of the original painting. These lovely Greek Goddesses or Charities of Fertility were named Aglaia (Whiteness or Splendor, Brightness, Shining One), Euphrosne (Joy, the Incarnation of Grace and Beauty), and Thalia ("to bloom"), according to Greek mythology. The lighting on these wax reproductions made them look lifelike with the tone of their beautiful skin glowing.

There was a piece which represented *Van Gogh (a self-portrait) and The Artists's Room at Arles* (Dutch, 1853-1890). The display was created by Italian artisans who had combined two of Van Gogh's paintings into one setting. The painters recreated a painting by Van Gogh as he saw himself, seated in *The Artist's Room at Arles* where he spent his most productive months. An erratic personality, Van Gogh is well known for an incident stemming from a fall where he sliced off part of his right ear. Van Gogh wrapped his head in a towel and delivered the severed ear to a girl in a brothel. An impressionistic painter, he depicted things simply as he saw them without great detail. He used wonderful hues and had a tremendous imagination for color. This set incorporated a wax figure of the painter sitting on a chair in his room at Arles, which is quite a noted picture in itself. The next piece we had was *The Man with the Golden Helmet* by Rembrandt Harmenszoon van Rijn (Dutch, 1606-1669). Being short of funds, Rembrandt asked his older brother to don a Renaissance helmet borrowed from a fellow painter and pose for this painting, which is now priceless. This masterpiece depicts a battle-worn soldier. The helmet in the Palace set reproduction was hand crafted in Spain. It was an exact duplicate of the helmet in Rembrandt's painting.

The Palace was fortunate to have an exact copy of the *Venus de Milo* (Greek, Circa 200 B.C.). The original was discovered in 1820 by a Greek peasant on the Agean Island of Milos, therefore it was named *Venus de Milo* (artist unknown). This is a priceless artifact from Grecian culture, thought to have been posed about 200 B.C. The statue was found in two sections but without the arms. Besides the flawless Louvre reproduction of the original, the Palace also presented the lovely Venus as she may have appeared while posing for the unknown sculptor. Her left hand was placed against the pillar for support, with her right hand holding her tunic to cover the lower portion of her body. Her classic profile was clearly captured in the wax likeness.

One particularly slow day at the Palace and the museum, Jack Collins was making the rounds. Jack entered the Palace from the museum through a special door that only the employees knew about. This door was a quick way to get from one building to the next. When Jack entered the Palace, he entered where the Venus wax figure and set was. He could immediately see that there was a man who had somehow gotten over the set's sensor which would have normally buzzed when someone went through it. Well, this fellow had walked right up to my wax figure of *Venus de Milo* and was down on his knees, and believe-it-or-not, he was actually sucking the wax figure's breast! The moment Jack realized what was happening, he shouted, "My *man*! What *are* you doing?" Scared and startled he flew out of that set and took off like a banshee, causing the buzzer to go off. Still, we never caught him.

Another classic display in the Palace was *The Blue Boy* by Thomas Gainsborough (English, 1727-1788). Purchased many years ago by the Huntington Gallery in Pasadena, California for $750,000, *The Blue Boy* was Gainsborough's most famous work. It is believed that *The Blue Boy* was painted in about 1770. This piece is now valued in the millions. This is one of the most beautiful portraits ever painted of a young boy. There was a large, beautiful reproduction of *The Blue Boy* on the left side, next to the set on the right which had the three dimensional figure of *The Blue Boy*. If you took a picture of both, you could not tell the difference.

There was a very interesting and famous American painting called *American Gothic* by Grant Wood (American, 1892-1942). Ironically, this was the only Grant Wood painting that gained fame. This one painting was famous to almost every American as a representation of the typical farm couple from the Midwest of the early 1900's. The man stands in front of the barn, the woman in front of the kitchen, each in his own domain. Grant Wood's sister, an Iowa dentist, was the woman who posed for the classic American painting. When Grant Wood's sister came to the Palace, she had heard we had created a wax representation of her brother's famous painting. She was very curious to see our set. When she saw it, she was so taken with it and thought it was just wonderful.

*Portrait of the Artist's Mother* by James McNeill Whistler (American, 1834-1903) was originally titled *"An Arrangement in Gray and Black"* but it has commonly come to be known as *Whistler's Mother*. Famous throughout the world as a tribute to motherhood, this was not the intention of Whistler, because he held great contempt for the interest the public had in sentimental anecdotes. He believed that what mattered was not the subject matter but how it was translated into color and form. The original piece hangs in the Louvre. They gave us a beautiful copy of this painting. Our set showed *Whistler's Mother* in her room, three dimensional and looking just like the painting.

Jack Collins was walking toward the *Whistler's Mother* piece one day in the Palace and was surprised by an older woman. He described this lady later on as looking "as if she had just come out of the back woods of Tennessee." This woman was standing over the old lady figure of *Whistler's Mother* and had the wax figure's dress pulled clear up over its legs. Jack exclaimed, "Madame! What are you doing in there?"

This hard-bitten old gal did not bat an eyelash when questioned by Jack. She did not even act as if she cared whether or not Jack had caught her. After a moment or two, she finally replied nonchalantly, "Well, I had always heard that this old lady carried a jug of booze under her dress and I just wanted to see if she had the jug under there!" Finding nothing, she dropped the dress and kind of shrugged, spryly stepping over the buzzer and walking right out of the museum with great gusto and grace, not saying another word. Jack just scratched his head, amused.

We also had a set of *Christ in the Garden of Gethsemane*. This is a famous painting by Heinrich Hoffman (German, 1824-1895). This inspiring scene portrays Christ praying to God the Father on the eve of his Crucifixion. Just like the painting, we had the wax interpretation with Jesus on his knees, leaning on a rock and looking up to the heavens, pleading that God spare him of this terrible ordeal, or at the least give him the strength to endure it.

As visitors continued through this area they would come upon the spectacular reproduction of Michelangelo Buonorroti's famous sculpture *La Pieta* (Italian, 1475-1564). On an adjacent wall were the *Stones from Jerusalem*. These special stones were presented to the Palace and were part of an ancient wall from the Church of the Holy Sepulcher. This church is said to have been erected on the actual site (Golgotha) where Jesus was crucified and also was buried. The original *La Pieta* resides in St. Peter's Basilica in Vatican City.

*La Pieta* is Michelangelo's most famous masterpiece and was sculpted in about 1500 when the artist was about twenty-five years of age. It is a haunting depiction of Mary, the mother of Jesus holding her son's dead body after the Crucifixion. Like the original at St. Peter's in Rome, the Palace's reproduction was carved from one flawless piece of Cararra marble. Recreated for the Palace by Pietrasanta artisans, the statue weighed over eight tons and took two years to complete to perfection. The sculptor's name was etched across the robe of the Virgin. It reads, "Michelangelo Buonarroti of Florence Made This." This was added after the statue had been completed and arguments had ensued over the true identity of the artist. It was the only one of his works that bore his name.

This piece was a fitting end to the tour of the beautiful and unique Palace of Living Art. Although the Palace of Living Art was a tremendous achievement, we have to give the fullest credit to the great artists who originally created their masterpieces for without them the Palace would never have existed. Finally, I want to say that working on the Palace was especially satisfying to me personally because of my training in classic art. I felt a real sense of accomplishment because we had created a serious but entertaining place where people could come and experience classic art in a new way. Whether you were an art buff or just an average person with little or no knowledge about art, this was a place you could learn something new and just maybe appreciate the talent these masters had and why their work remains timeless and unmatched to this day.

Logan's wax likeness of Rembrandt's masterpiece, *The Man with the Golden Helmet*. This was one of Logan's favorite pieces from the Palace of Living Art.

A replica of Michelangelo's *La Pieta* at the Palace of Living Art. *Photo by Ian Schapel, Adelaide, South Australia.*

# Part Three
# More Movieland Facts

**M**ovieland was opened in 1962 with a tremendous Hollywood opening that was discussed earlier. Later on, the world famous Madame Tussaud's Wax Museum in London followed Movieland's lead and saw the popularity of the movies as an application for wax museums. After a while they began to add more and more movie stars to their venue. Before that they mostly had historical figures in their museum.

While we're on the subject of Madame Tussaud (and to share a little more information on the origins of wax artistry), she had a very interesting history and start to her career. Her art training began in Paris in 1770 where she learned to model wax likenesses under her mentor, Dr. Philippe Curtis.

At age 17, she became art tutor to King Louis XVI's sister at the Palace of Versailles. However, when the monarchy was overthrown during the French Revolution, she was forced to show her allegiance to the rebels by making death masks of the aristocracy that were executed and beheaded by the guillotine.

After the Revolution, she was part of a traveling exhibition where relics from the war were displayed as well as wax figures of famous and infamous heroes and rogues of the Revolution. The exhibit found a permanent home in London and ultimately became Madame Tussaud's Wax Museum. The gruesome and macabre figures she had created years before led to the idea of creating a Chamber of Horrors, which became one of the main attractions of her museum and a fixture in almost every other wax museum that came after that. That is a brief introduction on how wax museums began.

One day at Movieland, Mr. Parkinson declared it to be "Keystone Kop Day." Out in front of the museum he had announced that they would feature "Mack Sennett's Keystone Kops." Mack Sennet owned a production company called "Film Company" which produced the Keystone Kops comedy series between 1912 and 1917. The Keystone Kops would be performing in front of the museum on this special day. It turned out to be quite an event and a rather impressive crowd showed up for this.

In front of the museum, instead of a Rolls Royce driving up, they had an old-time 1921 black Model-T. This was known as a Keystone Kop "buggy" and many of their pictures were made with this type of car. So they all pulled up in front of the museum followed by Mr. Parkinson in the Rolls Royce to greet them.

As Mr. Parkinson got out of his limo, the Keystone Kops all started to pile out of their car just as they used to do in the old, silent films. They started doing funny stunts, antics, arguing, talking, and running around. Among these Keystone Kops who were putting on quite a show was Mr. Parkinson's good, faithful old friend named Buster Keaton.

All of a sudden, in front of the entire group of Keystone Kops, there appeared a voluptuous and extremely sexy lady wearing tights and dressed up suggestively. She walked right up to the Keystones and really gave them a flirtatious eye. Then she kept right on walking past them, but Buster Keaton decided to run right after her, wild as ever, losing his hat. The others chased Buster Keaton and caught up to him, jumping on him and then piling on top of him, pretending to hit and slap him up. It was quite a funny sight to behold.

As Buster Keaton came out from underneath the pile of other Keystones, he stood up, dusted himself off, and put his flat hat squarely onto his head right as one of the other Keystones threw a great, big custard pie right into his face! Even funnier was when Buster grabbed another custard pie and retaliated, throwing it right into the face of the Kop who pied his face. Before you knew it, all the Keystone cops had joined in the action. There was pie flying everywhere! This was absolutely hilarious to watch and the crowd roared with laughter. This was truly one of the most entertaining and funny things that ever took place right out in front of the museum. Those Keystone Kops always knew how to deliver a good show.

On another day at Movieland, Mr. Parkinson decided to designate a special day at the museum was for the *Star Trek* cast and crew. This was a very special event set aside just for the *Star Trek* characters to dedicate their set inside the museum. The crew of the Starship Enterprise arrived in limousines and there were big banners up in front of the museum as usual. As the *Star Trek* actors stepped out of the limos there was quite a huge crowd there. Eugene Wesley "Gene" Roddenberry who was the creator of *Star Trek* and an American screenwriter, producer and futurist (1921-1991), was right there with the cast of his show. They all posed around the set figures and it turned out to be a great dedication.

At the back end of the Palace building, we created a very scary horror section. One of the sets in this section was *Alien (1979)*. They had asked me if I could make an alien monster and of course I told them I could but secretly wondered how I'd do it. I had some great photographs to work from and eventually I created a moving, working alien monster. It looked so real that it frightened the living daylights out of many people. When standing fully upright, this alien monster stood roughly over ten feet high. It was made out of all sorts of items including automobile body parts and automobile hoses. I used hot glue and other items. I created bones, hands and fingers out of aluminum foil. For the mouth, I made the teeth out of hot glue. Its moveable jaw and neck turned from side to side. It was quite a scary sight. The alien monster stood in a darker area of this horror section. We used to create a tremendous amount of "smoke" that addded to the eerie effect of the set. I'm quite proud of the scary alien monster that I created out of odds and ends. It was a fun project that turned out great.

It is interesting to note that Mr. Parkinson had two gold Rolls Royces. He was a real car buff and really loved cars. As mentioned before these luxurious vehicles were used to pick up stars and take them to and from their interviews, fittings, special trips, museum dedications and personal occasions of one sort or another. Mr. Parkinson was a very close friend with the Shah of Iran when he was in power. He used to go visit the Shah and they both shared a love of cars. The Shah had a little Ferrari and Allen Parkinson loved Ferraris. One day he told the Shah that he had an extra Rolls Royce and asked him if he might want to trade one Rolls Royce for the Ferrari, and the Shah gladly accepted because he had never owned a Rolls Royce.

I was working in my studio at the museum one day when I heard a loud noise, much like an engine gunning. I opened the door and there was Mr. Parkinson grinning like a Cheshire cat in his new little Ferrari. I asked him where he got it, and he told me that he traded the Shah of Iran one of his Rolls Royces for that Ferrari. He asked me to hop in the Ferrari for a spin. Allen loved to drive very fast. We had a huge, fenced parking lot around the museum. When I got in the car, Allen put the petal to the metal and we were up to 90 mph in an instant. He'd go right to the edge where the fence was and turn away, scaring the devil out of me! I was amazed at his nonchalant attitude about it. He did not flinch but I was a bit fearful at one point. He really knew how to maneuver and corner but I was quite nervous and excited at the same time. I was extremely happy to get back to work in my humble little studio after that spin around the parking lot!

During the 1980's we wanted to add President Ronald Reagan (1911-2004) to the wax museum. We contacted the White House to see if he would be interested in having a wax figure set displayed with other former actors since he had developed quite a respectable acting career on his own before moving into the world of politics. He was very receptive and had really enjoyed the wonderful memories of his acting in Hollywood; therefore, he was happy to oblige as long as his schedule permitted. In fact, President Reagan had told us we could come to the White House for the measurement session. This was very exciting and thrilling news to us.

The White House was in touch with the museum, and we were ready to schedule a date to travel to Washington, D.C., for the sitting. After some time, it was all arranged but eventually we received a phone call from the White House with the unfortunate news that the President had unexpectedly been called out of the country for some important meetings to attend. He was in fact quite disappointed that he would have to cancel our measurement session for his wax figure. I was also disappointed, for it would have been the highest honor to have met the President of the United States at the White House.

The representatives from the White House were in touch with us on several occasions as the President had offered to help us out any way we needed it. We received accurate measurements from the President's tailor in Hollywood. We also received one of President Reagan's suits directly from the White House, and his tailor spiffed it up to have it look in tip-top shape. We were given all the information that we needed to get his wax figure started and ended up making a very successful figure.

We decided to have President Reagan's wax figure in a set that looked like the Oval Office. Along with many photographs, our set designers got the exact dimensions, maps and information needed to recreate and build an authentic looking, smaller version of the Oval Office. There is a photograph of myself while this work was going on. It was very fun and interesting to partake in the building and creating of President Ronald Reagan's set for Movieland. It turned out quite nicely.

We sent Mr. Reagan photographs of the set and he really enjoyed them. Later on, we decided that President Reagan would also enjoy having another set and wax likeness created for him from one of the Western movies he made to which he was thrilled.

After you came upon the Western set with Ronald Reagan the actor, you would see the White House set with President Ronald Reagan. He wanted very much to come and see the sets at the museum and vowed to do so. But as his presidential schedule took over and world political situations arose, he just couldn't find the time to come to Movieland. We sent pictures to him after he left office before he fell ill with Alzheimer's and he let us know that he was very pleased.

Myrna Loy (1905-1993), an American actress who devoted her career to acting after some smaller roles in silent films, was one of the wax figures already in the museum when I joined it in 1964. Her set was the successful American detective comedy film called *The Thin Man* (1934) with the actor William Powell (1892-1984) and their popular Wire Fox Terrier named Asta.

Logan puts finishing touches on the wax likeness of President Ronald Reagan.

Myrna Loy was a very good friend of Mr. Parkinson's. She came to Movieland on many occasions and was particularly interested in her set, because we had incorporated Asta the dog. I never had the pleasure of meeting Mr. Powell although I believe he came to the museum also, but Ms. Loy was very delightful and told me that Asta was such a dear dog and he completed the set we made for *The Thin Man.*

Allen Parkinson had some television commercials shot for the museum to give it some exposure. He used experienced marketing and advertising agency folks from Hollywood to help handle the publicity for us.

One time we had a crew out to shoot a commercial of the very realistic Star Trek Enterprises' Bridge set which I mentioned earlier. This set was viewed by museum guests from a few feet above, so one would seem to be peering down into the control center of the ship. All the main characters from Star Trek were in this set, including Kirk, Spock, Bones, Chekov, Uhura, Scotty and others. It was fun to watch the commercial get set up with all the studio lighting and to watch the director find the right shots and angles. I was standing right next to the director and cameraman while this was happening and I got to take a quick peek into the camera. I could tell how realistic this set and the characters looked from the eye of the camera.

The director made a comment then that stood out in my mind and still does to this day. It was a huge compliment which summed up what I had been striving for during my entire career. He told me that he had also filmed the real actors for the actual television show *Star Trek* on the set of the Enterprise's bridge. He went on to say that viewing our wax museum set through his camera lens looked as real, if not more so, than when he shot the real actors in person. He was so amazed and could not believe his own practiced eyes. He then gave the go-ahead to shoot the scene; the commercial came out extremely well.

Several other commercials were shot for Movieland Wax Museum and the Palace of Living Art including one using *The Wizard of Oz*'s set. These commercials were quite successful and the exposure brought in a lot of revenue for the museum.

The complete Movieland set of the Oval Office with President Reagan.

# Part Four
## After Movieland

After Movieland was sold, I continued my career creating wax figures at other museums both in the US and overseas. Several years ago during this stage of my career I recall being asked by some of Oprah Winfrey's representatives to be on a television program that she produced. On the show there would be celebrity contestants who would come in and try to guess the occupations of people who were hand-picked by the producers. They were looking for people with somewhat unusual jobs to stump the celebrities. Of course, I had a very unique occupation, so I was ultimately selected to be on the show. The stars had only so much time to probe and ask us questions before they had to try to guess our occupations. If they guessed wrong, then we would win money. As time ran out and the buzzer went off, if the star hadn't figured out our occupation, we were instructed to finally divulge the truth. If the celebrities were adept at asking the right questions, they had a good chance of winning by ferreting out enough information to figure out our occupations.

I did not think it would be all that difficult to guess my occupation, and I was asked many questions. This went on for almost an hour, with four or five celebrities trying to figure out what I actually did for a living. They all had their chances and tried again and again, but they never asked the proper questions (even with Oprah's help) that would give them enough clues as to what I did. Finally, they simply ran out of things to ask me, and it was announced that I had won the contest. I was given $1,000 and was the only contestant who won that day.

Everyone seemed to be happy after the show. Naturally, Oprah and her producers wanted it to be interesting and with my turn on the show that was exactly what they got. The audience always rooted for the contestant to win and the celebrity to be stumped. The celebrities on the show had a great time, too. I was driven home in a very luxurious limo with a fully stocked bar. It was a great time, and I had a blast recapping the story to my family that evening.

Eventually, I created Oprah's wax figure for a museum in Missouri from pictures and measurements, but I never did get to take measurements of her in person. In spite of this, her figure turned out pretty nice. It was always an exciting challenge to create a realistic wax likeness of a special person whom I had never had the pleasure of meeting. I have to say, it was quite thrilling.

There was a wealthy Japanese investor who commissioned me to create several specific wax likenesses for a museum in Japan. He initially wanted me to create the wax figures for The Beatles, The Pope and Abraham Lincoln. This was also after Movieland and during the time I was freelancing as a wax artist, so I took his offer and started working on the figures he requested. I had completed the wax figures and was in a holding pattern, waiting for this investor to come to California to see my work. In the meantime, I had just started working on getting the costumes gathered for these figures.

One day, I got a phone call from this Japanese investor, out of the blue, that he was here in California and was on his way to our home to come and see the figures he was paying me to make for his collection! Having had no warning time whatsoever, my sons and I desperately scrambled to dig through our own closets and attic, trying to find any and every type of clothing that could possibly pass for attire to make these wax figures look acceptable, at least temporarily!

Can you imagine the mayhem and humor in trying to instantly outfit a Pope, a President and The Beatles from your own wardrobe? We did manage to scrounge up a few articles of 1960's or 1970's clothing that could be used to outfit The Beatles but we were at a total loss on what to do for the Pope and President Lincoln. With no time left, I believe we ended up putting some type of nice pajamas on Lincoln's figure just to have him dressed, and the Pope was outfitted in one of our bathrobes. It was hysterical and hilarious all at the same time. I kept thinking what our neighbors would think if they peered through the window. It would be strange enough to have The Pope, The Beatles and Abraham Lincoln all assembled together in one room...*but naked?* And then the spectacle of our family running around putting bathrobes and pajamas on a US President and a Pope while the Beatles stood there in the buff staring at this whole farce. Of course, I had planned on outfitting them properly soon enough, but I just did not have the costumes ready yet. Somehow we pulled it off and the Japanese investor was quite pleased with my work.

The same Japanese investor gave me another opportunity. I was able to create a wax likeness for the deeply respected and beloved Diana, Princess of Wales (1961-1997) during my career. Her likeness turned out beautifully, and many thought the photograph of it was really her. Her life was much too short, ending tragically in Paris during a car crash. Her figure was supposed to have been shipped to a museum in Asia, and sadly it fell and broke apart not once but twice, much too symbolic of her tragic ending. It remains broken in a safe place, and one thing I've wanted to do for quite some time is to finish it and give it a proper home.

I made many other wax likenesses of more modern-day celebrities in this later part of my career such as Tom Cruise (1962-present), Michael Jackson (1958-2009), Britney Spears (1981-present), Madonna, born Madonna Louise Ciccone (1958-present), and countless others that I either created or worked on, retouching and improving them.

One of the most unusual figures I ever had to create for another museum in Japan was a figure of Robert Pershing Wadlow (1918-1940), The World's Tallest Man Who Ever Lived. This man ended up being 8 feet 11.1 inches tall and weighed 439 pounds! I built this man's wax likeness in my garage with a very high ceiling. I made it in a very different way than I made most other wax figures due to his size. Instead of using the regular means, I had to create his basic body structure out of plywood and then fill it in later. I had to get all the information from the *Guinness Book of World Records*, including all the pictures, exact sizes and details. This was another wax figure I felt honored to have accomplished during my career, and it had been a fun and creative challenge.

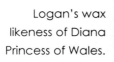

Logan's wax
likeness of Diana
Princess of Wales.

# Epilogue
## Final Thoughts on my Career

As mentioned earlier, there were close to a million visitors each year during the Museum's heyday. There were sometimes 6,000 to 8,000 people visiting the museum each day during the summer.

One particular day, right in the middle of summer, we got some amazing news from Movieland. Their one-millionth guest had just passed through the doors of the museum and this was a huge cause for celebration! The heads of the company decided to have a big, impromptu celebration that night for all the employees and their families. They threw a lavish party in the front office area. Everyone was enjoying champagne and celebrating together. I have a wonderful picture of this special event, and the memories of it will forever be emblazoned in my mind. It was one of the best and proudest moments in my career.

Over the years, Movieland enjoyed great success and had a long continuous run. If you think about all the time that Movieland was in business, there had to have been over twenty million people who came to visit the museum, and probably a lot more than that. People from all over the world visited us. We had become the third largest tourist attraction in the state of California at that time. With that type of notoriety, the word about Movieland spread globally. Since we were right next to Knott's Berry Farm and very close to Disneyland, it became a frequently visited spot by many a tourist.

I will always and forever look back so fondly on the days of my career with Movieland Wax Museum and the Palace of Living Art, where I learned to adapt to a host of interesting situations and work with so many different and fascinating people. My career was truly a gift and an honor, a way for me to give of myself to the world creatively, to express my artistic ability, and to experience so many once-in-a-lifetime adventures. I owe a huge amount of gratitude to Mr. Allen Parkinson, to my wife Liz and my family, and to all those stars who stood still before me.

Most of the Executive Team who ran Movieland Wax Museum and the Palace of Living Art at a dinner event, from left to right: Lt. Col. John H. Tomlinson USMC (now retired); Mr. Perez; Mona Poe; Mr. Allen Parkinson; Wanda Hartman; Joe Prevatil; Logan Fleming. (NOTE: Lovetta Kramer not pictured.)
*Photo by Peter Klein, Movieland Wax Museum.*

Logan works painstakingly long hours to create billboards for the Pacific Outdoor Advertising Company. This was shortly before he began his career with Movieland.

The End.

# Final Words of Praise

I recognized the magic of Logan Fleming's work the moment I first saw it. It was 1976 on the *Tony Orlando & Dawn* TV show as they premiered their wax likenesses from Movieland Wax Museum.

I was amazed at how realistic and expressive the effigies were. So I began collecting every brochure I could on Movieland. In 1983 I was an excited teenager on a family vacation, at the front doors of Movieland Wax Museum for the first time! I was now face-to-face with Logan's work. As I journeyed through the maze of Hollywood past and present, I was overwhelmed by the pure artistry of the figures.

Movieland did not feel like a wax museum, instead it was as if you were walking through frozen moments of Hollywood's greatest films. The faces radiated such life and expression, the poses were natural and true to the motion picture scenes. The hyper-realistic painting technique intrigued me most of all. Highlights and shadows painted in a way that photographed wonderfully and captured the celebrity the way film does. The painting finish became known as "The Movieland Look." Where most people would enjoy what they saw and move to the next exhibit, my thoughts were "Who made these?...Who is the artist?...Who is the genius behind this?"

It was through Movieland that the artist became my friend.

Over the years, Logan Fleming and I had a wonderful friendship. We talked for hours about his work and career. He taught me his craft and trade secrets. I treasured every conversation and immediately wrote them down while they were fresh on my mind. To truly appreciate the art...you must know the artist.

Just as Logan captured great Hollywood moments and made you feel like you were right there in the movie, Suzanne Sumner Ferry has captured the wonderful life and career of the genius of the wax world. Anytime I need inspiration while working on a project, I can join Logan at a photo shoot or experience the nerves at a wax premiere and it's as if I'm standing right there with him.

**Movieland Wax Museum was Logan Fleming and Logan Fleming was Movieland.** Thanks to Suzanne Sumner Ferry, both Mr. Fleming and Movieland live within the pages of this book and continue to inspire.

*Mr. Shannon Schrum*
*Schrum Studios*

# Index

## A

*Alien* 207
*American Gothic* 143, 202
Ammannati, Bartolomeo 193
Angkor-Vat Shrine 192

## B

Baer Jr., Max 91, 95, 96
Barrymore, John Drew 85
Beatles, The 212
Beatty, Warren 71
*Ben-Hur* 101, 102, 113
Benny, Jack 177, 178
*Beverly Hillbillies, The* 91-96, 114, 168, 169
Bijou Theatre 108
Bishop, Mr. 101
Blocker, Dan 121, 122
Bolger, Ray 168
*Bonanza* 121, 122
Bonaparte, Napoleon 194
Bond, Ward 97 137, 138
"Bones" (Dr. McCoy) 26, 210
Borgnine, Ernest 79
Boyd, Steven 113
Browning, Elizabeth Barrett 194

Burke, Billie 168
Burnett, Carol 179-182
*Butch Cassidy and the Sundance Kid* 123-25
Buttons, Red 105, 168
Byrnes, Edd 71

## C

Cantinflas, Mario Moreno 148
Chamber of Horrors 205
Chandler, Helen 44
Charisse, Cyd 187
Chekov 25, 210
Church of the Holy Sepulcher 203
Clark, Roy 139, 140, 142
Collins, Jack 22, 81, 140, 143, 159, 198, 201, 202
Connors, Mike 171, 172
Cooper, Gary 148
Cruise, Tom 213
Curtis, Dr. Philippe 205

# D

Davis, Jr., Sammy  37-42
De Champaigne, Philippe  194
del Gioconda, Marquis  194
Di Vinci, Leonardo  193, 194
Diana, Princess of Wales  213
Disneyland  XVIII, 215
Doohan, James  26
Douglas, Donna  91
Douglas, Kirk  114, 117-120
*Dracula*  44
Duffin, Allan T.  IV

# E

Eastwood, Clint  185, 186
Ebsen, Buddy  91, 168

# F

Ferry, Suzanne Sumner  IV, 20, 220
Fields, W.C.  155, 156
Fleming, Craig  IX, 127
Fleming, Kevin  IX, XV, 127
Fleming, Liz  VI, IX, XI, XIII, 2, 6, 11, 12,
    17-20, 127, 167-169, 185, 186, 187, 216
Fleming, Miles  IX, XI, XV, 18, 127, 188
Fonda, Peter  71
Ford, Glenn  169
Ford, John  138
Foxx, Redd  143-145, 169
*Frankenstein*  34, 45, 75-77
Franklin, Benjamin  194

# G

Gable, Clark  4, 135, 136
Gabor, Zsa Zsa  186
Gainsborough, Thomas  194, 201
Garland, Judy  105, 168, 188,
General Foods, Inc.  72
Geritol  130
Gogh, Vincent Van  201
Golden Globe Awards  101, 102, 168, 185-
    189
Goldwyn, Samuel  168

*Goldwyn's Follies*  168
Golgotha  203
*Gone with the Wind*  135, 136
Grant, Cary  156
*Great Caruso, The*  148
Griffith, D. W.  31, 107, 117
*Guinness Book of World Records, The*  213
*Guns of Navarone, The*  79, 80

# H

Haley, Jr., Jack  105, 168
Hals, Frans  200
Hamilton, Margaret  168
Hardy, Oliver  55, 56, 107-109
Head, Edith  156, 158
Hearst, William Randolph  50
Hearst Castle  50
Herbert Jepson Art Institute  1
Herod, King  196
Heston, Charlton  101, 102, 113
Hoffman, Heinrich  202
Hogan, Hulk  183, 184
Holden, William  147
*Hondo*  137, 138, 141
Hope, Bob  177, 178
Hope, Delores  177, 178
Hopkins, Telma  114
Horton, Robert  138
*House of Wax*  61, 64
Hudon, Jean Antoine  193, 194
Hudson, Rock  45
Huertas, Jon  VI, XV, Back Cover
Hunter, Jeffrey  71
Huntington Library  194

# J

Jackson, Michael  213
Jarrod, Professor Henry  61
John the Baptist  196
Johnson, Brad L.  XV
Jurras, Ty  151, 153, 154

# K

Keaton, Buster 57, 206,
Kelley, DeForest 26, 210
Kelly, Gene 103, 124, 187
Kennedy, John F. 71, 72
King Louis the XIII 195
King Louis the XIV 195
King Louis XVI 205
Kirk, Captain James T. 23 - 30, 210
Klein, Mr. 34, 75 , 76
Knotts Berry Farm 215
Koenig, Walter 25, 26, 210
Keystone Kops 6, 22, 45, 46, 55, 81-83, 101, 107, 156, 172, 199, 206
Kramer, Lovetta 21-23, 33, 37, 38, 67, 128, 151, 169
Kubrick, Stanley 119

# L

La Moulin Rouge 196, 198
Lahr, Bert 168
Lanza, Mario 148
Larsen, Peter VI, XV
*Lassie* 138
Laughton, Charles 98
Laurel, Stan 55, 56, 107-109
*Laurel & Hardy* 55, 56, 107-109
Lawrence, Sir Thomas 194
Leigh, Vivien 135, 136
Lemmon, Jack 188
Lewis, Jerry 33 - 35, 37
*Limb Shot* 114
Lincoln, President Abraham 195-197
*Little Caesar* 148
*Little Rascals, The* 173, 174
Lloyd, Harold 175
Lollobrigida, Gina 45 - 47, 148
London 20, 195, 200, 205
Loren, Sophia 59, 60, 97, 111
Los Angeles County Museum of Art 200
Louvre 17, 192 - 195, 201
Loy, Myrna 208, 209
Lugosi, Bella 44

# M

*Mad Wednesday* 175
Madonna 213
*Mannix* 171, 172
Margret, Ann 165, 166
Martin, Dick 49-51, 53
Martin, Tony 187
Mears, Mr. Jim 191
Merrill, Dina 72
Metropolitan Museum of Art 196
Meyer, Duffy 169
Michelangelo 16, 191-193, 199, 203, 204
*Miss Polly* 103
Mitchum, Robert 186, 187
Montmartre 198
Moulton, Sarah Barrett 194
Munchkins 168
Muscle Beach 117, 118, 156, 163
*My Little Chickadee* 155
Myers, Ida XV

# N

National Gallery in London 195
Ness, Eliott 75
Newman, Paul 123-125
Nimoy, Leonard 26, 27, 29, 30
Norton Simon Foundation 200

# O

Olivier, Sir Lawrence 114
Oval Office 208, 210
Oxsen, Jo Ann (formerly Gordon) VI, XV

# P

*PT109* 71, 72
Pacific Outdoor Advertising Agency 1-4, 7, 217
Page, LaWanda 143 - 145
Palace of Living Art XIIII, XVIII, XX,15-17, 20, 22, 25, 191-199, 201-204, 207, 210, 215, 216
Palmer, Arnold 128

Paris 17-20, 192-195, 198, 200, 202, 205, 213
Parkinson, Allen XVIII, 5-7, 9-11, 13 - 22, 31, 34, 55, 57, 59- 61, 73, 85, 97, 101, 103, 105, 107, 108, 111, 123, 124, 139, 140, 147-149, 156, 158, 167, 169, 173, 191, 192, 206, 207, 209, 216
Perez, Mr. 43, 44, 216
Pietrasanta Artisans 16, 191, 203
Pickford, Mary 59
Pitts, Zasu 55, 59, 103
Poe, Mona 5 - 7, 61, 62, 162, 216
*Poncho* 200
*Poppy* 155
Post, Marjorie Merriweather 72
Powell, William 208, 209
Pozzo, Padre Andrea 192
Prevatil, Joe 29, 158, 160 - 163, 177, 178, 216
*Poseidon Adventure, The* 79
*Private Life of Henry VIII, The* 98

## Q

Queen Elizabeth 20
*Quixote, Don* 200

## R

Ravenswood 152
Reagan, President Ronald 19, 207- 210
Redford, Robert 123-125
Reeve, Christopher 67-69
Reni, Guido 196
Reynolds, Burt 65- 68
Reynolds, Debbie 114
*Rifleman, The* 99, 100
Rigaud, Hyacinthe 195, 200
*Road to Bali, The* 177
Robertson, Cliff 71, 72
Robinson, Edward G. 148, 149
Roddenberry, Gene 23, 29, 206
Rogers, Will 114
Rowan, Dan 49, 51, 53, 54
Ryan, Irene 91, 92

## S

St. Peter's Basilica 203
*Safety Last* 175
*Salome* 196
*Sanford and Son* 143 - 145
Scala, Gia 80
Schapel, Ian XV, XIX, 196, 197, 199, 204
Scotty 26, 28, 210
Selleck, Tom 183
Sennet, Mack 206
Shah of Iran 207
Shatner, William 23 -30, 210
*She Done Him Wrong* 156, 163
*Si Yo Fuera Diputado* 148
Simmons, Jean 114
Sinatra, Nancy 85-87, 89
*Singin' in the Rain* 103, 124
*Singing Nun, The* 114
Smothers, Tom and Dick 89
*Smothers Brothers, The* 89
Snoey, Mr. & Mrs. Jan 101, 102, 185
*Spartacus* 114, 117-119
Spears, Britney 213
Spock 26-30, 210
Stack, Robert 75, 76
*Star Trek* 23-30, 206, 209, 210
Stars Hall of Fame VI, XIV, XV, 73, 74, 92, 95, 129, 130, 135, 167-170
Starship Enterprise 23, 26-28, 206
*Strange Bedfellows* 45
Strode, Woody 114, 117
Summerville, Slim 5-7, 59, 103
Sumner, Bob XV
*Sunset Blvd.* 147, 167
Swanson, Gloria 147, 167

## T

Tacca, Pietro 192
Takei, George 27, 28, 210
*Teahouse of the August Moon* 169
*That Girl* 97, 98, 114
*Thin Man, The* 208, 209
Thomas, Danny 105, 168-170
Thomas, Marlo 97, 98, 114

Tomlinson USMC (retired), Lt. Colonel
    John H.   VI, XV, 77, 135, 169, 216
*Tony Orlando & Dawn* 114, 115
Toulouse-Lautrec, Henri de 196, 198
Turpin, Ben 156
Tussaud, Madame 205
*Two Women (La Ciociara)* 97, 111

# U

Uhura, Lt. 28, 29, 210
Uloa, Hilda 101
*Untouchables, The* 75

# V

van Eyck, Jan 195
van Rijn, Rembrandt Harmenszoon 196,
    200, 201, 204
Varin, Jean 194
Vatican City 203
Versailles 18, 195, 205
Von Stroheim, Eric 147

# W

Wadlow, Robert Pershing 213
*Wagon Train* 97, 137, 138
"Walter, Wax" 82, 83
Wayne, John 13, 14, 45, 137, 138, 141
Welk, Lawrence 127-133
West, Mae 151-163
Western Costume 74, 122, 156-158
Westmore, Wally 117-119
Whistler, James McNeill 202
White, Gene 79
White House, The 71, 207, 208, 210
Widmark (start of wax likeness), Richard
    Front Cover
*Wild Angels, The* 85, 87
Wilson, Joyce Vincent 114
*Winds of War, The* 186, 187
Winfrey, Oprah 211, 212
Winters, Shelley 79, 188
*Wizard of Oz, The* 105, 114, 115, 168, 210
Wood, Grant 143, 202

Christ in You
Colossians 1:27

# Fully Alive
## *and*
# Finally Free

## Knowing God
## As Father

David Howell

## Your Identity In Christ

**Christ in You**
*Colossians 1:27*

This title may be purchased in bulk for educational
and evangelical purposes. Please contact the
publisher for more information:

David Howell
P O Box 571977
Houston, Texas 77257

prisonevangelism.com
davidhowell@aol.com
info@HowtobeaChildofGod.com
www.HowtobeaChildofGod.com

Research and editing by Leigh McLeroy

Art direction and book graphic design by
John Magee, Houston, Texas • JohnMageeDesign.com

All illustrations by Randy Rodgers,
The Woodlands, Texas • artistguy@att.net

Christ in You
Colossians 1:27

*N*ow is the time to introduce this piece for those Christians who know Jesus, but don't know much about victorious Christian living. It is two booklets in one. The first section originally called *Fully Alive and Finally Free* is a narrative explanation of the rest of the gospel and explains your co-crucifixion, co-burial, co-resurrection and co-seating with Christ in the heavenly places that takes you into the new life. It is new information for most every believer. The second part called Quiet Time is a devotional that takes you through scriptures and explanations with pictures and reiterates this same message of the cross. The teaching is biblical, but not widely taught in the church.

In the Billy Graham Evangelistic Association's *Steps to Peace with God* tract, we are asked to:
1. Admit your need. (I am a sinner.)
2. Be willing to turn from your sins. (repent).
3. Believe that Jesus Christ died for you on the cross and rose from the grave.
4. Through prayer, invite Jesus Christ to come in and control your life through the Holy Spirit. (Receive Him as Lord and Savior.)

The sinner's prayer on the next page follows:

*Dear Lord Jesus,*
*I know I am a sinner, and I ask for Your forgiveness. I believe You died for my sins and rose from the dead. I turn from my sins and invite you to come into my heart and life. I want to trust and follow You as my Lord and Savior.*
*In Your Name, Amen.*

As a new member counselor in a large church for thirty years, I have used that tract and prayer as countless numbers of persons have come to know Jesus Christ. Invariably, these new believers walk away thinking and maybe knowing they are going to heaven when they die. But what about now? What about a better life as a Christian? What about the victory in Jesus the hymns sing about? What about the abundant life? The first section of this book will take you through the truth through narrative. The devotional part is designed to reaffirm the narrative through illustrations and scripture. That is my hope.

– David Howell

Therefore, since we have been justified through faith, we have peace with God through our Lord Jesus Christ, through whom we have gained access by faith into this grace in which we now stand. And we boast in the hope of the glory of God. Not only so, but we also glory in our sufferings, because we know that suffering produces perseverance; perseverance, character; and character, hope. And hope does not put us to shame, because God's love has been poured out into our hearts through the Holy Spirit, who has been given to us. Romans 5:1-5 NIV

*Christ in You*
Colossians 1:27

# Fully Alive *and* Finally Free

## Your Identity in Christ

*W*ho doesn't want a richer, deeper, more meaningful life? Whether you are 16 or 70, chances are you've asked yourself "Isn't there something more than this?" The things you've sought – security, peace, love, acceptance – have either come to you, or not, but in either case you're likely less than satisfied. You've tried the things men and women have tried through the ages to make life more fulfilling: prestige, popularity, education, a good job, money, possessions, relationships, and you still sense that something is missing. No matter what you do, you can't fully escape feelings of inadequacy, depression, fear, loneliness, or futility. You may imagine you are alone in this – but you are not. In fact you are among the majority who, in spite of their own striving, live less than "fully alive." But that can change. It should change. Because the life you are meant to live is an abundant, free, victorious life.

This booklet is meant to help you experience that full, abundant life – and it begins by explaining why it remains elusive for so many.

## We all start here.

*A*ll human beings are, by design, made up of three parts: **body, soul** and **spirit.** This three-part identity is referenced in the Bible in I Thessalonians 5:23 ("… may your spirit and soul and body be preserved complete…") and in Hebrews 4:12 ("piercing as far as the division of **soul** and **spirit,** of both joints and marrow…"). With our bodies, we engage our physical surroundings. With the soul, or personality, we relate to others, using our minds, our wills, and our emotions. With our spirit, or God-consciousness, we relate to eternity, transcending our temporal abilities, limitations and circumstances. One writer has distinguished these facets of our essential nature in this way: "Man *is* a spirit, he *has* a soul, and he *lives* in a body."[1] In the context of this three-part nature we live, move and act.

All human beings are made up of three parts; body, soul and spirit. In this three-part context, we live, move and act. Our bodies interact with the environment, our soul or personality with others, and our spirit with God.

---

[1]Charles R. Solomon, *Handbook to Happiness.* Tyndale House Publishers, Inc., Carol Stream, IL. P. 14

*E*very man or woman shares not only this three-part nature, but a common heritage as well. We are born as descendants of Adam, the first man, and we share his finite, flawed humanity. In the same way that physical characteristics are encoded in our DNA and passed down to us from our ancestors, sin is encoded into our spiritual DNA and every generation since Adam has inherited his original bent to sin. As Adam's heirs, we have bodies and souls that are "awake and oriented" toward life; but because of the sin that entered the human race through him, our spirits are "awake and oriented" toward death. These orientations are not static; we are all going somewhere. If human life could be viewed as a line extending out from birth uninterrupted, that line would end in death and hell. The Bible says in Romans 3:23, "all have sinned and fall short of the glory of God," and in Romans 6:23, "the wages of sin is death." Unless God intervenes, we are all destined by our birth to sin and death.

Our lineage going back to Adam. *"For everyone has sinned; we all fall short of God's glorious standard."* Romans 3:23 NLT

*"When Adam sinned, sin entered the world. Adam's sin brought death, so death spread to everyone, for everyone sinned."* Romans 5:12 NLT

# And some of us get this far.

Apart from God, the natural man is centered upon himself, operating in his own power and depending upon his own strength and ability to become the person he wants to be. His identity rests in the external and the material – those that can be seen and approved by himself and other men.

*U*ltimately, no matter how materially successful such a person may become; the fruit of this self-oriented life is death – and often (in spite of worldly achievement) frustration, failure and a sense of futility along the way. So long as self is in control with its emotions, attitudes and problems, the conflicts of our soul – (inferiority, insecurity, inadequacy, anger, guilt, worry, doubt, fear) will continue. In fact, these soul issues can become health issues, making us physically sick as well as psychologically afflicted.

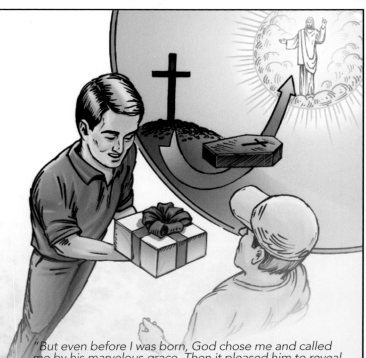

*"But even before I was born, God chose me and called me by his marvelous grace. Then it pleased him to reveal his Son to me, so that I would proclaim the Good News about Jesus to the Gentiles."* Galatians 1:15-16 NLT

While every man or woman born starts out with the same nature (body, soul, and spirit) and the same heritage (a descendant of Adam and inheritor of sin), some experience a life-changing event that awakens their spiritual self and reorients the trajectory of their life. Since we are born spiritually dead or dead to God, then our greatest need must be spiritual awakening, rebirth, or regeneration. Thankfully, the God who made us makes provision for just the kind of life we most need! God may send a messenger or proclaimer. It might be your spouse or a friend or by way of an event like a funeral, a loss or some form of revelation that God might use to wake you up and make you aware of His presence and His calling on your life. When the time is right and your heart is right, the message of the gift of God's grace will be clear.

You may have heard this new life called many things. Salvation, conversion, being born again, being saved, trusting Christ, accepting Christ, and receiving Christ are all terms for the same thing: new spiritual life through the sacrificial death and resurrection of Jesus Christ, God in flesh.

To be reborn spiritually, we must come to the end of self; self-reliance and self-absorption: confess ourselves as born sinners who, by the outworking of our nature, have continued to commit deadly sins. Then we must accept Jesus as Lord and God – who became a man, lived a perfect life, and died as a perfect sacrifice for the sins of every man. The death penalty for sin must be paid, and in Christ it was paid in full. He lived, died, and was raised to life again, enabling all who believe to follow Him from death into life. No wonder this message is often called the good news!

Many who come to hear this message of salvation in Christ do believe, and are spiritually reborn. They may pray a prayer something like this, asking God to apply the sacrifice of Christ to their own sin, faults and character defects and inviting him to come in and take control of their lives:

*"Dear God, I know that I am a sinner. I believe that you sent your Son, the Lord Jesus Christ, to die for my sins, that He was buried, and that He rose from the dead. I surrender now and turn from a life of sin and self-centeredness and trust the Lord Jesus Christ to forgive my sins and to be my life. Thank you for saving me, for Jesus' sake. Amen."* [2]

At the moment we pray such a prayer, we are saved and become children of God. The Bible says "If you openly declare that Jesus is Lord and believe in your heart that God raised him from the dead, you will be saved. For it is by believing in your heart that you are made right with God, and it is by openly declaring your faith that you are saved." (Romans 10:9-10 NLT)

---

[2]Charles R. Solomon, *Handbook to Happiness*. Tyndale House Publishers, Inc., Carol Stream, IL P. 19

Say with your mouth and believe in your heart that Jesus died, was buried, and came back to life. Trust in Him that He is God in flesh and become a child of God.

*A*nd when we are saved, we are fundamentally and irrevocably changed. The down hill trajectory of our lives is disrupted, and we are no longer destined for death and hell, but for eternal life with Christ beginning now and continuing in heaven after our physical death. We are immediately transferred from the spiritual lineage of Adam to the family of God. At the cross of Christ, we too, are crucified with Him, buried with Him, and resurrected spiritually with Him into a new life.

The Bible describes it like this: "Do you not know that all of us who have been baptized into Christ Jesus were baptized into his death? We were buried therefore with him by baptism into death, in order that, just as Christ was raised from the dead by the glory of the Father, we too might walk in newness of life." (Romans 6:3-4)

In Christ we have been made spiritually alive – with the potential of manifesting Christ's life in every aspect of our being: body, soul and spirit. But for so many, this is as far as they will go. While they receive forgiveness, unconditional love, and salvation in Jesus Christ, they fail to receive, appropriate, and live in the power of His living risen life! Their ultimate destiny is secure, but their present lives are frustrating, flat and joyless. One writer describes such an existence: "Most people's Christianity is like an old iron bed: firm at both ends and sagging in the middle. On one end you trust Christ as Savior and get your sins forgiven. On the other end, one day you will go to heaven. In between, it gets pretty desperate. You have lots of questions that all boil down to one: Where is the life? Where is the abundant life that Jesus promised?"[3]

---

[3]Dan Stone and David Gregory, *The Rest of the Gospel*. One Press, Corvallis, OR. P. 15

Many believers attempt to have one foot in the lineage of Adam or the world of our earthly family and the other foot in the family of God. The result is inner conflict and spiritual turmoil. Failing to make a clear choice leaves us confused and short of the victory and abundant life God has for us.

## Where is the life?

When we receive Christ, we receive all that we need to live a full, abundant life in body, soul, and spirit, and even our family tree is miraculously changed! We are now considered co-heirs with Christ in line to inherit all that is His, no longer descendants of Adam that stand to inherit nothing but a sinful nature and spiritual death. (Romans 8:16)

Incredibly, it is possible to receive all this and still miss out on the full, abundant life God intends for his children. After we are saved, our soul life may prosper and our personality may improve, but we may continue to seek the quality of life we desire not from Christ, but from the same externals we depended upon before. We may assume our new Christian identity in name, but still live out of the same wounded, unregenerate self whose inevitable end was death and defeat. Sadly, some even "accept the Lord Jesus Christ as Savior and Lord and then spend the rest of their lives trying to get him to accept them."[4] Is it any wonder that we keep on asking ourselves – after being saved and born anew – "Is *this* all there is?"

---

[4]Charles R. Solomon, *Handbook to Happiness*. Tyndale House Publishers, Inc., Carol Stream, IL P. 21

Jesus confidently stated, "I came that they may have life, and have it abundantly." (John 10:10) Christ didn't just die for our sins; He died to give us a new quality of indwelling life – His life! The fact that our sins are forgiven in Christ and we are reconciled to God is an essential, precious truth, but we must appropriate the abundant life that is now ours in Christ as a result. Unsure of how to do so, many of us go back to what we've done all along: living life by our own efforts, trying to "be Christian" in our body and soul without surrendering to the empowering life of Christ now residing in us! But there is another, better way to live. And to discover it, we must go back to the cross of Jesus Christ, and understand what truly happened there.

**Back to the cross.**
At the cross Jesus died. And He was not alone. You were with Him. The apostle Paul understood this when he wrote "I have been crucified with Christ; and it is no longer I who live, but Christ lives in me; and the life which I now live in the flesh I live by faith in the Son of God, who loved me and gave Himself up for me." (Galatians 2:20)

When you ask Jesus Christ to take over your life, His very spirit, the Spirit of God enters you; and you become whole with body, soul and spirit now alive to God. You now have Christ's eternal life, which is forever in the past and forever in the future. This eternal life allows you to go back 2000 years to the cross where your old self is crucified with Him. This is where Jesus deals with our old sinful nature once and for all. The old self dies and the new you becomes one with Him, united with Christ forever!

This co-crucifixion, co-burial, co-resurrection and co-ascension with Jesus Christ is the gateway from human striving into the full and free Christ-empowered life. Pastor Charles Stanley has said, "The life crucified, buried and resurrected with Christ Jesus is the answer to whatever you are facing. Your life can never be the same."

At the cross the person whose sins are forgiven, who is born again, is "crucified with Christ" and the new, regenerated man or woman becomes a partaker in His life – eternal life. This eternal life has no beginning, and it has no end. It is not just forever in the future, but forever in the past and forever in the future. The apostle Paul describes our shared experience with Jesus Christ in his death, burial and resurrection – and the implications of it – in this way: "How can we who died to sin still live in it? For if we have been united with him in a death like his, we shall certainly be united with him in a resurrection like his. We know that our old self was crucified with him in order that the body of sin might be brought to nothing, so that we would no longer be enslaved to sin. For one who has died has been set free from sin." (Romans 6:2, 5-7)

We cannot inhabit two lives at once. If we are no longer in Adam and subject to Adam's consequential death, then we are in Christ and can experience his saving, sustaining, fulfilling life. But the good news doesn't stop there.

In Ephesians chapter two Paul writes "But God, being rich in mercy, because of His great love with which He loved us, even when we were dead in our transgressions, made us alive together with Christ (by grace you have been saved), and raised us up with Him, and seated us with Him in the heavenly places in Christ Jesus." (Ephesians 2:4-6)

In other words, we have not only been crucified with Christ, we have already died and gone to heaven in the spiritual sense. Forevermore, we live from a different place. The eternal life we received at salvation is Christ's life… now operating in us. We were crucified with him, buried with Him, raised with him, and are even now seated with him in the very presence of God! But just as we had to be convicted of our sin to accept God's gift of salvation, we must be convicted of our pride and self-centeredness in order to reject the self-life and begin to experience the resurrection life of Christ.

We must die so that he can live. We must admit that we've failed at running the show and that we have not

*"… And just as Christ was raised from the dead by the glorious power of the Father, now we also may live new lives. Since we have been united with him in his death, we will also be raised to life as he was."* Romans 6:4b, 5

been able to meet our own needs our own way.

The Lord Jesus Christ is waiting for us to acknowledge what actually took place when we died with Him. He longs for us to know that His experience is our own experience! He wants to impart to us not simply right standing with God and the promise of heaven, but His own powerful, resurrected life – here and now. Our spirit is united with Him, seated at the right hand of the Father in heaven, even as our body and soul continue to dwell on this earth. When we grasp this great truth, we can surrender our self-striving ways, and know the joy of His life, the life of Jesus Christ lived in and through us.

This exchanged life ushers in a radical new lifestyle for the Christian. And we can expect further changes to come, not the least of which are:

- A new relationship with other people, because we are no longer dependent upon them for our identity or our self esteem.

- Victory over besetting sins or lingering habits, because in Christ, the power of sin over us is broken. If we continue to sin in Christ, it is not because we don't have the power to resist Satan (we do!), but because we have chosen sin over obedience.

- An abandonment of demanding my rights, because I yield my rights to the love and leadership of Jesus Christ. As someone has once said, "A man on a cross has no future plans."

- A restful reliance on Christ for everything that concerns me. He has taken responsibility for my life, and he will accomplish his purposes in me. (Ephesians 2:10)

- A sustained joy and peace, regardless of my circumstances. My life will not be trouble-free. Jesus promises just the opposite! But he himself will be a steadying peace in the midst of every troubling circumstance.[5]

In order to understand what actually happened to us in a spiritual sense, we must mentally let God take us by the hand and lead us back to the cross, to the place where we died with Christ, so that we might be raised with Him. So oriented, we can actually welcome the things that used to trouble and terrify us because they become the very things that drive us back to the cross again and again, and back to the power of the living, risen, resurrected Christ who now dwells in us.

Because you died with Christ, the threat of death no longer has mastery or influence over you. The old self died and came back to life as a reborn child of God.

---

[5]Paraphrased from Charles Stanley's sermon, "Live in Christ"

*A* new courage and a new boldness come with this new eternal life. Christ died for our sins, but we died with Him to get rid of

"If you are a Christian, God created a union between you and Christ, [and] because of this union, you died with Christ, when he died. Because you died, you are now free from

our old self or sin nature. We now have the freedom of choice to do things our way or God's way. We did not have that choice before.

As we grow in Christ and our soul is transformed, we and others will see the changes. We will begin to experience the full more abundant life that God had in store for His children.

Pastor John Piper writes,

the guilt and power of sin in your fullest and truest identity, that is, in your union with Christ. And because of this unshakable position and identity, you are already justified, and you are most certainly being sanctified, but you are not yet perfected.

"Therefore, confirm this great transaction by reckoning yourself to be what you really are in Christ."[6]

---

[6]John Piper, "United With Christ in Life and Death, Part 1", Desiring God Resource Library, www.desiringgod.org.

## Appropriating this truth

Chinese pastor Watchman Nee says we begin our Christian life by depending not on our own doing, but on what Christ has already done. "The Lord Jesus has done everything for us, and our need is now to rest confidently in him. He is seated on the throne, so we are carried through in his strength. Sitting describes our position with Christ in the heavenlies. Walking is the practical outworking of that heavenly position here on earth."[7]

How can you "confirm this great transaction"? By confirming what God says is already true about your identity in Christ. Just as many express their salvation with a prayer, perhaps an "identification prayer" might help Christians to acknowledge both their co-crucifixion with, and their new life in Jesus Christ. It might go something like this:

Dear God,

I accept by faith my crucifixion with Christ. I accept by faith my death, my burial, and my resurrection. And as a result, I further accept the truth that Christ now lives in me, and desires to live his life through me. From this moment on, I embrace this truth, and want to have your Son Jesus Christ live "the life that I now live in the flesh." I consider myself dead to sin and alive to you, and I am counting on the Holy Spirit to convict me when I attempt to live in my own power apart from Christ. I choose to yield all that I am to you as an instrument of righteousness, allowing no part of me to be used in sinful and selfish activity. Thank you for making Christ and his life real to me in every experience of life. Glorify yourself through the Christ in me, who is my hope of glory. In Jesus' life changing name I pray. Amen.

[7]Watchman Nee, *Sit, Walk, Stand*. Tyndale House Publishers Inc., Carol Stream IL, p. 15, 16

*C*hange your thinking as most everything begins in the mind. Visualize what has happened to you. The old self died on the cross with Christ and the new reborn spiritual self is now residing in Christ in the heavens. Imagine that! It all begins in the mind. "Set your minds on things above, not on earthly things. For you died, and your life is now hidden with Christ in God." (Colossians 3:2-3 NIV)

So how does a "sitting" Christian learn to walk? The Apostle Paul's instruction to the Colossian Christians points the way: "If then you have been raised with Christ, seek the things that are above, where Christ is, seated at the right hand of God. Set your minds on things that are above, not on things that are on the earth. For you have died, and your life is hidden with Christ in God." (Colossians 3:1-3) And to the church at Rome he writes, "Do not be conformed to this world, but be transformed by the renewal of your mind, that by testing you may discern what is the will of God, what is good and acceptable and perfect." (Romans 12:2)

"Don't copy the behavior and customs of the world, but let God transform you into a new person by changing the way you think. Then you will learn to know God's will for you, which is good and pleasing and perfect." Romans 12:2 NLT

The key to living this transformed life – to living out of our true position in Christ – is to renew our minds…to replace our human thoughts with the truths of God. Our feelings are not the truest barometer of our position and progress in the Christian life. Satan can deceive us by manipulating our feelings, but he cannot manipulate the word of God. So we must choose to set our minds on God's truth, regardless of our own feelings or the lies of the enemy.

We renew our minds by learning to recognize the lies and condemning thoughts of Satan, then refusing to accept those thoughts as true. When Satan uses the old lures of sin and deceit to ensnare us, we can reckon ourselves dead to sin, resisting the lies of the evil one and replacing them with God's truth. Then we can rest in the fact that we are in Christ and He is in us, thanking Him for accepting and loving us, and for seating us in heaven with Him.

*"For he raised us up from the dead along with Christ and seated us with him in the heavenly realms because we are united with Christ Jesus."*
Ephesians 2:6 NLT

God has forever changed our status. We are sons and daughters of the King. Our sin and shame have been done away with, and our old self crucified on the cross with Christ. He has also changed our position. We are seated above with Christ, already experiencing eternal life. And we live abundantly here, now, being continually transformed by the renewing of our minds into the persons that Jesus intends us to be. **Remember:** Your salvation was also the scene of your co-crucifixion with Jesus

Christ. With him you died, you were buried, and you have been raised to new life. With him you are anchored in the very heavenlies – in the eternal presence of the Father – and his life now resides permanently in you. As a result, "you will know that I [Jesus] am in my Father, and you are in me, and I am in you." (John 14:20) This is the secret to abundant life: not just Christ for you, but Christ in you. "Not your life but His. Not you producing His life, but you expressing His life, as you by faith, trust Him to live through you, as you."[8]

*"Since I live, you also will live. When I am raised to life again, you will know that I am in my Father, and you are in me, and I am in you."*
John 14:19b, 20 NLT

---

[8]Dan Stone and David Gregory, *The Rest of the Gospel.* One Press, Corvallis, OR P. 85

*T*his identification with Christ – His crucifixion, His resurrection, His mind, His heart – is the abundant life, not just in heaven, but right now, right here on earth. And Christian, it belongs to you. Jesus Christ lives in you. Where you go, He goes.

Be totally surrendered to the Christ in you. His desire is to live His life through you and in you. We are the body of Christ and He desires to use us to reach others.

## What Happened to You at the Cross?

- *You were justified – completely forgiven and made righteous.* **(Romans 5:1)**
- *You were crucified with Christ, and the life you now live is Christ's life.* **(Galatians 2:20)**
- *You died with Christ and died to the power of sin's rule in your life.* **(Romans 6:1-6)**
- *You were made alive together with Christ.* **(Ephesians 2:5)**
- *You were redeemed and forgiven of all your sins.* **(Colossians 1:14)**
- *You became free from condemnation forever.* **(Romans 8:1)**
- *You received the Spirit of God, so that you might know the things freely given to you by God.* **(I Corinthians 2:12)**
- *You became a co-heir of Christ.* **(Romans 8:17)**

## What is Yours as a Result?

- *You have been blessed with every spiritual blessing.* **(Ephesians 1:3)**
- *You have been made a recipient of God's lavish grace.* **(Ephesians 1:7-8)**
- *You have been given direct access to God through the Holy Spirit.* **(Ephesians 2:18)**
- *You have been given a spirit of power, love and self-discipline.* **(2 Timothy 1:7)**
- *You have the right to come boldly before the throne of God, to find mercy and grace in your time of need.* **(Hebrews 4:16)**
- *You have been given the exceedingly great and precious promises of God, in order that you might become a partaker of His divine nature.* **(2 Peter 1:4)**

## Galations 2:20

*I have been crucified with Christ and I no longer live, but Christ lives in me. The life I now live in the body, I live by faith in the Son of God, who loved me and gave himself for me.*

# Knowing God As Father

*Father.* It's a word that's meant to say to us, "provider, leader, mentor, supporter, and friend." It's meant to make us feel loved, accepted, wanted, cared for.

For many of us—maybe most of us—it doesn't. The word *father* gives us mixed feelings, at best. Really bad feelings, at worst. Many of our fathers were alcoholics, or drug users, or in prison. They didn't support our family well and weren't there for us. Some of our fathers abused us. Some of them abandoned or neglected us. Many of our fathers were removed from us through divorce. For many of us, our parents were never married. We may have known who our father was and seen him occasionally, or we may not have known him at all. Stepfathers or boyfriends were the male figures we had in the home. Most of them never lived up to what a father should be or what we needed a father to be.

If we came from such a childhood, the word *father* doesn't produce warm feelings in us. Just the opposite. And even if we had a dad who was there physically, we may not have good feelings about *father.*

# Knowing God as Father

### A Cycle of Brokenness

So many of our problems start here, don't they? Boys and girls needing a strong, healthy father figure to love them and show them they are loved. To lead and guide them, helping them make good choices and giving them a sense of hope and meaning in life. Fathers, through what they say and do, are supposed to tell us who we are in the world. They are supposed to teach us why we are here, and how to best live our lives.

But so many of us didn't get that. Whether it was their fault or not, we didn't get what we needed from a father.

God offers us something even better. He offers us a perfect *heavenly* Father.

So we face the world on our own. We may be angry or bitter about what we didn't get. We feel empty. There is a hole in our hearts that we don't know how to fill. So from an early age, we try to fill the hole through relationships, alcohol, drugs, and sex. To one degree or another, our lives end up broken. Our brokenness affects the lives of those around us. And the cycle passes down to the next generation, and the next, and the next.

**The Way Out of the Cycle**
There is a way out of the cycle, though. And there is a way our broken lives can be put back together beyond what we ever imagined. It is something we have all longed for, but we probably gave up on long ago.

That way is to have a perfect father.

No, not a perfect earthly father. For us, as adults, it's too late for that. And even if we did have a dad around growing up, and he did his best, he could never be perfect. None of us are. God offers us something even better. He offers us a perfect *heavenly* Father.

From the very start, God intended that *He* would be our Father. Our earthly dads were, at best, imperfect, temporary stand-ins for Him. The Bible tells us that:

> There is one Lord, one faith, one baptism, and one God and Father, who is over all and in all and living through all.
> (Paul's Letter to the Ephesians, chapter 4, verses 5 and 6)

**The Apostle Paul wrote:**
… I fall to my knees and pray to the Father, the Creator of everything in heaven and earth. (Ephesians 3:14-15)

**The prophet Isaiah declared:**
O Lord, you are our Father. We are the clay, and you are the potter. We all are formed by your hand. (Isaiah 64:8)

**God told us His eternal plan for us by saying:**
And I will be your Father, and you will be my sons and daughters, says the Lord Almighty. (2 Corinthians 6:18)

**Jesus Himself echoed this, saying:**
And don't address anyone here on earth as "Father," for only God in heaven is your spiritual Father… (Matthew 23:9)

God *especially* wants to be Father to those who never had an earthly father, or whose earthly father wasn't really there for them. In the Bible, He specifically calls Himself a "father to the fatherless" (Psalm 68:5).

God planned that He would be our real Father for all of eternity. But many of us may wonder, "Is that good news? Based on my own experience, I'm not sure I really want a heavenly Father." Our question really comes down to this: how do I know that God is the kind of father I would want to have? It's a great question. Fortunately, it's one that God has already answered for us.

## Jesus Shows Us the Father

We all have a certain image of God, as to what He is like. This image is almost always shaped by the people who helped raise us. Deep in our hearts, we think of God as a stern judge, or a pleasant grandparent, or a never-there father.

But all of our images of God are off the mark, either by a little bit or by a lot. There's one place where we can go, though, and never have to wonder again what God is really like. We can know for sure. That place is the life of His only Son, Jesus Christ.

Say with your mouth and believe in your heart that Jesus died, was buried, and came back to life. Trust in Him that He is God in flesh and become a child of God.

According to the Bible, when we look at Jesus, we see *exactly* what God is like. Speaking of Jesus, the New Testament says that:

> The Son radiates God's own glory and expresses the very character of God ... (Hebrews 1:3)

**Another Bible version translates it:**
> And He [Jesus] is ... the exact representation of His [God the Father's] nature ... (Hebrews 1:3, New American Standard Bible)

The exact representation! That means that when we look at Jesus, we see exactly who God is. Jesus Himself said this to His disciples before He went to the cross. Philip, one of Jesus's close companions, asked Jesus to show them God the Father.

> Jesus replied, "Have I been with you all this time, Philip, and yet you still don't know who I am? Anyone who has seen me has seen the Father! So why are you asking me to show him to you?" (John 14:9)

We know we need God's grace, and in Jesus we find more of it than we could imagine.

So what do we see when we look at the person of Jesus? We see someone who is full of love, compassion, grace, and acceptance. He actually wants to be with people. That's why all the people who knew they weren't perfect, who thought they had blown it, and who were down-and-out were drawn to Jesus. They knew they needed God's grace, and in Jesus they found more of it than they could imagine.

The four New Testament gospels (Matthew, Mark, Luke, and John) give us eyewitness accounts of what Jesus actually said and did when He walked on the earth. Since Jesus perfectly shows us who the Father is, how Jesus treated people, how He responded to them, and the things He said to them must be how God the Father is toward us.

## What Kind of Father Does Jesus Show Us?

I'd like us, then, to do a little thought experiment. Imagine you are a boy growing up. You live in a small house with a small yard. You go to school. You play basketball. (These may not have been your circumstances growing up, of course, but we are just imagining here—it's the people that are important, not

How would your life look, if Jesus were your father?

the circumstances.) Your father is Jesus. Only, he's just a normal dad to you. What would he be like?

If we look at the gospel accounts in the Bible, I think we have a very good idea what kind of father Jesus would be. Let's simply bring those gospel stories into the present day. How would those stories look if Jesus were your father? Looking back on your childhood, I think you would tell a story like the following.

*I had the greatest dad ever. He was kind, and smart, and a genuinely good man who treated people with love and dignity. When I got old enough to know what the word "integrity" meant, I realized my dad was a man of integrity.*

*I guess the thing I appreciated most about Dad growing up was that he was always available. He always had time for me. He actually wanted to be with me. He would take me fishing, or out to shoot hoops, or to a ballgame, just so we*

*When I wanted his advice, he would give me his advice.*

could be together. He had a shop in our little backyard where he liked to make things. We spent hundreds of hours there together. He would teach me to make things out of wood like he did. And he would teach me about life, too.

I felt like I could talk to Dad about anything. When I had blown it, it was safe to go to him and talk about it. When I was struggling with something at school, he was ready to patiently help. When I had friendship issues, he would always listen. When I wanted his advice, he would give me his advice. But he never forced it on me. Sometimes, when he thought I was going down a wrong path, he would let me know. But I always felt like he was saying it for my well-being, not so that I could live up to his expectations.

Dad always encouraged me to work hard at whatever I was involved with, like basketball. In sixth grade I was kind of small, but I was a good guard. I had a good jump shot. But after our first couple of games, I complained to him, "Dad, I can shoot rings around Jacob, but he gets to start games instead of me just because he's the coach's son. He'll never be as good as me."

Consider others first. Have integrity.

Dad put his arm around me. *"I'm proud of you for how hard you've worked on basketball. Remember, though, your good shooting—and everything else you accomplish—doesn't make you valuable. I'd love you as much if you couldn't hit a layup. And whatever gifts you have, like being able to shoot well, isn't something you earned. God gave you that ability. So just enjoy using it."* He smiled. *"And I'll enjoy watching you."*

Dad used to talk about the foundation I was laying for my life. *"You can build things the way the world builds them,"* he said. *"Put yourself first. Be a little dishonest if you have to. Always seek to get ahead. Or you can build the way God tells you to. Consider others first. Have integrity. Be humble, realizing that everything you have is a gift from God. Honor Him in all you do. Major storms hit in everyone's life. When the storms hit yours, you want your foundation to stand strong. You don't want what you've built to collapse."*

One time, in seventh grade, I got a C on a take-home paper for English. Dad saw

it and wondered why I got a C, since I usually got As or least Bs.

"I kind of ran out of time to write it," I answered, truthfully.

"Doing what?"

"Playing pickup football with the guys. But it's OK, I only needed a C to make an A for the six weeks."

"Uh-huh." He looked over the paper and all the red marks on it, and then handed it back to me. "Rewrite it so that it's an A. Then give it back to me to look at."

"But Dad," I objected, "the six weeks is over. The teacher won't even look at it again."

"You're not doing it for the teacher," he said. "You're doing it for you. You don't want to get into the habit of doing just enough to get by. You want to always do your best. Do everything for God's glory. He's the one you work for. And He's always happy with what you do, as long as you do it with a right heart."

Some people would say Dad was religious. I guess I never saw him that way. He wasn't into religious stuff that much. He was never into religious rules, that's for sure. But he knew God. Every day he would close the door to his room at home and spend time with God. Sometimes when I was little I would sneak in when it was early in the morning and he had forgotten to close the door. There Dad

would be, with an open Bible, talking to God. Sometimes I heard him talking to God about me, thanking Him for me, praising Him for His work in my life, agreeing with Him about what He wanted to do in my life. Somehow, hearing that always made me feel really secure.

Everywhere we went, Dad always noticed people in need. He seemed to have a radar that told him when people needed a handout, or encouragement, or just someone to be with. I can't say how many times we'd pass someone along the road asking for money and he would ask them, "Would you like to join us for lunch?" ...meaning, of course, that he would pay. Sometimes we'd go into a diner and he'd see someone at a table by themselves and he'd say, "Would you like some company?" If they said yes, we'd sit with them. Usually it was like bringing water to someone dying of thirst, how they started pouring out their life story once they had someone to listen to them.

Dad taught me practical things in life, like how to save money, and also the place of money in the grand scheme of things. One day I got my bank statement in the mail and said to him, "If I keep saving money at this rate, I'll never have to worry about a thing!" He glanced at the statement. "You're doing a great job saving, Son. Remember, though, where your treasure is, that's where your heart will be. God can be your God or money can be your god. You can't serve both."

Growing up, we never were rich, for sure. But Dad was always a good saver, and he was always generous with what we did have. One year, in ninth grade, a tornado came through town and destroyed a lot of homes and everything people owned. People we had known for years were penniless. We spent a lot of time helping people rebuild, and I noticed from time to time people thanking Dad for helping them out financially. I finally said to him one day, "It seems like we've been giving a lot of money away."

He simply nodded. *"People need help."*

*"How much have we given away?"*

*"Pretty much all of it,"* he said.

*I was silent for a minute. "So what about my college savings?"*

*He looked at me and answered candidly. "Saving for college is important, Son. But not as important as what these people need right now. They have no place to live, no clothes to wear, no food to eat. We can't say no to them, not if we can help them. If God wants you to go to college, He will provide."*

*As I got older I came to understand that my dad had had the opportunity to*

rise to the top of the company he had been a part of. All he had to do was overlook some underhanded dealings that were happening in the company. A lot of money was in the works for him. But he turned his back on it and resigned. He couldn't find a job for a while and we started to go through hard times financially. "Dad, are we going to have enough money?" I asked him one day at the breakfast table. "Are we going to have to sell the house?"

He looked at me very earnestly. "I don't know if we'll have to, Son. But I know this: God will provide for us. He says not to worry about what we will eat, or drink, or wear, that He will provide those things for us. He said rather than getting caught up in worry, we should focus on God's kingdom and His righteousness. God will take care of us."

And God did.

Dad used to tell me not to condemn other people. One day I came home from school, so mad that a friend of mine had cheated on a test and gotten an A and I had gotten a B. "I feel like telling the teacher!" I said. "Then he'll get a zero and a failing grade for the last six weeks."

He leaned across the table and said to me gently, "And then you will lose a friend, won't you? Which is more important? Don't judge others. Your friend will realize one day that cheating doesn't get him where he wants to go in life. Have you ever done anything dishonest?"

"Well ..." He knew what the answer to that was. "Yeah."

"Then focus on living your life honestly. One day, when he is ready, maybe you can help your friend live his honestly."

Another time I was complaining that something wasn't fair.

"Life isn't fair, Son," he told me. "So you'd better get used to it. What we have is better than fair. We have a God who always gives us infinitely more than we deserve."

Dad was that way, too, giving me more than I deserved. Once, in fifth grade, he got called to pick me up from the principal's office. I had been suspended for fighting with another kid. I wasn't sure which was worse, the black eye I got, being suspended, or the disappointment I expected Dad would feel when he picked

me up. He finally got to school and we walked silently to the car. Instead of driving home, however, he drove to the mall. Five minutes later we were standing in front of Marble Slab ice cream shop, my favorite.

"Double scoop today, Son," he said. "Or a large hot fudge sundae or banana split. Whatever you want."

We looked over the ice cream flavors, made our selections, and sat down a minute later to our treats.

"Dad," I finally asked, "Aren't you mad at me? For letting you down? Why are you taking me out for a treat?"

He smiled gently. "Because that's what God does with us. He offers us complete grace, no matter how badly we've blown it. And, because I love you."

After that, every time we passed Marble Slab, I was reminded: God offers us complete grace, no matter how badly we've blown it. And I didn't realize until I was older how much it meant that Dad would say, "I love you." He never stopped telling me that, even when I got to be a teenager and then a young man.

Dad was never about punishing me for the sake of punishing. He was always about doing what was best for me, and training me to be the kind of man I should be. Sometimes that involved disciplining me when I blew it. One time I lied to my basketball coach about why I didn't make a practice. Dad found out

and made me sit on the bench for three games. Three long games. I didn't lie to my coach again.

Sometimes Dad took the opposite approach. I was in youth group that Dad helped out with. Our group had a small bank account and I was the treasurer. One day, while the group was on a weekend campout, it came out that I had taken some of the money for my own personal use. They were furious and wanted to kick me out of the group for stealing. So Dad called all of us together around the campfire. He made me admit to all of them what I had done and apologize. They were still mad at me, I could tell. So Dad said to them, "You guys want to kick him out of the troop?" Over half of the guys nodded. "OK," he said. "If you've never stolen anything, or 'borrowed' something that you really didn't plan to give back, or taken something that you probably weren't supposed to when no one

was looking, then you have my permission to kick him out." I looked around at the guys, but no one said anything. "All right," Dad finally said. "Let's put this fire out and everyone get to bed."

As we were walking over to our tent, Dad simply said, "Son, don't steal anymore."

And I didn't.

You'd think that, with a father like my dad, I would have turned out pretty perfect. At least, I wouldn't have made any really bad mistakes in life. But I did. I went off to college and slowly drifted in with a wrong crowd, especially a girl I was crazy about who turned out to be bad news. One thing led to another, and the next thing you knew, I was being arrested for drugs.

I'll never forget what it was like when Dad came and got me out of jail. Not only

had I ruined my future, I had let Dad and my whole family down terribly. I couldn't imagine what he was going through as he posted bail and took me home.

What made it worse was knowing how the news was spreading. Dad was looked up to in our small community. He was friends with the very people that I was now in the hands of: the district attorney and the judge. I didn't have any choice but to just sit at home and wait for what would happen to me.

Then one day, not long after, Dad came home after work and said to me, "The charges against you have been dropped."

"What?" I couldn't believe it. "How did they get dropped?"

"I spent a lot of time talking with the D.A. and the judge. We worked things out." "So I'm free? I mean, I don't have to go to court?"

He smiled. "You're free, Son."

It was the greatest news I had ever heard. I was on cloud nine for about a week. Then I walked in on Dad packing a few things in a bag in his bedroom.

"Are you going somewhere, Dad?"

He nodded. "To the penitentiary."

"For what? Some kind of prison ministry?"

"No, Son. I'll be there the next few years. Your record is clean. I didn't want your mistakes to ruin your whole future. So I pled guilty to the charges myself." He walked over and hugged me tightly, tears in his eyes. "I'll miss you terribly. But we can write and you can come visit. I'll still be there for you. But I want you to move on with your life. Finish your studies. Pursue the career you've dreamed of. Find a good young woman." He smiled. "And I'll be back for my first grandchild."

These are the kind of things Jesus did with people when He walked on earth. (The Bible verses that this story is based on are listed at the end.) They show us His heart toward us, and how He relates to us. In turn, Jesus shows us exactly the kind of father God will be toward us. Who wouldn't want a father like that?

The great news is that we can have a father like that, forever, starting today. We are born into the world with God as our *Creator*. But we have the incredible privilege of choosing to become part of God's eternal family and have Him as our perfect *Father*—one who will always be there for us, always lead us, always care for and provide for us, and give us an inheritance forever beyond anything we could imagine. Ultimately, only a heavenly Father who loves us unconditionally, forgives us completely, and gives us eternal life with Himself can fill the void that we all carry in our hearts.

## Choosing God as our Father

So how do we get God as our Father? We receive it—we receive Him—as a free gift. There is nothing we can do to earn getting God as our perfect Father. There is nothing we can do to be good enough to have God as our perfect Father. How could we, as imperfect, sinful people, ever be good enough to earn such a thing? And that's exactly what the Bible tells us.

But now God has shown us a way to be made right with him without

keeping the requirements of the law… We are made right with God
by placing our faith in Jesus Christ. And this is true for everyone who
believes, no matter who we are. For everyone has sinned; we all fall short
of God's glorious standard. Yet God, in his grace, freely makes us right in
his sight. He did this through Christ Jesus when he freed us from the
penalty for our sins. For God presented Jesus as the sacrifice for sin.
People are made right with God when they believe that Jesus sacrificed
his life, shedding his blood. (Romans 3:21-25a)

We are made right with God, and God becomes our Father, when we chose to
receive His free gift. And how do we do that? By faith. Faith is simply the word the
Bible uses for receiving. We accept God's free gift by trusting Him.

And what exactly are we trusting? We are trusting that He Himself has already
done everything we need to be made right with Him. We were born into this
world sinners, rebels against God, living independently of Him, trying to make
life work on our own. The Bible says that we were spiritually dead. We were
separated from a holy God because of our sins. We were headed for an eternity
separated from Him. That was what our sins had earned us. And there wasn't
anything we could do to earn our way back to Him.

But because God loves us so much, He did for us what we could not do, at
incredible cost to Himself. He sent His own Son, Jesus Christ, who is God
Himself, to live a perfect life and die on a cross to pay the penalty for our sins.
The Creator is greater than all of His creation, which means that Jesus, the
Creator, was able to take human form and, through His death, pay the price for

all of our sins. God the Father then raised Him from the dead, signaling that the price had truly been paid.

What this means is that the door to joining God's family and having God as our perfect Father is wide open to us. All we have to do is choose to receive the free gift.

> For the wages of sin is death, but the free gift of God is eternal life through Christ Jesus our Lord. (Romans 6:23)

We receive this free gift by placing our personal trust in Jesus Christ. Jesus said:

> "For this is how God loved the world: He gave his one and only Son, so that everyone who believes in him will not perish but have eternal life." (John 3:16)

The Bible says:

> If you openly declare that Jesus is Lord and believe in your heart that God raised him from the dead, you will be saved. (Romans 10:9)

What happens, then, when we place our trust in Jesus? We become God's own child.

Everyone who believes that Jesus is the Christ has become a child of God. (First John 5:1).

But to all who believed [Christ] and accepted him, he gave the right to become children of God. They are reborn—not with the physical birth resulting from human passion and pain, but a birth that comes from God. (John 1:12)

Have you been born with the birth that comes from God? Have you placed your trust in Jesus as your Lord and Savior? If you haven't, you can right now become God's child forever by placing your trust in Jesus and His death and resurrection for you. We become God's child through faith, not through prayer, but here is a prayer that can show your choice to place your trust in Jesus:

Jesus, I recognize that I have sinned and that I need your forgiveness and the life you offer. Thank you for dying for my sins and rising from the dead on my behalf, so that you could give me true life. I receive you by faith as my Savior and Lord and trust you to join me to yourself forever, making me one with you, and coming to live within me.

If you have chosen to put your trust in Jesus, congratulations! You are a forever child of God. God is now your heavenly Father. He will always love you, care for you, and guide you. His love for you will never change, no matter what you do. You are His, and He is yours.

## What Happens When God Becomes our Father

So what happens to us when we become a child of God—when He becomes our Father? A whole lot of incredible things. Here are five of them.

**First,** our sins are completely forgiven.

> God made you alive with Christ, for he forgave all our sins. He canceled the record of the charges against us and took it away by nailing it to the cross. (Colossians 2:13-14)

Notice that the Bible says that God forgives *all* of our sins—past, present, and future. Jesus completely did away with the sin issue between us and God. That issue is taken off the table. God doesn't deal with us according to what our sins deserve anymore. He always deals with us in His love, to *always* achieve His best for us.

I love you Lord. I did it. Thank you for saving me. Change me!

God is love … perfect love expels all fear. If we are afraid, it is for fear of punishment, and this shows that we have not fully experienced his perfect love. (First John 4:16,18)

**Second,** when we place our trust in Jesus, God actually does a heart transplant deep down inside us, in our spirit. Long ago, He told the Hebrews that one day He would do this, when the Messiah came.

And I will give you a new heart, and I will put a new spirit in you. I will take out your stony, stubborn heart and give you a tender, responsive heart. (Ezekiel 36:26)

All of us are born with that stony, stubborn heart.

As for you, you were dead in your transgressions and sins …, gratifying the cravings of our flesh and following its desires and thoughts. Like the rest, we were by nature deserving of wrath. (Ephesians 2:1-3, New International Version)

That's who we used to be—God's enemies at heart. But when we put our faith in Christ, God does a heart transplant on us. In the depths of our being, we become a completely new person, one born by the Spirit of God. Jesus said:

"Flesh gives birth to flesh, but the Spirit gives birth to spirit." (John 3:6, NIV) The Holy Spirit gives birth to a completely new "us." As a result,

… anyone who belongs to Christ has become a new person. The old life is gone; a new life has begun! (Second Corinthians 5:17)

The new person that we are is in the depths of our being, in our spirit. We can still *feel* many of the same feelings we used to. We can still *think* negative things. We still have the freedom to make wrong choices. But in our deep inner being, we are now on the same page with God. He has given us a new heart. We truly

want what He wants.

So when God becomes our Father, our sins are completely forgiven, and we are given a new heart, righteous and holy (Ephesians 4:24).

**Third,** when we have God as our Father, He Himself (through His Holy Spirit) comes to live within us. That is the real reason Jesus went to the cross, not only to forgive us of our sins, and not only to give us a heart transplant, but to actually join Himself to us, coming to live in us, and living His life through us. That has been His plan all along.

The Apostle Paul, who spread the message of Christ in the first century more than anyone else, said that:

> God has given me the responsibility of serving his church by proclaiming

his entire message to you. This message was kept secret for centuries and generations past, but now it has been revealed to God's people ... And this is the secret: Christ lives in you. (Colossians 1:25-27)

God's great secret, revealed to those who have placed their trust in Jesus, is this: Christ lives in us! Jesus said to His disciples:

When I am raised to life again, you will know that I am in my Father, and you are in me, and I am in you. (John 14:20)

The Apostle Paul knew that it was Jesus living in him. He wrote:

My old self has been crucified with Christ. It is no longer I who live, but Christ lives in me. So I live in this earthly body by trusting in the Son of God, who loved me and gave himself for me. (Galatians 2:20)

What does this mean in our daily lives? That we depend on Him to live this life of glorifying God and loving others. We know that we can't pull it off ourselves. But Jesus lives in us, and He always loves and glorifies the Father!

We now have this light shining in our hearts, but we ourselves are like fragile clay jars containing this great treasure. This makes it clear that our

great power is from God, not from ourselves. (Second Corinthians 4:7)

**Fourth,** when God becomes our Father, we are on equal footing with Jesus before God. Jesus is God's Son. Now we, too are His sons and daughters.

So now Jesus and the ones he makes holy have the same Father. That is why Jesus is not ashamed to call them his brothers and sisters. (Hebrews 2:11)

As incredible as it may sound, this means that the Father loves us as much as He loves Jesus, His own Son. Before He went to the cross, Jesus prayed for all of those who would come to believe in Him (including us). He said to the Father,

I have given them the glory you gave me, so they may be one as we are one. I am in them and you are in me. May they experience such perfect unity that the world will know that you sent me and that you love them as much as you love me. (John 17:22-23)

The Father loves us as much as He loves Jesus! In an amazing passage of the Bible, here is how the Apostle Paul describes the love the Father has for us, His children:

What shall we say about such wonderful things as these? If God is for us, who can ever be against us? Since he did not spare even his own Son but gave him up for us all, won't he also give us everything else? ...

**Victory in Jesus**

Can anything ever separate us from Christ's love? Does it mean he no longer loves us if we have trouble or calamity, or are persecuted, or hungry, or destitute, or in danger, or threatened with death? … No, despite all these things, overwhelming victory is ours through Christ, who loved us. And I am convinced that nothing can ever separate us from God's love. Neither death nor life, neither angels nor demons, neither our fears for today nor our worries about tomorrow—not even the powers of hell can separate us from God's love. No power in the sky above or in the earth below—indeed, nothing in all creation will ever be able to separate us from the love of God that is revealed in Christ Jesus our Lord. (Romans 8:31-39)

Because of our heavenly Father's love for us, we will never be abandoned or neglected again. Our heavenly Father will never fail us. Significant people in our lives may have done this to us, but our heavenly Father never will. He says to us directly:

"I will never fail you. I will never abandon you." So we can say with confidence, "The Lord is my helper, so I will have no fear. What can mere people do to me?" (Hebrews 13:5-6)

Fifth, because we are God's sons and daughters, we are now His heirs. We may or may not have much on earth, but in eternity we will be given the whole thing—God's entire inheritance.

And because we are his children, God has sent the Spirit of his son into our hearts. Now you are no longer a slave but God's own child. And since you are his child, God has made you his heir. (Galatians 4:6-7)

So you have not received a spirit that makes you fearful slaves. Instead, you received God's Spirit when he adopted you as his own children. Now we call him, "Abba, Father." For his Spirit joins with our spirit to affirm that we are God's children. And since we are his children, we are his heirs. (Romans 8:15-17)

As a result, God says, as His children "all things are yours" (First Corinthians 3:21, New American Standard Bible). In God's eyes, everything is ours, for all of eternity. We do not see that yet today. But one glorious day we will.

## Our Next Steps as God's Child

So, if we have received Christ into our hearts by placing our trust in Him and His death and resurrection for us, what do we do now? What are our next steps?

**First,** we simply enjoy our new relationship with God. We talk to Him. We tell Him what we are thinking and feeling and our heart's desires. We praise Him for the loving God that He is. We ask Him to show us every day how much He loves us. He speaks to us especially through His Word, the Bible. (The Gospel of John is a great place to start).

**Second,** we trust Him to lead us. The Bible says that

all who are led by the Spirit of God are children of God. (Romans 8:14)

This doesn't mean that if we don't feel led, we aren't a child of God. Rather, it's a promise: The Holy Spirit, who lives in us, *will* lead us. Calling those who have trusted Him His sheep, Jesus said,

"My sheep listen to my voice; I know them, and they follow me. I give them eternal life, and they will never perish. No one can snatch them away from me, for my Father has given them to me, and he is more powerful than anyone else. No one can snatch them from the Father's hand." (John 10:27-29)

This tell us two things. First, Jesus does lead us. We do hear His voice to us, when we are quiet to listen for Him. Second, our new relationship with God the Father and Jesus (God the Son) is permanent. No one—not even ourselves—can snatch us away from God. He has us, and He has us forever.

**Third,** it is very helpful to make a choice to leave our old, earthly family behind, and fully embrace that we have a new Father, and a new family. Our earthly parents were in our lives for a time—maybe a very short time. God is now our Father forever. Jesus is our Brother forever. And we have a host of new brothers and sisters all across the world, and through eternity. It's completely right for us to say goodbye, at least within ourselves, to our earthly family. We are choosing to trade our temporary, imperfect earthly family for an eternal, perfect family.

Jesus Himself had done this by the time He started His earthly ministry.

As Jesus was speaking to the crowd, his mother and brothers stood outside, asking to speak to him. Someone told Jesus, "Your mother and yours brothers are outside, and they want to speak to you." Jesus asked, "Who is my mother? Who are my brothers?" Then he pointed to his disciples and said, "Look, these are my mother and brothers. Anyone who does the will of my Father in Heaven is my brother and sister and mother!" (Matthew 12:46-50)

We can say within ourselves,

> Mom and Dad (whether you knew him or not), I appreciate how God used you in my life to get me to this point. Mom, you cared for me and loved me as best you could. Dad, _____ (you have to fill in the blank; he may have loved and cared for you too; he may have just conceived you). Now God has become my earthly Father. Jesus is my Brother, and I have a new, eternal family. On the inside, I am trading families. I am part of God's family now. My allegiance and my loyalty are to Him.

Doing this doesn't mean we are rejecting anyone. Just the opposite. We can still love our family as before—even be more loving toward them. It's simply saying what is true, that we do have a new family. For years, our earthly family has told us who we are and how we are to live. Now, we receive that from God. He tells us who we are now (new creations in Christ). He tells us how we are to live (by depending on Jesus to live His life through us). He tells us how incredibly loved we are. He tells us what our future holds (we are His heirs).

**Fourth,** saying goodbye to our earthly family almost always involves forgiving them (and others) for how they have hurt us or let us down. We have all been hurt by others, even by those who love us. None of the people in our lives have been perfect; they have all offended us in some way. God calls us to forgive them.

> Be kind to each other, tenderhearted, forgiving one another, just as

God through Christ has forgiven you. (Ephesians 4:32)

God forgave us a debt much larger than the debt anyone owes us. We had sinned against an infinitely holy God. He had to give the life of His own Son to pay the price for our forgiveness. Now, we turn around and forgive others, even if they have hurt us badly. Jesus will give us the power to do it. He has already given us His nature. We have a forgiving heart now, even if we don't realize it yet.

Forgiving others is not for their sake. It is for ours. Holding onto bitterness and resentment poisons our hearts. It *always* prevents us from fully experiencing God's love. We have to get it out of our hearts.

Forgiving someone doesn't mean that they didn't really hurt us, or that what they did or didn't do doesn't matter, or that we are doormats and they can go ahead and hurt us again, or that we feel forgiving. We almost never *feel* forgiving.

Rather, forgiveness is us saying *to God*:

> Father, I know that _____ wronged me, and that wrong hurt. But in Christ you have given me a forgiving nature. I choose to forgive _____ of his/her offense against me. I choose to release them from that debt and not hold it against them anymore. They are free from that debt. I am no longer judging them for it. I am free to act toward them with the love of Christ. I entrust to you, Father, the consequences of their wrong against me. I give it completely to you to handle as you see best. I trust that you are working all things, even this offense, for good in my life, even if I don't understand that good right now. I am not depending on _____ to change in any way for my needs to be met. I trust you, Jesus, to be the one who meets all my needs. Thank you that you are my very life, Jesus.

Jesus promises that He really is enough to meet all our needs:

> Jesus replied, "I am the bread of life. Whoever comes to me will never be hungry again. Whoever believes in me will never be thirsty." (John 6:35)

And God does tell us that He is big enough to use everything in our life, even the hard things, for good:

> And we know that God causes everything to work together for the good of those who love God and are called according to his purpose for them. (Romans 8:28)

The highest good for us is that we become more and more like Jesus:

> For God knew his people in advance, and he chose them to become like his Son, so that his Son would be the firstborn among many brothers and sisters. (Romans 8:29)

Our final "next step" is just to relax into getting to know God as our heavenly Father and Jesus, God the Son, as our heavenly Brother. The Apostle Peter told people who had placed their trust in Jesus to

> grow in the grace and knowledge of our Lord and Savior Jesus Christ. (Second Peter 3:18)

God wants us to know Him better and better. He wants us to know His love more and more. Ask Him every day to reveal His love. Jesus has come to live in us. He lives His life through us. He wants us to bring everything in our lives to Him. He wants us to trust all the details of our lives to Him. If everything doesn't seem to go right (and it never does), we trust Him. He is working it all for good. We give Him thanks in every circumstance, for everything, even the difficult things.

> Be thankful in all circumstances, for this is God's will for you who belong to Christ Jesus. (First Thessalonians 5:18)

As we trust Him, He reveals Himself to us more and more. And as we know Him more, we experience more and more of what Jesus said He came to give us: true abundant life.

**BIBLE VERSES**

The story about Jesus as our dad is drawn largely from the following Bible passages (several other passages mentioned in the book are here as well):

*Colossians 3:23-24* Work willingly at whatever you do, as though you were working for the Lord rather than for people. Remember that the Lord will give you an inheritance as your reward, and that the Master you are serving is Christ.

*1 Corinthians 4:7* What do you have that God hasn't given you? And if everything you have is from God, why boast as though it were not a gift?

*1 Corinthians 13:4-7* Love is patient and kind. Love is not jealous or boastful or proud or rude. It does not demand its own way. It is not irritable, and it keeps no record of being wronged. It does not rejoice about injustice but rejoices whenever the truth wins out. Love never gives up, never loses faith, is always hopeful, and endures through every circumstance.

*Ephesians 2:1-3* Once you were dead because of your disobedience and your many sins. You used to live in sin, just like the rest of the world, obeying the devil—the commander of the powers in the unseen world. He is the spirit at work in the hearts of those who refuse to obey God. All of us used to live that way, following the passionate desires and inclinations of our sinful nature. By our very nature we were subject to God's anger, just like everyone else.

*Ephesians 2:4-9* But God is so rich in mercy, and he loved us so much, that even though we were dead because of our sins, he gave us life when he raised Christ from the dead. (It is only by God's grace that you have been saved!) For he raised us from the dead along with Christ and seated us with him in the heavenly realms because we are united with Christ Jesus. So God can point to us in all future ages as examples of the incredible wealth of his grace and kindness toward us, as shown in all he has done for us who are united with Christ Jesus. God saved you by his grace when you believed. And you can't take credit for this; it is a gift from God.

*Ephesians 4:24* … and to put on the new self, which in the likeness of God has been created in righteousness and holiness of the truth. (New American Standard Bible)

*Hebrews 12:4-11* After all, you have not yet given your lives in your struggle against sin. And have you forgotten the encouraging words God spoke to you as his children? He said,

"My child, don't make light of the Lord's discipline
, and don't give up when he corrects you.
For the Lord disciplines those he loves,
and he punishes each one he accepts as his child."

As you endure this divine discipline, remember that God is treating you as his own children. Who ever heard of a child who is never disciplined by its father? If God doesn't discipline you as he does all of his children, it means that you are illegitimate and are not really his children at all. Since we respected our earthly fathers who disciplined us, shouldn't we submit even more to the discipline of the Father of our spirits, and live forever? For our earthly fathers disciplined us for a few years, doing the best they knew how. But God's discipline is always good for us, so that we might share in his holiness. No discipline is enjoyable while it is happening—it's painful! But afterward there will be a peaceful harvest of right living for those who are trained in this way.

*James 1:17* Whatever is good and perfect is a gift coming down to us from God our Father, who created all the lights in the heavens. He never changes or casts a shifting shadow.

*John 8:1-11* Jesus returned to the Mount of Olives, but early the next morning he was back again at the Temple. A crowd soon gathered, and he sat down and taught them. As he was speaking, the teachers of religious law and the Pharisees brought a woman who had been caught in the act of adultery. They put her in front of the crowd.

"Teacher," they said to Jesus, "this woman was caught in the act of adultery. The law of Moses says to stone her. What do you say?"

They were trying to trap him into saying something they could use against him, but Jesus stooped down and wrote in the dust with his finger. They kept demanding an answer, so he stood up again and said, "All right, but let the one who has never sinned throw the first stone!" Then he stooped down again and wrote in the dust.

When the accusers heard this, they slipped away one by one, beginning with the oldest, until only Jesus was left in the middle of the crowd with the woman. Then Jesus stood up again and said to the woman, "Where are your accusers? Didn't even one of them condemn you?"

"No, Lord," she said.

And Jesus said, "Neither do I. Go and sin no more."

*1 John 3:16-18* We know what real love is because Jesus gave up his life for us. So we also ought to give up our lives for our brothers and sisters. If someone has enough money to live well and sees a brother or sister in need but shows no compassion—how can God's love be in that person? Dear children, let's not merely say that we love each other; let us show the truth by our actions.

*1 John 4:8-10* But anyone who does not love does not know God, for God is love. God showed how much he loved us by sending his one and only Son into the world so that we might have eternal life through him. This is real love—not that we loved God, but that he loved us and sent his Son as a sacrifice to take away our sins.

Before daybreak the next morning, Jesus got up and went out to an isolated place to pray. (Mark 1:35)

**Matthew 5:42** "Give to those who ask, and don't turn away from those who want to borrow."

**Matthew 6:19-24** "Don't store up treasures here on earth, where moths eat them and rust destroys them, and where thieves break in and steal. Store your treasures in heaven, where moths and rust cannot destroy, and thieves do not break in and steal. Wherever your treasure is, there the desires of your heart will also be. Your eye is like a lamp that provides light for your body. When your eye is healthy, your whole body is filled with light. But when your eye is unhealthy, your whole body is filled with darkness. And if the light you think you have is actually darkness, how deep that darkness is! No one can serve two masters. For you will hate one and love the other; you will be devoted to one and despise the other. You cannot serve God and be enslaved to money."

**Matthew 6:25-34** "That is why I tell you not to worry about everyday life—whether you have enough food and drink, or enough clothes to wear. Isn't life more than food, and your body more than clothing? Look at the birds. They don't plant or harvest or store food in barns, for your heavenly Father feeds them. And aren't you far more valuable to him than they are? Can all your worries add a single moment to your life? And why worry about your clothing? Look at the lilies of the field and how they grow. They don't work or make their clothing, yet Solomon in all his glory was not dressed as beautifully as they are. And if God cares so wonderfully for wildflowers that are here today and thrown into the fire tomorrow, he will certainly care for you. Why do you have so little faith? So don't worry about these things, saying, 'What will we eat? What will we drink? What will we wear?' These things dominate the thoughts of unbelievers, but your heavenly Father already knows all your needs. Seek the Kingdom of God above all else, and live righteously, and he will give you everything you need. So don't worry about tomorrow, for tomorrow will bring its own worries. Today's trouble is enough for today."

**Matthew 7:1-5** "Do not judge others, and you will not be judged. For you will be treated as you treat others. The standard you use in judging is the standard by which you will be judged. And why worry about a speck in your friend's eye when you have a log in your own? How can you think of saying to your friend, 'Let me help you get rid of that speck in your eye,' when you can't see past the log in your own eye? Hypocrite! First get rid of the log in your own eye; then you will see well enough to deal with the speck in your friend's eye."

**Matthew 7:24-27** "Anyone who listens to my teaching and follows it is wise, like a person who builds a house on solid rock. Though the rain comes in torrents and the floodwaters rise and the winds beat against that house, it won't collapse because it is built on bedrock. But anyone who hears my teaching and doesn't obey it is foolish, like a person who builds a house on sand. When the rains and floods come and the winds beat against that house, it will collapse with a mighty crash."

*Matthew 20:1-16* "For the Kingdom of Heaven is like the landowner who went out early one morning to hire workers for his vineyard. He agreed to pay the normal daily wage and sent them out to work. At nine o'clock in the morning he was passing through the marketplace and saw some people standing around doing nothing. So he hired them, telling them he would pay them whatever was right at the end of the day. So they went to work in the vineyard. At noon and again at three o'clock he did the same thing. At five o'clock that afternoon he was in town again and saw some more people standing around. He asked them, 'Why haven't you been working today?'

"They replied, 'Because no one hired us.'

"The landowner told them, 'Then go out and join the others in my vineyard.'

"That evening he told the foreman to call the workers in and pay them, beginning with the last workers first. When those hired at five o'clock were paid, each received a full day's wage. When those hired first came to get their pay, they assumed they would receive more. But they, too, were paid a day's wage. When they received their pay, they protested to the owner, 'Those people worked only one hour, and yet you've paid them just as much as you paid us who worked all day in the scorching heat.'

"He answered one of them, 'Friend, I haven't been unfair! Didn't you agree to work all day for the usual wage? Take your money and go. I wanted to pay this last worker the same as you. Is it against the law for me to do what I want with my money? Should you be jealous because I am kind to others?'

"So those who are last now will be first then, and those who are first will be last." *Romans 5:6-8* When we were utterly helpless, Christ came at just the right time and died for us sinners. Now, most people would not be willing to die for an upright person, though someone might perhaps be willing to die for a person who is especially good. But God showed his great love for us by sending Christ to die for us while we were still sinners.

*Romans 8:1* So now there is no condemnation for those who belong to Christ Jesus.